T0336599

Analysis of the Development of Guangzhou in China

Editors-in-Chief: Qu Shaobing, Wei Minghai
Associate Editors-in-Chief: Zhang Qixue, Luo Jiaowan, Tu Chenglin

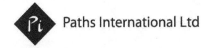

Paths International Ltd

社会科学文献出版社
SOCIAL SCIENCES ACADEMIC PRESS(CHINA)

Editorial Board

Tan Yuanfang, Xie Shouguang, Ding Yanhua, Ou Yangzhi, Wang Wenjiao, Li Wenxin, Huang Xu, Zeng Henggao, Li Yanling, Ren Wenwu, Ding Xuguang, Peng Xiaogang, Zeng Yonghui, Li Jiaxi, Wang Peng, Su Huaying, Zhao Ran, Tang Xuan, Liu Congmin, Ma Yuhong, Liang Huaxiu, Huang Juan, Yao Huasong, Liang Ningxin, Lv Huimin

Contents

I Economy

II Society

III Culture

IV Urban Development and Management

V Technological Innovation

Analysis of the Economic Situation in Guangzhou in 2016 and Prospects for 2017*

The joint research group of Guangzhou Development Research Institute of Guangzhou University and the General Affairs Office of Guangzhou Municipal Bureau of Statistics [1]

Abstract: In 2016, in the face of complicated economic situation, Guangzhou maintained steady economic growth by stabilizing economic growth, promoting reform, adjusting the structure and improving people's livelihood. In 2017, in the face of problems existing in economic operation, Guangzhou will achieve its target of economic growth by opening wider to the outside world, strengthening regional cooperation, vigorously developing the real economy, increasing effective investment, tapping more consumption potentials and accelerating innovation-driven growth.

Keywords: Guangzhou, economic situation, prospects

I. An Analysis of Guangzhou's Economic Operation in 2016

Since 2016, in the face of the complicated economic situation at home and abroad, the whole city has adhered to the basic principle of steady improvement, committed to stabilizing growth, promoting reform, adjusting the structure, and improving people's livelihood, and has been vigorously advancing the supply-side structural reform. As a result, the city's economy has seen steady progress and a better structure, the economic operation is generally stable, reform and innovation are accelerated, the economic structure is being optimized and the benefits of economic development have been steadily improved.

*This research report is a fruit of the collaboration between Guangzhou Development Research Institute of Guangzhou University - a provincial key research base for humanities and social sciences, "Guangzhou Studies" Collaborative Innovation and Development Center under Guangdong Provincial Development of Education, and the decision-making consultancy and innovation team for integrated development of Guangzhou - a provincial university innovation team of Guangdong.

[1] Heads of the research group: Tu Chenglin (researcher, doctoral supervisor), Huang Pingxiang (deputy director). Members: Zhou Lingxiao (associate professor), Tan Yuanfang (professor, Ph.D.), Ouyang Zhi (Distinguished Professor), Jiang Nianyun (researcher), Wang Wenjiao (Ph.D.), Feng Jun (division chief), Chen Wanqing (deputy division chief), and Li Jun (section chief). Written by: Zhou Lingxiao, Li Jun.

1

i. Basic judgment: the overall economic operation was smooth, and the contribution of the tertiary sector to GDP continued to rise

Preliminary accounting shows that in 2016, the city's GDP reached RMB1,961.094 billion, a year-on-year increase of 8.2%, basically the same as that of 2015 (8.4%). The trend of stable growth continued. It was 1.5 percentage points and 0.7 percentage point higher than the national GDP growth (6.7%) and the provincial GDP growth (7.5%), respectively, and up by 0.1-0.2 percentage point from the first three quarters (8.1%), the first half of the year (8.0%) and the first quarter (8.0%), respectively. As to the three major sectors, the primary sector generated added value of RMB24.004 billion, down by 0.2%, the secondary sector RMB592.587 billion and the tertiary sector RMB1,344.503 billion, up by 6.0% and 9.4%, respectively. Their industrial structure composition ratio was 1.22:30.22:68.56. In particular, the proportion of added value created by the tertiary sector increased by 1.45 percentage points from the previous year and it contributed to 77.0% of the economic growth, maintaining the over-70% contribution rate since 2015.

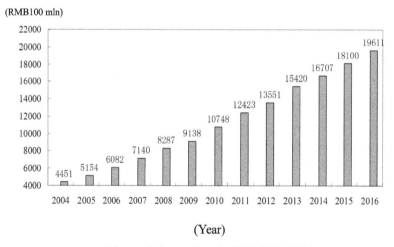

(RMB100 mln)

(Year)

Figure 1 Guangzhou's GDP 2004-2016

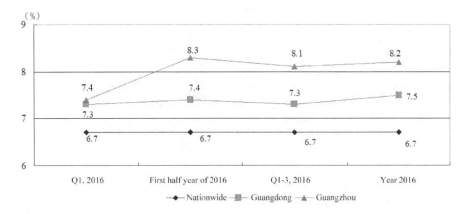

Figure 2 Quarterly Accumulative GDP Growth for China, Guangdong and Guangzhou in 2016

ii. As to production areas, agricultural production grew steadily, industrial production grew steadily with better quality, and the service industry developed rapidly

In 2016, the added value of agriculture in Guangzhou reached RMB26.03 billion, a year-on-year increase of 0.1%. The output of agricultural products was basically stable: the fruit output increased by 1.5%, in particular the sugarcane output up by 3.5%, the meat output fell by 4.6%, but the beef output rose by 8.4%.

In 2016, the city's gross output value of industrial enterprises above the designated size reached RMB1,955.625 billion, an increase of 6.5% over the previous year. The trend of steady growth continued from 2015 (6.4%). The economic development was mainly boosted by the pillar industries. The gross output value of the three pillar industries registered RMB969.348 billion, up by 7.6%, a 0.2 percentage point increase from the previous year. Among them, the automobile manufacturing industry continued to recover under the impetus of product structure optimization and upgrading, with its gross output growing by 12.6%, an increase of 4.7 percentage points from the previous year. The vehicle output was 2.6288 million and the sales volume was 2.6259 million, up 19.0% and 17.2% respectively, 4.5 and 3.5 percentage points higher than the national growth rate of vehicle production and sales respectively.

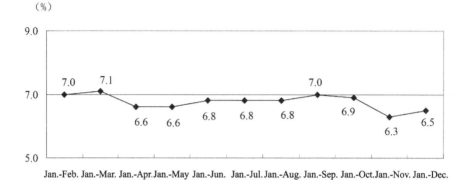

（%）

Jan.-Feb. Jan.-Mar. Jan.-Apr.Jan.-May Jan.-Jun. Jan.-Jul. Jan.-Aug. Jan.-Sep. Jan.-Oct.Jan.-Nov. Jan.-Dec.

Figure 3 Monthly Accumulative Output Growth for Industrial Enterprises above the Designated Size in Guangzhou in 2016

First, the function of international transport hub was enhanced. In 2016, Baiyun International Airport ranked the third in the country with the passenger throughput of 59.7766 million. Guangzhou Port was among the world's busiest ports with the cargo throughput of 544 million tons and the container throughput of 18.8497 million standard containers. The cargo turnover, freight volume, passenger turnover and passenger traffic increased by 62.6%, 11.6%, 7.0%, and 6.8% respectively from that in 2015.

Second, financial services for the real economy were strengthened. The added value of the financial industry reached RMB180 billion, accounting for 9.18% of GDP, increasing by 0.18 percentage point from the previous year, and up by 11.1%, outgrowing the GDP. As of the end of December 2016, the volume of domestic and foreign currency deposits and loans of financial institutions continued expand, with the balance of deposits and loans amounting to RMB4,753.02 billion and RMB 2,966.982 billion, up by 10.9% and 8.7% respectively from the previous year.

iii. In term of demand, consumption rose steadily, investment grew slowly but steadily, and foreign trade increased steadily.

In 2016, the total retail sales of consumer goods reached RMB870.649 billion, up 9.0% year-on-year, an increase of 0.4 percentage point over the previous three quarters, including 9.2% for wholesale and retail sales, 7.7% for the accommodation and catering industry. Retail sales related to quality improvement of consumer consumption grew rapidly. Retail sales of articles for daily use, cosmetics and western and traditional Chinese medicines above the designated size increased by 22.9%,

4

16.6% and 12.9%, respectively;   online consumption remained hot, and the retail sales of online shops above the designated size increased by 20.7%. The growth momentum of travel commodities was sound. The retail sales of automobiles were up 9.6%, and increased quarter by quarter; that of petroleum and its products declined by 1.1% due to the price fall of crude oil, but at a slower rate from quarter to quarter.

（%）

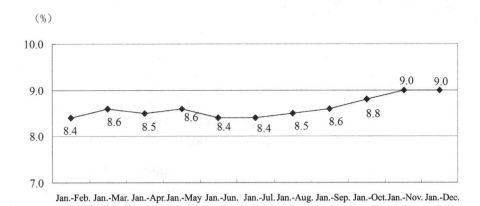

Jan.-Feb. Jan.-Mar. Jan.-Apr. Jan.-May Jan.-Jun. Jan.-Jul. Jan.-Aug. Jan.-Sep. Jan.-Oct. Jan.-Nov. Jan.-Dec.

Figure 4 Monthly Accumulative Retail Sales Growth of Consumer Goods in Guangzhou in 2016

In 2016, the total investment in fixed assets was RMB570.359 billion, an increase of 8.0% over the previous year. Specifically, the industrial investment throughout the year was RMB71.392 billion, an increase of -5.4%. Investment in real estate development maintained a rapid growth, amounting to RMB254.085 billion, up by 18.9%. Investment in electronic information manufacturing and automobile manufacturing, two of the three pillar industries of Guangzhou, increased by 14.8% and 13.7% respectively; that in producer service industries such as transportation & warehousing and postal service, rental & commercial services, increased by 20.2% and 55.4% respectively.

（%）

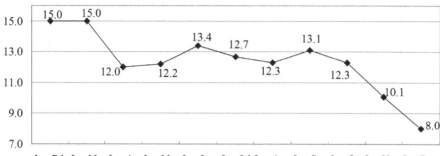

Figure 5 Monthly Accumulative Growth of Fixed-Asset Investment in Guangzhou in 2016

In 2016, the total value of imports and exports reached RMB856.692 billion, up 3.1% from the previous year, slightly lower than the growth rate in 2015 (3.5%). The total import value was RMB337.987 billion, an increase of 3.3%, higher than that the national growth rate of 0.6% and the provincial growth rate of 0.01% of Guangdong. The total export value was RMB518.705 billion, up 3.0%, compared to the national growth rate of -1.9% and the provincial rate of -1.3%.

（%）

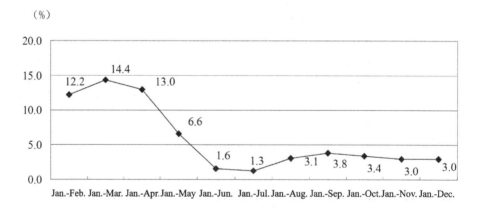

Figure 6 Monthly Accumulative Growth of Exports of Guangzhou in 2016

iv. In terms of the operating efficiency and environment, fiscal revenue and expenditure was balanced, corporate operating efficiency was good, and the price level was stable.

In 2016, Guangzhou's general public budget income was RMB139.385 billion, up 5.2% on a year-on-year basis. Specifically, the tax revenue was RMB106.227 billion, up by 5.5%. The business tax and personal income tax increased rapidly, by 41.3% and 15.7% respectively, the corporate income tax increased by 8.3% while the value added tax decreased by 5.2%.The general public budget expenditure was RMB194.368 billion, an increase of 12.5% over the previous year.

（%）

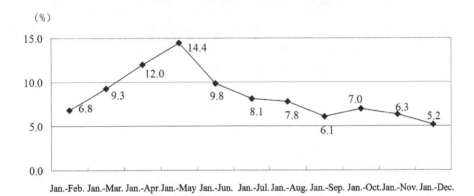

Jan.-Feb. Jan.-Mar. Jan.-Apr.Jan.-May Jan.-Jun.　Jan.-Jul. Jan.-Aug. Jan.-Sep. Jan.-Oct.Jan.-Nov. Jan.-Dec.

Figure 7 Monthly Accumulative Growth of General Public Budget Income of Guangzhou in 2016

First, the profit growth of industrial enterprises was relatively good, and the percentage of loss-making enterprises was reduced. From January to November, the total profit of industrial enterprises above the designated size reached RMB103.016 billion, up 8.0% over the previous year, and up 7.0% over the same period of the previous year. The percentage of loss-making enterprises was 20.24%, 1.26 percentage points less than that of the previous three quarters (21.50%). In particular, the automobile manufacturing industry, chemical raw materials and chemicals manufacturing industry, electricity and heating generation and supply industry realized profits of over RMB10 billion.

Second, the profits of service enterprises increased rapidly. From January to November, operating profits of services enterprises above the designated size increased by 27.1% year-on-year, of which profits for rental and commercial services increased 19.4%, those for information transmission, software and information

7

technology services increased 27.8%, and those for transportation, warehousing and postal service increased 62.8%. The operating profits of the above three industries accounted for over 80% of the total.

In 2016, the city's consumer price index (CPI) rose 2.7% year-on-year, an increase of 0.1 percentage point from the previous three quarters. Specifically, the price of consumer goods and services rose 2.7% and 2.8% respectively. The price of eight major commodities went up for six of them while down for two of them. Clothes, food, tobacco & alcohol and housing commodities saw the highest price growth, 5.9%, 4.4% and 2.9%, respectively, while the price for daily necessities & services and transportation & communications went down by 0.4% and 0.3%, respectively.

The decline in industrial prices continued to slow down. The industrial producer purchasing price index (IPI) was down 1.5% year-on-year and the producer price index (PPI) down 1.2%, for the 11 and 12 consecutive months, respectively.

（%）

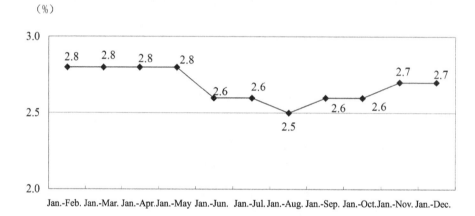

Jan.-Feb. Jan.-Mar. Jan.-Apr.Jan.-May Jan.-Jun. Jan.-Jul. Jan.-Aug. Jan.-Sep. Jan.-Oct.Jan.-Nov. Jan.-Dec.

Figure 8Monthly Accumulative Growth of Urban Consumer Prices in Guangzhou in 2016

v. Reform and innovation were accelerated, and efforts of cost reduction and efficiency increase paid off

First, market vitality was strengthened. The number of newly registered enterprises increased rapidly. In 2016, the number of newly registered domestic enterprises reached 242,100, an increase of 17.6% over the previous year, with an average of 663 enterprises registered each day. The registered capital reached RMB770.255 billion, an increase of 42.5% over the previous year. Guangzhou introduced a total of 16 projects of the world's top 500 companies, with an investment of RMB27.2 billion, and housed the headquarters of COSCO Shipping Bulk and China Tunnel Group as well as Cisco Innovation Center.

Second, micro and small-sized enterprises grew rapidly. Tax and fee reduction policies played out to give more financial support to the real economy, and thanks to that, micro and small enterprises remained active. The total industrial output value of micro and small enterprises above the designated size was RMB435.885 billion, up by 7.7% from the previous year, which was 1.2 percentage points faster than that of industrial enterprises above the designated scale, and accounting for 22.3% of the industrial output of enterprises above the designated scale.

Third, the construction of Nansha New Area and Pilot Free Trade Zone made positive progress. There were 14,200 newly-established enterprises with a registered capital of RMB159.05 billion, an increase of 87% and 65% respectively, 910 of which were financial and quasi-financial enterprises. China Communications Construction Co., Ltd., China Railway Engineering Corporation and China Railway Construction Corporation moved their functional headquarters there and GAC-Toyota started its Phase III construction project. It produced more than 100 reform and innovation outcomes, led the country with its market supervision and business information & credit platform, and 31 of its practices including the "single counter" for international trade were promoted province-wide.

Since 2016, the city has issued a 1+5 policy document on the supply-side structural reform, vigorously pushing forward the five major tasks of "reducing excessive production capacity, stock and cost, de-leveraging, and making up for weakness", and making new progress in all fronts of the supply-side reform. As of the end of November, 2016, the asset-liability ratio of industrial enterprises above the designated scale was 51.4%, down 1.3 percentage points from the same period last year. On the one hand, industrial enterprises above the designated scale saw their finished goods stock down 2.9% from the same period last year. The profit of enterprises increased rapidly. From January to November, the total profit of industrial enterprises above the designated scale reached RMB103.016 billion, an increase of 8.0%; the profit margin of principal business income was 6.6%, up 0.2 percentage point from the same period last year. The total profit of service enterprises above the designated scale reached RMB85.388 billion, with a growth rate of 27.1%. On the other hand, the burden on industrial enterprises was obviously eased. From January to November, the income of industrial enterprises above the designated scale increased by 4.7%, while the total tax decreased by 5.2% from the previous year, accounting for 0.5 percentage point less of the revenue from principal business (4.8%) from the same period of last year.   The policy of replacing the business tax with the value added tax (VAT) took effect and reduced the tax burden on service enterprises as a whole, with the total of business tax and additional and payable VAT decreasing by 2.7% from the same period of last year.

The scheme to double the amount of fiscal input and the number of incubators went on smoothly, building nearly 190 high-tech business incubators with a total area of over eight million square meters. In 2016, the growth rate of the output value of industrial high-tech products above the designated scale (7.3%) was faster than the industrial average (6.5%), accounted for 1.0 percentage point more of the output value of industrial enterprises above the designated scale than the previous year (45.0%), and contributed to 3.0 percentage points of output growth of industrial enterprises above the designated size.

vi. The new economy led industrial optimization and promoted industrial transformation and upgrade.

In 2016, that advanced manufacturing industry and the high-tech manufacturing industry developed steadily, and their added value increased by 6.6% and 7.5% respectively, 0.1 and 1.0 percentage point higher than that of added value of industries above the designated scale. The output value of high-tech products accounted for 46% of that of industries above the designated scale. Eight industrial sectors, namely automobile, electronics, petrochemical, electricity & heating, electrical appliances & machinery, general and special equipment, railway, ship, aviation & aerospace equipment, and pharmaceuticals, continued to expand in size, with the combined industrial output value accounting for 70.9% of the city's total, up by 0.4 percentage point from the previous year. The modern service industry related to software, commerce and technology maintained rapid growth. From January to November, the business income of research & development, software and information technology services and commercial services above the designated scale increased by 32.5%, 26.6% and 16.2% respectively. The new business forms of the Internet economy led the growth of service industry, and the business income of Internet and related services above the designated scale increased by 97.2%.

In 2016, equipment products increased remarkably. The output of mobile communication base station equipment increased by 17.0%, the output of industrial automatic control instruments and control systems and industrial robots reached 435,700 sets and 2,287 sets respectively, up by 44.4% and 31.7% respectively from the previous year. The output of new energy vehicles (NEVs) and sports utility passenger vehicles (SUVs) registered 4,869 and 1,093,900, a year-on-year increase of 86.3% and 63.7% respectively. The output of optoelectronic devices and optical cables, among information technology products, increased 1.4 times and 43.0% respectively, and that of lithium-ion batteries increased 24.5%.

In 2016, the growth of online retail sales above the designated size reached 20.7%, 11.7 percentage points higher than the city's total retail sales growth of consumer goods. Cross-border e-commerce imports and exports amounted to RMB14.68 billion, up 1.2 times over the previous year, with exports up 1.5 times and imports up 83.2%.

In 2016, investment in automobile manufacturing and electronic information manufacturing increased by 13.7% and 14.8% year on year, respectively. The investment in new energy and energy-saving and environmental protection industries was RMB9.437 billion, up by 17.6%.In the service sector, investment increased by 69.0%, 55.4% and 12.7% respectively in education (RMB11.943 billion), rental and commercial services (RMB20.913 billion) and culture, sports &entertainment (RMB5.928 billion).

II. Noteworthy Issues in Economic Operation

Generally speaking, in 2016, Guangzhou maintained relatively stable and healthy economic development, with improvements in both quality and efficiency, but there were also issues that deserved our special attention.

First, the downward pressure on industrial enterprises should not be ignored.

In 2016, the output value of industrial enterprises above the designated scale in Guangzhou grew only by 6.5%, down 0.7 percentage point from the previous year (7.2%), and the growth rate of the three pillar industries was low. From January to November, the total output value of the three pillar industries increased by 7.5%, 12.0% for automobile manufacturing, 8.1% for electronics manufacturing and 0.2% for petrochemical manufacturing, respectively. In particular, the figure was at the bottom low for electronics manufacturing in recent couple of years and the fall is still continuing for petrochemical manufacturing. Among the top 100 industrial enterprises that accounted for over 60% of the total industrial output value, 30% of them experienced negative growth and indicated poor potential for industrial growth. The downward pressure on production should not be ignored.

Second, the investment growth was insufficient.

In 2016, the investment in fixed assets in Guangzhou was RMB570.359 billion and increased by 8%, less than 10.6% in 2015. It paled by comparison to the investment amount in Chongqing (RMB1,736.112 billion) and Tianjin (RMB 1,462.922 billion).

The growth of industrial investment was negative, and that of private investment fell back. In 2016, private investment grew by 5.3% to RMB251.977 billion, 2.7% lower than the city average, and even much lower than the growth rate of 35.8% in 2015. Compared with Shenzhen, Tianjin and Chongqing, Guangzhou suffered from more prominent decline in private investment and should pay more attention to it. The construction progress of some key projects was slow. Only few projects boasted both huge investment and high quality. The stock of projects worth more than RMB100 million was small. The problem was still outstanding for stabilizing investment growth.

Table 1: Status of Fixed-Asset Investment in Guangzhou in 2016

Indicator	Accumulative total (unit: RMB10,000)	Increase (%) from the same period of last year
Total investment in fixed assets	57035860	8
Investment in real estate development	25408549	18.9
Investment in fixed assets by units under central and provincial governments	9115511	25.8
Investment in fixed assets by units under the municipal government	47920349	2.4
Private investment in fixed assets	25197721	5.3
State-owned investment in fixed assets	13109710	0.7
Newly-increased fixed-asset investment in 2016	21570430	-33.8
Investment in fixed assets in the primary industry	211577	-37.4
Investment in fixed assets in the secondary industry	7320025	-6.1
Investment in fixed assets in the tertiary industry	49504258	10.8

Table 2: Investment Growth of Major Chinese Cities in 2016

City	Investment in Fixed Assets (RMB100 million)	Growth rate (%)	Investment in the secondary industry (RMB100 million)	Growth (%)	Investment in the tertiary industry(RMB100 million)	Growth (%)	Private investment (RMB100 million)	Growth (%)	Real estate investment (RMB100 million)	Growth (%)
Guangzhou	5703.59	8.0	732.0	-6.1	4950.43	10.8	2519.77	5.3	2540.85	18.9
Beijing	8461.7	5.9	722.9	6.8	7639	6.1	2766.0	-5.6	4045.4	-4.3
Shanghai	6755.88	6.3	982.69	2.5	5769.11	7.0			3709.03	6.9
Tianjin	14629.22	12.0	3940.48	6.5	10376.6	14.0	9896.69	11.2	2300.01	22.9
Shenzhen	4078.16	23.6	695.47	19.1	3382.6	24.6	2097.16	61.5		
Chongqing	17361.12	12.1	5666.36	13.4	11136.7	11.9	8858.50	11.0	3725.95	-0.7

Data source: sorted based on local statistical data, with some data missing

Third, the consumer goods market was lackluster.

As consumption hotspots cooled downs, the growth rate of consumer goods retail sales in Guangzhou was 9.0%, down by 2.0 percentage points over the previous year, lower than the national (10.4%) and provincial (10.2%) average, but higher than that of Beijing, Shanghai, Tianjin and Shenzhen. The retail sales of large-sized traditional department stores were flat. The retail sales of 32 department stores with the retail sales volume over RMB10 billion such as Grand buy and Guangzhou Friendship Store were falling.

Table 3: Total Retail Sales of Consumer Goods in Major Chinese Cities in 2016

City	Total consumer goods retail sales (RMB100 million)	Growth (%)	Retail sales of online stores above the designated size (RMB100 million)	Growth (%)
Guangzhou	8706.49	9.0		20.7
Beijing	11005.1	6.5	2049	20.0
Shanghai	10946.57	8.0	1249.77	15.8
Tianjin	5635.81	7.2	383.14	44.6
Shenzhen	5512.76	8.1		
Chongqing	7271.35	11.7	245.99	45.3

Data source: sorted based on local statistical data, with some data missing

Fourth, the development of the new economy was to be pushed.

Although the new economy has been growing fast, its size is too small and its infusion insufficient. First, the new economy was still small in size. For example, the output of NEVs accounted for only 0.19% of Guangzhou's total automobile output. Second, the integration of new and old economies was insufficient. Taking "Internet +" business as an example, only a few traditional department stores had online sales, and online retail sales only took up a small portion of the total retail sales. Third, compared with Beijing, Shanghai, and Shenzhen, Guangzhou needed to strengthen its technological innovation ability.

Table 4: Statistical Table of Invention Patent Applications Handled in Some Chinese Cities in Recent Three Years

City	Year 2014	Year 2015	Year 2016
Beijing	78129	88930	104643
Shanghai	39133	46976	54339
Guangzhou	14595	20087	31892
Shenzhen	31097	40028	56326
Tianjin	23391	28510	38153
Chongqing	19418	35086	19981
Hangzhou	14800	17814	25009
Nanjing	28050	27825	31556
Xi'an	21383	14244	18569
Chengdu	22096	29791	39431

Source: Sorted based on the statistics data of the State Intellectual Property Office.

Table 5: Statistical Table of Authorized Invention Patents in Some Chinese Cities in Recent Three Years

(Year)

City	2014	2015	2016
Beijing	23237	35308	40602
Shanghai	11614	17601	20086
Guangzhou	4597	6626	7669
Shenzhen	12032	16956	17665
Tianjin	3279	4624	5185
Chongqing	2321	3964	5044
Hangzhou	5559	8298	8666
Nanjing	5275	8268	8705
Xi'an	4379	5992	6686
Chengdu	4021	6206	7190

Source: Sorted based on the statistics data of the State Intellectual Property Office.

III. Prospects for 2017 and Countermeasures

i. Analysis of the Economic Environment in 2017

Trade growth was slowing worldwide, and the UN's World Economic Situation and Prospects predicted the global economy to grow only 2.2% in 2017, maintaining a low rate of growth. Global trade was at a historically low level and investment growth slowed significantly in both major developed and developing countries. The Federal Reserve announced to raise interest rates by 25 basis points rates and released signals of further rate hikes next year, fueling fears over global economic recovery.

At home, the supply-side structural reform was struggling and experiencing the pain of structural adjustment, but the performance of leading indicators was encouraging. In December 2016, the Purchasing Manager's Index (PMI) of the Chinese manufacturing industry was 51.4%, growing for the 5th consecutive month, and that of the high-tech manufacturing industry and the equipment manufacturing industry was 53.8% and 52.0%, respectively, still above the average level of the manufacturing sector, meaning that the new impetus was playing a strong role in boosting growth in the manufacturing sector. The PPI continued to grow in that month, with a year-on-year decrease of 1.4%, which was down 3.8 percentage points from 2015, reflecting the steady growth of industrial production and market demand, and gradual improvement of the supply-demand relationship. In Q4 of 2016, the People's Bank of China's Entrepreneur Expectation Index (EEI) was 54.2%, up 3 and 8.2 percentage points from the previous quarter and the same period last year, respectively.

In the case of Guangzhou, its economic development faces both opportunities and challenges. Guangzhou was voted the best commercial city in Mainland China for the third consecutive time by Forbes, topped the country in terms of cross-border e-commerce imports and exports, and beat other sub-provincial cities in terms of comprehensive tourism competitiveness. The construction of the Nansha New Area Free Trade Zone went on well, the Guangdong-Hong Kong-Macau Greater Bay project was included into the national strategy, and efforts to build three international strategic hubs started to pay off. It's fair to say that Guangzhou is facing historic opportunities for its opening up and the new momentum is gathering for economic development.According to the leading indicators, industrial power consumption increased steadily and industrial product prices continued to rise. In December 2016, the PMI of Guangzhou's manufacturing industry reached 54.8%, indicating that the city's manufacturing industry continued to maintain a steady growth. But we should also see that, restricted by the global landscape for economic development and the city's ongoing transition between new and old momentums, Guangzhou still suffers from a prominent weakness in technological innovation, and faces an arduous task of adjusting the economic structure and transforming the development mode. In response, it needs to continue to pursue steady progress, accelerate the supply-side structural reform on all fronts, foster and grow the three major new economies, increase market demand, actively release policy dividends and make utmost efforts to ensure sustainable and sound economic operation.

ii. Countermeasures

1. Seizing the historic opportunity of opening to the outside world and regional cooperation to create new momentum for economic development

Guangzhou shall make full use of the historic opportunities brought by the Belt and Road Initiative, the Guangdong-Hong Kong-Macau Greater Bay project and the Nansha Free Trade Zone, and open a new chapter in opening up to the rest of China and the world. The Greater Bay project was formally elevated to the level of national strategy, in which Nansha enjoyed a unique geographical advantage. Guangzhou should make it its top priority to seize this historic opportunity and make strategic planning and layout in advance for the Greater Bay project.

First, Guangzhou shall continue to further in-depth collaborative development of Guangdong, Hong Kong and Macau and liberalize service trade with Hong Kong and Macau. It will strengthen cooperation with cities along the Pan-Pearl River Delta and high-speed railways, and speed up the formation of infrastructure connectivity. It shall promote higher-level integration of Guangzhou and Foshan, Guangzhou and Qingyuan, accelerate the construction of the Guangzhou – Foshan – Zhaoqing – Qingyuan – Yunfu - Shaoguan economic circle, and focus on major cooperation projects regarding transportation facilities, industrial parks, environmental improvement and public services.

Second, Guangzhou should actively seek to establish the inter-city coordination mechanism of the Greater Bay area, find its position in the labor division of cities, and do a good job in industrial upgrading, talent pooling, and regional innovation. In particular, it should deliberate on Nansha's strategic positioning in the future development of the Greater Bay area, scientifically lay down Nansha's functional plan, development goals & path, transportation hub and urban infrastructure construction plans.

Third, Guangzhou should give play to its role as a national central city and actively participate in the allocation of global resources. It should strive to gather global technological, human and capital resources. It shall adopt the import-export optimization strategy, build international procurement and distribution centers, and continuously strengthen the international supply chain. It shall also explore more platforms for external exchanges and collaboration and integrate into the global innovation network through opening up and collaboration.

Fourth, Guangzhou should strive to maintain the steady development of foreign trade. It shall implement policies to stabilize foreign trade development and organize activities to explore the overseas market. It shall carry out pilot projects such as market procurement and service trade innovation, build a national comprehensive pilot zone for cross-border e-commerce, and promote the customs clearance reform and the development of "single counter" for international trade and digital ports. It shall encourage and support local enterprises to go global and invest in and help build industrial parks in other countries and regions along the Belt and Road. It shall strengthen economic and trade exchanges and cooperation with South Pacific island countries and African countries, explore emerging overseas markets for exports and increase both imports and exports.

Fifth, Guangzhou shall promote high-level international cooperation. It shall seek to expand its international influence and bring its international cooperation and exchange to a higher level via high-profile events such as 2017 Fortune Global Forum, 2017 Guangzhou International Innovation Festival, the 25th Guangzhou Fair, the 6th China (Guangzhou) International Finance Expo, Guangzhou Annual Investment Conference, Guangdong 21st Century Maritime Silk Road International Expo, Guangzhou-Auckland-Los Angeles Tripartite Economic Alliance Summit (Guangzhou), Global Annual Meeting of the International Financial Forum (IFF) and World Cities Day activities.

2. Focusing on the development of real economy and building a high-end, high-quality high-tech industrial system

Guangzhou shall focus on advancing the supply-side reform, place more emphasis on the development of real economy, channel more resources and factors into the real economy, foster emerging industries, employ new technology and business forms to upgrade traditional businesses, and improve enterprises' development quality and core competitiveness.

First, vigorously developing advanced manufacturing. It shall strengthen the city competitiveness by developing the manufacturing industry, and elevate the level of industrial development along the high-end value chain. By optimizing industrial planning and layout, it shall build advanced manufacturing bases, international spare auto parts bases, Internet industrial clusters and integrated circuit industrial ecosphere in Huangpu, Nansha and Zengcheng, and develop industrial clusters for intelligent equipment and robots, energy-saving and new energy vehicles, bio-pharmacy and health care.

Second, cultivating and strengthening emerging industries and new business forms of strategic significance. It shall attract more investment in high-tech and strategic emerging industries and achieve technological absorption and innovation through international capital cooperation. It shall make strenuous efforts to make up for weaknesses and develop advanced manufacturing and modern service industries, and strive to attract a number of high-quality projects at the upper end of the industrial chain, technology chain and value chain. It shall promote high-quality and efficient development of service industries and vigorously develop producer service industries such as commercial services, conventions & exhibitions, science & technology, information and logistics. It shall also strive to set up a national demonstration zone for green finance and promote the establishment of a number of financial institutions and financial platforms, to better serve the real economy.

Third, strongly supporting the development of private manufacturing. Guangzhou shall comprehensively examine the difficulties and weaknesses facing the development of private manufacturing, formulate and comprehensively implement targeted countermeasures to promote the development of the private economy, and cultivate a number of leading private manufacturers. It shall vigorously support the development of high-growth private enterprises, increase support for micro, small- and medium-sized enterprises, and cultivate a number of highly competitive small- and medium-sized enterprises. It shall establish a list of key private enterprises for reform and support, and build a demonstration base for the commercialization of innovation outcomes by private enterprises (small- and medium-sized enterprises).It shall also speed up the construction of Sino-foreign cooperation areas for small- and medium-sized enterprises engaged in advanced manufacturing, and support enterprises to pool talent, technology and capital from worldwide for innovation.

Fourth, encouraging and supporting inter-business strategic cooperation and cross-sector and cross-regional mergers, acquisitions, and restructuring to form a number of central, backbone enterprises. Guangzhou shall strengthen the reform of state-owned enterprises and promote the reform and innovation of mixed ownership. It shall implement measures to promote the development of business clusters and vigorously cultivate and attract corporate headquarters. It shall increase efforts to attract foreign investment, land a number of world-class innovation projects, better play the important role of foreign-funded enterprises in promoting the development of the real economy, and strive to make Guangzhou the first-choice investment destination and the heaven for business development for global companies.

3. Increasing effective investment while staying oriented toward industrial upgrade

Aimed at the transformation of the economic development mode and industrial transformation and upgrading, Guangzhou shall on the one hand, through the progress of key projects, increase investment and the momentum of growth, and on the other hand, actively guide and support private capital and channel it to key areas of economic and social development.

First, making utmost efforts in ensuring the progress of key projects, in particular the construction of the three major international strategic hubs. Guangzhou shall guarantee land, capital and other resources for these projects, urge local governments to accelerate the progress of key projects, in particular the construction of the international shipping hub, the expansion of deep-water channel of Guangzhou Port, and the construction of the Phase IV project of Nansha Port, international general-purpose terminals, Nansha international cruise terminals, and the port railway. It shall promote the construction of the international aviation hub, in particular the expansion of Baiyun Airport and the development of the commercial aviation service base at Baiyun Airport. It shall facilitate the development of air-bound economic demonstration zone and boost air logistics, aviation maintenance, aviation manufacturing, aviation finance, freighter conversion and other air-bound industries. It shall push ahead the construction of the international technological innovation hub, lure industrial companies to the technological innovation corridor and the innovation belt along the Pearl River, and advance the construction of key projects such as the innovation and startup park for academicians and experts and the Phase III project of the software business incubator.

Second, promoting the national railway project, inter-city rail project, subway project, expressway project, national (provincial) trunk road projects and a number of urban road projects to build Guangzhou into an international comprehensive transport hub and a national demonstration city of integrated transport hub. Guangzhou shall push ahead the development of Pazhou Internet Innovation Agglomeration Zone and accelerate the construction of the takeoff zone of the international financial city to improve the image and environment of the economic, innovation and landscape belts along the Pearl River. It shall also plan the second central business district with the international financial city - Huangpu Airport Economic Zone as the heart, and facilitate the development of Bai'etan Central Business District.

Third, supporting the healthy development of private investment, implementing opinions on encouraging social investment in key areas, and launching a number of public-private partnership (PPP) pilot projects. Guangzhou should open public services to private investment when appropriate, guide and encourage private capital to invest in infrastructure and public utilities through PPP and other modes, to inject momentum and vitality for the sustainable growth of investment.

4. Promoting the integrated development of new economy and the release of consumption potential

Guangzhou shall speed up the integration of traditional industries and new business models and foster new business models in the consumption sector.

First, as the market share of traditional commercial trade enterprises is gradually eroded by e-commerce, Guangzhou shall, through policies and capital support, guide competent traditional commercial trade enterprises such as department stores, chain stores and specialty markets to develop e-commerce based on their offline resources and promote online-offline integration.

Second, efforts should be made to adjust the consumption supply structure, speed up the reform of public institutions providing education, healthcare and cultural services, lower the threshold for private capital, ease supply constraints and release service consumption potential. Besides a regulatory system shall be established and perfected to strengthen the sustainable development of new business forms.

Third, Guangzhou shall stimulate consumption by multiple means, hold the international shopping festival, international food festival and other thematic exhibition and marketing activities, deepen domestic trade circulation system reform, carry out traditional retail experience consumption, launch the e-commerce demonstration project, and promote public service platforms for the transformation and upgrade of specialty markets.

5. Guangzhou shall speed up the implementation of the innovation-driven development strategy, realize industrial upgrade and foster emerging industries.

First, implementing innovative policies and measures to optimize the environment for innovation and entrepreneurship. Guangzhou shall significantly streamline the process of technology management, improve the way of allocating resources for technological innovation, and create an environment that encourages innovation and tolerates well-intended failure. It shall reform the right to use, dispose of and benefit from R&D results in institutions of higher learning and research institutes, and develop institutions for the commercialization of R&D results. It shall carry out the demonstration project for state intellectual property pledge financing and the pilot project of operating intellectual property rights in key industries to promote the deep integration of technological innovation and finance. It shall also accelerate the pooling of leading talents, adopt more open-minded policies for the recruitment and retaining of human resources, protect and stimulate the entrepreneurial spirit, and attract talents in various fields to settle in Guangzhou.

Second, building a major innovation platform and cultivating technological innovation enterprises. Guangzhou shall speed up the development of the national homegrown innovation demonstration zone, adjust the regional scope of the demonstration zone, and make it a high ground for the agglomeration and development of innovative enterprises. It shall improve the service ability and specialization level of incubators and group innovation spaces, and develop Guangzhou standards. It shall actively build new research institutes through partnership and seek for national laboratories, state key technological infrastructure and provincial laboratories.

Third, planning future industries and strengthening the R&D and commercialization of transformative, key technologies. Guangzhou shall track and serve the backup high-tech enterprises in relevant fields to cultivate technological innovation enterprises. It shall support the growth of micro and small enterprises, little giant companies, and model companies in technological innovation in related fields. It shall also support the establishment of R&D centers by industrial enterprises above the designated size in relevant fields, and increase the efforts of technological transformation.

Practice and Reflection on Review and Oversight of Budgets and Final Accounts by Guangzhou Municipal People's Congress

Ouyang Zhi   Chen Bilian*

Abstract: The review and oversight of budgets and final accounts by the people's congress plays an important role in modernizing the country's governance system and governance capacity. This paper summarizes the practice and experience of Guangzhou Municipal People's Congress in the review and oversight of budgets and final accounts in recent years, and puts forward suggestions for further strengthening the review and oversight against existing problems.

Keywords: National governance, budget, review, oversight

In recent years, Guangzhou Municipal People's Congress and its standing committee, from the perspective of national governance, has proactively acted to satisfy the new requirements of socialist democracy reform and meet people's new expectations, focused on solving problems, made innovations in the way of oversight, and established a long-term mechanism to effectively strengthen the review and oversight of all governmental budgets and final accounts by the people's congress, and promote the establishment of a modern fiscal system and law-based budget, with remarkable results achieved.

I. Improve the People's Congress Organizational Mechanism for Review and Oversight of Budgets and Final Accounts

The standing committee of Guangzhou Municipal People's Congress has always taken the review and oversight of budgets and final accounts as a major task in making plans, and intensified efforts to strengthen the development of organizations and improve the review mechanism. In October 2012, the Budget Working Committee

* Ouyang Zhi, President of the Research Association for Guangzhou Study and Guangzhou Grand Series, Guest Professor of Guangdong Provincial Party CommitteeSchool, Guest Professor of Guangzhou University; former member of the Standing Committee of Guangzhou Municipal People's Congress, former chairman of the Budget Committee of the Standing Committee of Guangzhou Municipal People's Congress; once served as Deputy Secretary-General to Guangzhou municipal government, Mayor of Baiyun District, and Secretary of Conghua Municipal Party Committee. Chen Bilian, Head of the Publicity Division of the Research Office of the Standing Committee of Guangzhou Municipal People's Congress.

under the standing committee of the municipal people's congress was set up; in February 2015, the Budget Committee of the municipal people's congress was established. The organization, coordination and other specific work related to review and oversight of budgets and final accounts is undertaken with the Budget Committee and the Budget Working Committee at the core. The Budget Committee is staffed with two members for each representative group, that is, there are a total of 22 members for 11 groups. When formulating rules of procedure for the Budget Committee, members of the Budget Committee were required to attend the meeting and take the lead in the discussion. The professional team of representatives and the panel of experts of the Budget Committee were reconstituted to provide professional advice for the review and oversight of budgets and final accounts. According to decisions of the director meeting of the standing committee of the municipal people's congress, the Budget Working Committee should take the lead in organizing other special committees of the municipal people's congress, the standing committee and other working committees under the standing committee to bring into full play their advantage in being familiar with corresponding organizations and operations in their respective field, to jointly carry out pre-review of budgets and final accounts, and to create a strong synergy for conducting oversight within the people's congress. With the joint efforts between the standing committees of people's congress at municipal and district levels, relevant working committees at the district level are systematically arranged to participate in budget reviews and special investigations organized by the standing committee of the municipal people's congress, so as to guide and promote the standing committees of people's congress at the district level to raise the level of budget review and oversight. In order to further enhance the participation of deputies to the people's congress in the budget review, the "three examinations" system for budgets and final accounts and the "1+1" model under which each group of deputies specifically reviews one department's budget and one draft plan for government-invested project were established. The "three reviews" system of budgets and final accounts means that the Budget Working Committee takes the lead in organizing the pre-review, the Budget Committee implements the preliminary review, and the municipal people's congress or the standing committee of the municipal people's congress gives approval after review. It will make intervention in the preparationof budget, so that reasonable suggestions put forward by deputies can be taken and adopted as far as possible.

II. Implement Review and Oversight of All Government Budgets and Final Accounts

"Full coverage, whole process, all aspects" were highlighted in the review and oversight of the government budgets and final accounts. "Full coverage" means to gradually expand the review and oversight scope of budgets and final accounts by the people's congress in accordance with the principle that all revenue and expenditures of the government should be included in the budget. Since 2008, all departmental budgets have been submitted to the people's congress for review. By 2014, the five categories of government budgets, namely, the general public budget, the budget for governmental fund, the budget for state capital operations, the budget for social insurance fund, and the budget for special fiscal account management fund, had all been submitted to the people's congress for review. Since 2016, the final accounts of all departments, together with the draft final accounts of the city, have been submitted to the standing committee of the municipal people's congress for review. In the meantime, constant efforts have been made to ensure that budgets and final accounts are being worked out in greater detail and in a transparent way. At present, the government budgets and final accounts and the municipal-level departmental budgets and final accounts, including all public spending on official overseas visits, official vehicles, and official hospitality, are publicized simultaneously on the government and department websites. "Whole process" means the focus of oversight should be extended from the status of budget balance to expenditure budget and policy, so as to promote the implementation of the Party committee's major decisions and arrangements and urge the government to improve the work throughout the entire budget cycle, and achieve whole-process oversight of budget preparation, implementation, adjustment, and evaluation on final accounts and performance. "All aspects" means full involvement of the oversight entities, which not only exerts the leading role of the standing committee of the people's congress, but also brings into full play the leading role of deputies. It gives play to the role of the people's congress in review and oversight and pays attention to mobilizing the government functions of management and supervision. It not only attaches great importance to the oversight on budget by state institutions, but also actively supports and properly guides the media supervision. Before the convention of the municipal people's congress in 2016, the standing committee organized nearly 300 deputies to participate in the pre-review, and also jointly prepared *Government Budget Interpretation (2016)* with the municipal Finance Bureau to support deputies' budget review.

III. Highlight and Strengthen the Oversight of Key Financial Expenditure

Following the principle of "standardization, transparency, performance, accountability" and focusing on key expenditures and difficulties, the government is urged to improve relevant work system and mechanism and fundamentally regulate its fiscal revenue and expenditure. **Strengthen the review and oversight of government-invested projects.** The standing committee of the municipal people's congress independently formulated the *Regulations of Guangzhou Municipal Government on Investment Management*, impelling the municipal government to promulgate rules for the implementation of the regulations. In addition, it coordinates with the Municipal Development and Reform Commission and the Municipal Finance Bureau to strengthen the coordination of plans for government-invested projects and budgetary fund arrangement. **Strengthen oversight of local government debt.** Issues of government debt were included in the oversight plan of the standing committee of the municipal people's congress. The plans for debts and repayment of the municipal government shall be submitted to the standing committee of the municipal people's congress for approval. From 2015, the government debt at the municipal level has been incorporated into the budget adjustment and submitted to the standing committee of the municipal people's congress for approval according to the budget law. **Strengthen oversight of financial transfer payment.** Special investigation was conducted on the allocation and utilization of the municipal financial transfer payment funds, and the Municipal Finance Bureau was urged to formulate *Administrative Measures for Municipal-to-District Financial Transfer Payment in Guangzhou*. In 2016, a total of RMB1.45 billion for 30 projects were changed from special transfer payment to general transfer payment. The transfer payment plans were prepared based on different regions and projects, and released to districts in advance. **Strengthen oversight of special fiscal funds.** The municipal government was urged to implement the requirements of the central and provincial governments for standardizing and strengthening the management of special financial funds, and the municipal financial bodies were driven to comprehensively overhaul and integrate special financial funds at the municipal level, which reduced the original 214 items involving RMB23.07 billion to 58 items involving RMB13.69 billion at the end of 2015. **Strengthen oversight of financial interim funds.** The municipal government is urged to gradually overhaul and reduce financial interim funds, and the Municipal Finance Bureau is pushed to formulate *Administrative Measures for Financial Interim Funds at the Guangzhou Municipal Level*. In 2014, "zero interim payment" was realized at the municipal level.

IV. Strictly Regulate the Budget Adjustment

Great importance was placed on strengthening rigid constraint of budget to ensure that the budget be strictly implemented. The *Measures for Oversight of Budget Review and Approval by Guangzhou Municipal People's Congress* has further specified in detail and standardized the budget adjustment and listed six situations, including using excess revenue, into budget adjustments that must be submitted to the standing committee of the municipal people's congress for approval. In order to avoid "rush spending" at the end of the year and change the previous conduct of reporting the budget adjustment plan to the standing committee of the municipal people's congress at the end of the year, it is required that a budget adjustment be submitted for approval immediately. From 2014 to 2016, based on making good use of government funds at hand and the debt-converting bonds issued by the provincial government, the municipal government was urged to submit the budget adjustment plan to the standing committee of the municipal people's congress three times a year, so that financial funds can be arranged and utilized timely and reasonably.

V. Strengthen the Whole-Process Oversight of Budgetary Performance

The requirements on performance were implemented throughout the preparation and execution of budgets, and the review and oversight of final accounts to promote efficiency of budget implementation and financial fund utilization. The standing committee of the municipal people's congress basically hears and reviews the performance of financial expenditure at the municipal level annually. In view of the low efficiency of budget implementation, it conducted special inquiries and follow-up oversight, which has effectively improved the efficiency. With the active promotion of the Budget Working Committee under the standing committee of the municipal people's congress, since 2013, the Municipal Finance Bureau has commissioned the third party to carry out performance appraisal for utilization of special funds for some of the government's key programs and others aiming at promoting people's wellbeing, and then to submit the results to the standing committee of the municipal people's congress for review. In 2014, the Municipal Finance Bureau issued the *Administrative Measures of Guangzhou for Budgetary Performance*. From that year onward, departmental project expenditures must set an objective for performance and carry out comparative inspections when reviewing the implementation of budget. In 2016, the Municipal Finance Bureau continued to expand the scope of assessment by the entrusted third party, and it was the first time for the standing committee of the municipal people's congress to independently entrust a third party for performance appraisal of special financial funds.

VI. Intensify Efforts in Oversight of Rectification of Problems Identified in the Audit

Importance was attached to the application of audit results, promoting effective rectification of problems found in the audit and improving the working mechanism for reporting the implementation of rectification to the people's congress. In 2014, all members of the standing committee of the municipal people's congress were organized to conduct special inquiries of all departments and units involved in the audit report, with live broadcast on Dayoo.com. In accordance with relevant requirements of the Standing Committee of the National People's Congress, in May 2016, the standing committee of the municipal people's congress heard and reviewed the reports on the municipal-level budget implementation and the rectification of problems identified in the financial revenue and expenditure audit for the first time. The report changed the written form to oral speech delivered by secretary general of the municipal government at the meeting. Heads of key audited departments were required to attend and listen to opinions and answer inquiries. At the same time, the audit department was required to timely disclose the report on rectification to the public, and the audited department should publish the results of rectification to the public for social oversight. From 2016, after the standing committee of the municipal people's congress heard and reviewed the audit work report in September, the municipal government should make an oral report to the standing committee of the municipal people's congress in December of that year on the rectification of problems found in the audit, which has further enhanced the timeliness of oversight of rectification after audit.

VII. Steadily Push Forward the Building of the Budget Oversight Network

Under the guidance of the people's congress and adhering to the principle of "giving prominence to ourselves and for our own use", we should make full use of information technology to innovate ways of oversight. Since 2014, in accordance with the requirements of the people's congress on oversight of budgets and final accounts, the standing committee of the municipal people's congress has independently developed and designed functional modules and gradually realized whole-process electronic transmission of budget reports, statements, policies and regulations by accessing data of the financial authorities, which helped the people's congress to review and oversee the budgets and final accounts in a more targeted and timely manner. The budget oversight network is not only to meet the work requirements of budget oversight, but also to expand into a shared system facilitating the oversight by the people's congress. In addition to the financial department, the network will gradually be expanded to authorities of development and reform, state-owned assets, human resources and social security, and even cover all budgetary organizations. Users of the budget oversight network are not limited to the Budget Working Committee of the standing committee of the municipal people's congress. With the setting of classified permission, the system will be gradually open to leaders of the standing committee of the municipal people's congress, its members, its working committees, and all deputies to the municipal people's congress. The first phase of the system was completed and tested in January 2016.

On the whole, Guangzhou Municipal People's Congress and its Standing Committee has made some achievements in strengthening the review and oversight of budgets and final accounts. However, there remain problems, for example, the government budgetary system is not sound, complete or detailed, the mechanism of the people's congress for reviewing and overseeing budgets and final accounts is not sound, and it is difficult to investigate the violations of the budget law. There is still a large gap from requirements of the people's congress on substantive review and oversight of budgets and final accounts, the budget law and the establishment of a modern financial system. Therefore, the following suggestions are put forward:

Firstly, the review and oversight system of the people's congress on all government budgets and final accounts should be improved. The review procedures of the people's congress need improvement, particularly, the pre-review of budgets should be enhanced, and the report and feedback mechanism for pre-review be established. In accordance with requirements of the whole-process budgetary performance oversight, the review of performance in budget preparation should be strengthened, and the results of performance review should be used as an important reference for budgetary arrangement. The focal points in the review and oversight of the five categories of government budgets and final accounts (the general public budget, the budget for governmental fund, the budget for state capital operations, the budget for social insurance fund, and the budget for special fiscal account management fund) should be further clarified, and separate voting for each budget category and major investment project should be gradually implemented. The guidance on the review and oversight of government-invested projects and government debts should be strengthened. The building of the budget oversight network should be sped up to further clarify the oversight requirements, highlight the focus and enhance the effectiveness. A modification mechanism for the people's congress reviewing drafted budget should be established. The system for summarizing budgets and final accounts and putting on record the government consolidated financial reports should be improved, so as to constantly deepen and refine the review and oversight of all government budgets and final accounts by the people's congress. The practice that chief responsible persons of the government's financial departments make oral reports on budget implementation at the people's congress should be recovered at an appropriate time, and the time for budgetary review by deputies to the people's congress should be appropriately increased.

Secondly, the formulation of procedures for the review of departmental budgets and final accounts by the people's congress should be expedited. Over the past decade or so since the departmental budget reform was implemented, almost all related departments have submitted their budgets to the people's congress for review and approval. According to the Ministry of Finance's *Notice on Issuing the Management System for Departmental Final Accounts* (C.K. [2013] No.209), departmental final accounts should be submitted by the government to the standing committee of the people's congress for review and approval after being reviewed by the finance department. But so far, in many regions, the departmental final accounts have not been submitted to the standing committee of the people's congress. There remain problems such as the inconsistency between departmental final accounts and budgets, and the revised budget law has not clearly clarified the power and procedures of the people's congress in review and approval of departmental budgets and final accounts, which urgently requires further improvement of relevant laws and regulations.

Thirdly, the people's congress shall strengthen their review and oversight of government investment and government debt. On the one hand, the people's congress shall reinforce their review and oversight on government-invested projects. The report of the plan and the plan draft submitted by the government to the people's congress should mainly include the principles for government-invested projects and explain relevant expenditure policies, and further annual draft plan for government-invested projects should be prepared in detail, and the specific projects in the annual overall financial budget draft and departmental budget draft should be specified correspondingly. The annual report of the plan and the draft plan, the report on the plan implementation for the first half of the year should mainly report the implementation of government-invested projects to the standing committee of the people's congress. The adjustment of government-invested projects should be reported to the standing committee of the people's congress for review and approval. The people's congress can organize deputies to intervene in the preparation of plans for government-invested projects in advance, so as to strengthen the scientific basis, democracy and feasibility of decision-making for government-invested projects.

Follow-up oversight of the implementation of government-invested projects should be strengthened. As to major problems identified in the project implementation, questioning, inquiries, and investigation on specific problems can be conducted when necessary, and the legislation on government investment should be further strengthened and improved. On the other hand, the people's congress should standardize its mechanism for review and oversight of local government debts. Pursuant to the requirements of the Financial and Economic Affairs Committee of the National People's Congress on approving *The Proposal of the State Council on Imposing Ceilings on Local Government Debt in 2015*, key content, main reference indexes and data calibers should be further clarified for local people's congress to review the government debt at the same level and government debts in the budgets and final account drafts. The financial department should report the management of local government debts to relevant special committees and working committees of the standing committee of the people's congress at the same level in writing form once half a year. Based on local conditions, it is proposed to give sub-provincial capital governments the power to independently issue debt-converting bonds under the premise of risk control and with reference to the practice in municipalities with independent planning status.

Fourthly, the participation of deputies to the people's congress and all sectors of society in the oversight of budgets of final accounts should be expanded. In accordance with the budget law and relevant provisions of the State Council and the Ministry of Finance, the government and its financial departments should be urged to prepare budgets and final accounts in detail, publicize relevant reports and statements pursuant to laws, and vigorously increase the level of detail, openness and transparency of budgets and final accounts. Channels should be further expanded, and opinions of representatives and all walks of life on oversight of budgets and final accounts ought to be heard through various channels and forms, such as the sub-district working committee of the people's congress, the community station for liaison with deputies. The standing committee of the people's congress at the community level are encouraged and supported to carry out participatory budgeting and continuously expand the participation of representatives and people from all walks of life in the oversight of budgets and final accounts.

Fifthly, the accountability for violations of the budget law should be reinforced. A prominent feature of the revised budget law is the legal responsibilities are more specified, but it does not make it clear who will be in charge of investigation and how to investigate the breach of the budget law. As the people's congress assumes the responsibility of reviewing and overseeing the government budgets and final accounts, it should be the entity to investigate the legal liability of the government in violation of the budget law. Meanwhile, other supervisory bodies' duties in investigation into the accountability should also be defined. The main body for accountability should be further clarified, the procedures for accountability for violations of the budget law should be improved, and the rectification and the investigation into accountability concerning problems identified in audit should be enhanced, so that legal responsibilities stipulated in the budget law can be fulfilled.

Study on Measures for Eradicating "Fake Trade Fairs"

------Take Guangdong as an example

Tan Yuanfang

Abstract: Fake trade fair refers to the spurious trade shows that emerge alongside official trade fairs and make profits mainly through selling booths and shoddy products, which does great harm to the society. The number of trade fairs in Guangdong Province has ranked second in the country for a long time, and fake trade fairs are not rare. Taking the "Fake Maritime Silk Road Expo" in Dongguan in 2016 as an example, it can be seen that the fake trade fair had features such as taking a free ride, false publicity, poor quality and inferiority, being difficult for investigating into accountability. The mechanism for its appearance includes such two aspects as inertia in innovation and resonance of destruction. The main solutions are to enhance the government regulation, curb the collusion of expo venue owners and trade fair organizers, and strengthen media publicity.

Keywords: Fake trade fair; exhibition economy; government regulation

Since the implementation of reform and opening up, China's exhibition sector has seen rapid development and become one of the important driving forces for economic development and industrial upgrading. In the new century, Beijing, Shanghai, Guangzhou and other mega cities have proposed to vigorously develop the exhibition sector and hope to enhance regional competitiveness by creating clusters of exhibition sector. At the same time, trade fairs have sprung up all over the country. According to statistics of the Ministry of Commerce in 2016, "the exhibition sector in China continued to expand in scale, with over 10,000 trade fairs held for the year and the exhibition area exceeding 100 million square meters."[1] Along with the numerous exhibition activities, "fake trade fairs" tread on the heels and produce a vicious "free riding" effect on the exhibition economy, which leads to mix-ups in the market, severely undermines the order of the socialist market economy, affects the image of the government, causes obvious negative impacts on local economy and the city's

---

[1] The Ministry of Commerce, 2016 Business Review XXXII: The Exhibition Sector Maintains Stable and Rapid Growth and Market Vitality is Further Released
.http://www.mofcom.gov.cn/article/ae/ai/201702/20170202516648.shtml, cited on February 16, 2017.

brand effect. This should arouse high attention of relevant departments.

I. Features of "Fake Trade Fairs": Based on the Case in Guangdong Province

On November 1, 2016, *Yangcheng Evening News* exposed the fraudulent "Fake Maritime Silk Road Expo" in Dongguan, triggering wide discussion in all sectors of society. The fake trade fair was held over the same period and at the same venue as the "21st Century Maritime Silk Road International Expo" sponsored by Guangdong Provincial Government. Not only the trade fair names were similar, but the entrance and exit of the exhibitions were intertwined, which was extremely confusing, therefore, many consumers were deceived and suffered enormous loss. Moreover, the fake trade fair took advantage of the national "Belt and Road" Initiative, and caused serious damage to the government's credibility.

According to *Yangcheng Evening News*, on October 30, 2016, a Guangzhou citizen purchased a jadeite with RMB120,000 at the so-called "Maritime Silk Road Expo", which was identified as "fake jade made with bleaching filling and dyeing technique". The citizen immediately went to the exhibition hall to find the merchant, but the stall became empty. After investigation, the police found that the so-called "2016 Maritime Silk Road Crafts Trade Fair of Belt and Road Initiative in Dongguan" was the "Fake Maritime Silk Road Expo" held by Dongguan Huimeng Exhibition Co., Ltd. During the Expo, high counterfeiting technology was adopted and many foreigners were hired to attract customers, confusing and deceiving a large number of customers, with a huge amount involved. Moreover, "exhibitors" selling fakes disappeared overnight, and the organizer of the "Fake Maritime Silk Road Expo" which set no threshold for exhibitors eventually bore no joint liability. It not only caused a great sensation among the public, but also brought significant negative impacts on the "21st Century Maritime Silk Road International Expo" which had been hosted by Guangdong Provincial Government for three years and enjoyed excellent reputation.

In fact, in recent years, the exhibition sector in some cities of Guangdong Province has witnessed lots of counterfeit trade fairs, shoddy and inferior commodities, disguised apportionment, unreal data, and redundant construction of exhibition halls, which not only damaged the reputation and image of the industry, but also became huge obstacles to sound development of the exhibition economy.

Table 1 Some cases in Guangdong Province exposed by the media in the past five years

Time	Title	Content	Reported by
2016-11-04	Way-out for the exhibition economy in Zhongshan in face of concerns and challenges	Highly redundant exhibitions in Zhongshan City	*Southern Daily*
2016-11-01	Fake jade at the international expo? - early inkling of the "fake expo"	Fake jade purchased at fake expo with RMB120,000	*Yangcheng Evening News*
2016-05-18	Uncover secrets of frauds at Guangzhou trade fairs	Deceptive trade fairs in Guangzhou's exhibition sector	*Sohu*
2015-04-27	"Chaos" behind the prosperous exhibition sector needs urgent adjustment and upgrade	Numerous bogus companies in Foshan trade fairs	*China Business Herald*
2012-08-06	Lack of supervision of local exhibitions leads to chaos	Foshan cultural industry expo does not go through the approval procedures	*China Economic Net*

Generally speaking, the chaos in the exhibition sector in various cities of Guangdong Province mainly shows the following features:

First, "free riding". Some immoral enterprises in the field of trade fair, taking advantage of government-sponsored trade fairs and non-government-sponsored brand exhibitions that are highly recognized at the market, hold similar trade shows which mislead and deceive consumers and exhibitors.

Second, mendacious publicity. Some trade fair organizers deliberately exaggerate the venue level, area, scale, number of exhibitors and specialized enterprises, falsified data, misuse the "international" label, and conspire with foreigners to further confuse and mislead consumers.

Third, inferior quality. Some trade fairs carry out tacky publicity by means of raffling, performances, contests, etc., which greatly reduce the cultural quality of the exhibition sector and degrade social morality. A large number of fake and shoddy products are displayed at exhibitions. Some unauthorized exhibitors have long lurked in the exhibition sector and threaten organizers with "damaging the reputation of the trade fair" to force them to relax the supervision and even defraud in collusion with them.

Fourth, difficulty in accountability. Due to the neglect of management by competent authorities, government agencies often fail to strictly examine the qualification of trade fair organizers. In the meantime, some exhibition venue owners are mercenary, lacking a basic review mechanism for qualification examination and follow-up accountability of trade fair organizers. For example, after the exposure of fraud cases such as "Fake Maritime Silk Road Expo", none of the exhibitor recruiter, the exhibition venue owner and the government agency had contact information of the exhibitors, making it impossible to protect the legitimate rights and interests of consumers.

According to the investigation, fake trade fairs are primarily in two forms. One is trade fair traps in which the organizer defrauds exhibitors and exhibitors in turn defraud consumers with shoddy products. The other is the so-called "lean-on trade fairs" in which the organizer, in collusion with exhibitors, holds a trade show that is confusingly similar to the well-known shows held by government agencies or other organizations, at the same time and a nearby place. In both kinds of trade fairs, the economic loss of exhibitors can be compensated by cheating consumers, and consumers are the ultimate victims. It can be said that the lack of supervision by relevant departments has led to excessively low criminal cost for trade fair organizers and exhibitors and made it difficult to investigate into accountability, which is an important reason for frequent "fake trade fairs".

II. Formation Mechanism and Case Analysis of "Fake Trade Fairs"

In recent years, with the attention and support of governments at all levels, the exhibition sector has gradually become the highlight and new growth area of urban and regional economic development. However, while taking measures to promote the rapid development of the industry, local government fails to pay due attention to the its regulation, thus "fake trade fair" has become the "canker" in the exhibition sector, and has gradually festered and spread, which has aroused wide concern and criticism in the society. The extensive report and criticism by nationwide media such as *Yangcheng Evening News* and *Beijing Evening News* have constituted an obvious negative "landscape of resonance". Especially in the era of We-Media, "fake trade fairs" often attract massive "onlookers" and develop into cyber group incidents due to the wide coverage and the large number of deceived people. There are many reasons for the increasingly intensified "chaos". As to cases in Guangdong Province, the causes can be summed up as follows:

First, there is a severe lack of government regulation. In recent years, local governments in Guangdong have attached great importance to the driving force of the exhibition sector on economy, and have rolled out policies to support its development. However, such policies focus on support but place less emphasis on the regulation of the industry. Exhibitions are often regarded as the image of the city, and attention is paid to the levels of participating leaders, the exhibition scale, the number of exhibitors, the volume of transaction, while supervision over exhibition, protection of legitimate rights and interests of exhibitors and consumers are neglected. With insufficient regulation, the "fake trade fair" becomes increasingly rampant.

Second, the exhibition venue owners are mercenary. In 2016, Dongguan "Fake Maritime Silk Road Expo" was held in Modern International Exhibition Center in Houjie Town. The exhibition center undertook both the "21st Century Maritime Silk Road International Expo" and the "Fake Maritime Silk Road Expo", so it can hardly shirk the responsibility. It is because the venue owners are mercenary and conduct no qualification examination on exhibitors and reach no necessary liability agreement with them that the "fake trade fair" emerges repeatedly. "Fake exhibitions" that took place in Guangdong in recent years show it is not rare for venue owners to collaborate with exhibition organizers. Local governments, for their pursuit of political achievements, build redundant large-scale exhibition halls in the same area, deteriorating the competitive environment of venue owners, which is another reason for the "conspiracy" of venue owners with trade fair organizers.

Third, the trade fair organizers deceive people. Currently, the low entry threshold for the exhibition sector in Guangdong Province has resulted in varying quality of trade fair organizers. Some organizers are accustomed to exploiting legal loopholes and evading the supervision by relevant authorities, and they rent venues on their own, attract exhibitors and hold trade fairs with false information of the exhibition area and scale. The trade fair organizers neither conduct any qualification examination nor check product certifications of exhibitors, and exhibitors can attend and display their products as long as they pay the exhibition fee. In the event of frauds, the organizers often shirk responsibilities with reasons such as losing contact with exhibitors, or can only assist in the police investigation. Some trade fair organizers, lacking social responsibility and moral conscience, even attract exhibitors with fake information and abscond with large sums of deposit paid by the exhibitors.

Fourth, the media's effort in guiding is insufficient. Though *Yangcheng Evening News* and other local media in Guangzhou have been supervising and reporting "fake trade fairs" for years, which reflect the social conscience and guidance consciousness of the media, they lack direct report on government-sponsored trade fairs and other brand trade fairs developed over years. Moreover, their efforts in exposing trade fair organizers and names involving "fake trade fairs" are not enough. Instead, they merely mention "an exhibition company", "some trade fairs" in a brief way. This greatly weakens the supervision function of the media. As a result, consumers only have heard of the matters, but are unaware of the subjects and possible fraud venues, thus unable to distinguish fake trade fairs from professional ones, and easy to be misled to misjudgment.

III. Some Countermeasure Proposals for Eradicating "Fake Trade Fairs"

After nearly 30 years of development, China's exhibition sector has formed a pyramidal development pattern, with three major exhibition clusters, namely. Beijing, Shanghai and Guangdong, formed[2]. Unlike Beijing's government-sponsored trade fairs and Shanghai's high-profile international trade fairs, Guangdong mainly holds import and export trade fairs featuring Canton Fair and some specialized shows in Dongguan and Shenzhen. Compared with Beijing and Shanghai, the exhibition sector in Guangdong features large quantity, miscellaneous types, and great difficulties in supervision. This means that the supervision of the exhibition sector in Guangdong faces more severe challenges. According to statistics, although the overall scale of China's exhibition sector continued to expand in 2015, the growth rate was merely 1.2%, with an obvious slowdown[3]. It can be concluded that the "intensive and meticulous mode" will gradually become the new normal in the exhibition sector. It also indicates that governments at the provincial and municipal levels should provide more guidance and support for and implement more intensive supervision over the exhibition sector, so as to effectively promote the transformation and upgrading from extensive operation to refined development, with quality and efficiency enhanced, and give full play to the important role of the exhibition sector in stabilizing the growth, promoting the reform, adjusting the structure and benefiting people's livelihood.

First, relevant government agencies should pay high attention to and include "fake trade fairs" into the rectification of the market order. From reports of *Yangcheng Evening News* in recent years, it can be seen that the prominent feature of "fake trade fairs" is that they emerge repeatedly despite the ban. It is not only because fake trade fairs are organized in various forms, making it difficult to investigate, but also because relevant government agencies are merely concerned about political achievements and often turn a big problem into a small one and a small problem into

---

[2] Refer to: Fang Zhongquan, Spatial agglomeration characteristics and influencing factors of Guangzhou's exhibition enterprises, *Acta Geographica Sinica*: Issue 4, 2013.

[3] China's exhibition scale increased by 1.2%, *Ningxia Daily*: January 15, 2016.

nothing in the punishment. Governments at all levels should pay great attention to the consequences of "fake trade fairs", incorporate the eradication of "fake trade fairs" into the rectification of market order and the improvement of the government image, and build a long-standing mechanism to curb "fake trade fairs".

Second, vigorous measures should be taken for the top-level design and system building, and the outdated management regulations of the exhibition sector should be revised as soon as possible. In 2015, the *Opinions on Further Promoting the Reform and Development of the Exhibition Sector* (the "Opinions") promulgated by the State Council clearly states that "the reform of the system and mechanism for the exhibition sector in China lags behind, and the marketization has been sluggish. There are problems such as irrational structures, imperfect policies, and weak international competitiveness", which requires optimized market environment and enhanced policy guidance. The Opinions require governments at all levels to "take innovative regulatory measures, and include the fight against infringement and fake commodities into the overall plan and emergency plan for trade fairs". The severe negative impacts of the "Fake Maritime Silk Road Expo" in Dongguan in 2016 were due to the lack of necessary regulation and post-disposal plans.

Third, strict pre-review and emergency plans shall be worked out to curb "fake trade fairs" from the source. At present, in the regulations for management of the exhibition sector in China, there is a severe lack of government regulation. For instance, the *Opinions on Strengthening the Management of the Exhibition Sector in Guangzhou* and the *Codes of Practice for the Exhibition Sector in Guangzhou (Trial)* introduced by Guangzhou ten years ago require the industry association to regulate the chaos of "fake trade fairs" and require the industry association, as the supervising body, to handle consumer complaints, and "suggest relevant government agencies to impose punishment pursuant to provisions". In fact, the provision has absolved relevant government agencies from responsibilities and makes it difficult to effectively manage the increasingly fierce fake trade fairs. Relevant government agencies should intervene as early as possible to introduce more feasible management measures for the exhibition sector and practically fulfill the regulatory responsibilities of the administrative law enforcement agencies.

Fourth, the qualification of the trade fair organizer should be strictly examined to impose "one-vote veto" on fake trade fairs. The root cause of "fake trade fairs" lies in the premeditated planning and deliberate fraud of the trade fair organizer. However, the reason for the organizers' serious frauds is the lax supervision by relevant government agencies and the lack of self-discipline mechanism in the industry association. Under the guidance of the opinions issued by the State Council, government agencies should establish a coordination mechanism to conduct qualification examination of exhibitors and trade fair organizers. In particular, the "one-vote veto system" should be imposed on organizers that once held "fake trade fairs" and have poor business credit records, and exclude them from the exhibition sector. In case of severe violations, the legal representatives shall be enjoined from engaging in the exhibition sector and related industries for a number of years.

Fifth, the exhibition venues should be strictly managed to maintain the social credibility of government-led exhibitions. The social impact of the "Fake Maritime Silk Road Expo" in 2016 in Dongguan was extremely severe because the official exhibition it modeled after was the government-sponsored "Maritime Silk Road International Expo" with a high reputation. The "fake trade fair" severely "consumed" the credibility of the government, resulting in great damage to the reputation of organizers including Department of Commerce of Guangdong Province, Guangzhou Municipal Government and Dongguan Municipal Government. In view of that the exhibition venue owner can gain a high reputation from government-sponsored exhibitions, the owner should sign an agreement with the administrative authority to share both the reputation and responsibilities. Meanwhile, government agencies should strengthen the normative guidance on the exhibition venue and require all other trade fair organizers to strictly define the liabilities for "soliciting fake exhibitors" and "selling fake goods" in contracts. And it should be strictly forbidden from holding trade fairs under the same name and over the same period with government-sponsored trade fairs or brand exhibitions in the nearby place.

Sixth, the guidance for media publicity of the exhibition sector should be strengthened to reverse the "stigmatization" trend of the exhibition economy. In recent years, the chaotic phenomenon of "fake trade fairs" in China has emerged repeatedly, which has caused the "stigmatization" trend of the exhibition economy. This trend mainly concentrates in Guangdong Province, but there are already signs of its spreading all over the country, therefore it is imperative for the media to exert its guidance function. It should strengthen positive coverage of government-sponsored trade fairs and compliant non-government-sponsored ones, which exhibitors and consumers can rely on. In addition, the media should increase efforts to expose "fake trade fairs" and introduce government measures on combating "fake trade fairs". Thus, a good environment and image of the exhibition sector can be formed through the government intensified supervision and the vigorous publicity by the media.

Analysis of the Social Situation in Guangzhou in 2016 and Prospects for 2017[1]

The research group of Guangzhou Development Research Institute,
Guangzhou University[2]

Abstract: In 2016, Guangzhou continued to place the improvement in people's livelihood on top of the agenda, applied the bottom-line thinking, delivered all the ten promises it made at the beginning of the year to improve people's livelihood,fully promoted the formation of inclusive and shared social security system, constantly strengthened the institutional innovation for social development and management, and made Guangzhou a safer place. It also maintained a steady growth momentum in several important fields concerning people's livelihood and social governance, e.g., improving the old-age services and facilities and innovating the social governance system. Looking into 2017, in the aspect of social development, Guangzhou will see accelerated integrated urban-rural development, a better social security network and public service system, rapidly growing community-level social organizations, and stronger ability in community-level social governance.

Keywords: Livelihood improvement, social governance, social organization, Guangzhou

I. Analysis of the Overall Situation of Social Development in Guangzhou in 2016

In 2016, facing the complicated economic situation at home and abroad, Guangzhou adhered to the general approach of seeking steady improvement by stabilizing growth, advancing reform, adjusting structure and benefiting the people, and vigorously pushed forward the supply-side structural reform, and as a result, the city's economy developed smoothly with better quality. In 2016, the city achieved a GDP of RMB19,610.94 trillion, a year-on-year growth of 8.2%, with the growth rate 1.5 and

[1] This research report is a fruit of the collaboration between Guangzhou Development Research Institute of Guangzhou University - a provincial key research base for humanities and social sciences, "Guangzhou Studies" Collaborative Innovation and Development Center under Guangdong Provincial Development of Education, and the decision-making consultancy and innovation team for integrated development of Guangzhou - a provincial university innovation team of Guangdong.

[2] Head of the research group: Tu Chenglin (researcher, doctoral supervisor). Members: Liang Ningxin (associate researcher, Ph.D.), Tan Yuanfang (professor, Ph.D.), Zhou Lingxiao (associate professor), Yao Huasong (Associate Professor, Ph.D.), Ou Yangzhi (distinguished professor), Zhou Yu (Ph.D.). Author: Liang Ningxin.

0.7 percentage points higher than that of the whole nation (6.7%) and that of the whole province (7.5%) respectively, and the regional per capita GDP exceeding USD20,000. The public finance budget revenue was RMB139.4 billion, up 5.2% over the previous year[3]. Stable economic operation and steady growth of local fiscal revenue laid a solid material foundation for the implementation of Guangzhou's policy of improving people's livelihood and the promotion of social development. As to social development in 2016, Guangzhou continued to place the improvement in people's livelihood on top of the agenda, applied the bottom-line thinking, delivered all the ten promises it made at the beginning of the year to improve people's livelihood,, fully promoted the formation of inclusive and shared social security system, constantly strengthened the institutional innovation for social development and management, and made Guangzhou a safer place. It maintained a steady growth momentum in several important fields concerning people's livelihood and social governance, e.g., improving the old-age services and facilities and innovating the social governance system.

i. Promoting the people-centered fiscal policy and the equalization of public services

In 2016, Guangzhou, aiming at improving weak links in social development and people's livelihood, continued to implement the people-centered fiscal policy. Over 70% of the government revenue was spent on improving people's livelihood to continuously promote the equalization of public services such as education and enhance people's happiness and sense of gain. In 2016, Guangzhou invested RMB5.08 billion in this regard, and addressed the 10 biggest concerns of the people rated by polls through various channels. It increased input to narrow the gap in public services such as education, medical treatment and health care in different regions, between urban and rural areas, and between groups, and push forward the equalization of public services. According to the United Nations Development Programme (UNDP), Guangzhou continued to lead Chinese cities in the Human Development Index (HDI) in 2016, close to the level of quasi developed countries[4].

-- The equalization of education was significantly promoted, and the delivery of compulsory education for children of the floating population began to make progress. In 2016, Guangzhou, aspiring to grow into a provincial model city in modern education, promoted balanced and high-quality compulsory education. Through

---

[3]   Source: Guangzhou Statistics Bureau and *2017 Guangzhou Municipal Government Work Report*. The data below, unless otherwise specified, is provided by the departments concerned.

[4]   *Guangzhou human development index ranks first in China*, Guangzhou Daily, December 5, 2016

resource input and institutional innovation, it built, renovated or expanded 129 primary and secondary schools in 2016, increasing the admission capacity by 160,000. At present, the city is 100% covered by standard public schools providing compulsory education, and the admission capacity of good schools is growing. Among them, the number of active students in provincial key and above vocational schools accounts for 80.59%, an increase of 12,600 students over 2011. The compulsory education in three sub-districts also saw balanced development. All the 11 districts in the city were rated as "Counties with Basically Balanced Compulsory Education in China". In the year, Guangzhou was listed a model city in educational modernization in Guangdong. By implementing the pre-school education action plan, Guangdong made its pre-school education more inclusive, benefiting more citizens. At present, 97% of the towns have at least one public standardized kindergarten, and there are 1,285 public and private kindergartens in total in the city, covering 74% of eligible children. In the meantime, Guangzhou introduced Measures on Compulsory Education for Children of the Floating Population in 2016, which is expected to be fully implemented in 2017, including introducing the points-based entrance system and subsidizing public and private schools taking children of the floating population, etc.. According to a series of polls on "Citizens' Evaluation of Guangzhou's Urban Situation" released by Canton Public Opinion Research Center[5], in 2016, 50% of the citizens were satisfied with educational services, an increase of six percentage points over 2015, and only 17% were "dissatisfied" or "not quite satisfied". High-income earners had higher satisfaction rate which was 57%, up nine percentage points from 2015, and the satisfaction level reached a new high of five years, higher than that for medical services (40%), elderly care (39%) and other livelihood services. In addition, the dissatisfaction with education fell below twenty percent for the first time (17%), reflecting citizens' affirmation of the equalization of educational services in Guangzhou.

-- The community-level medical service system was improved and the equalization of medical services promoted. In 2016, Guangzhou launched the "Community Health Service Promotion Project" to build medical service circles accessible within 15 minutes. Through the subsidy mechanism for pediatrics and standardized training of general practitioners and resident doctors, Guangzhou concentrated efforts to improve the service capacity of community-level medical institutions including township hospitals and village health stations. In 2016, Guangzhou improved the family doctor services and explored the incentive mechanism for contracted services in

---

[5]   Canton Public Opinion Research Center: *Public evaluation of social services is improving, most significant in public transport services*, http://www.c-por.org/index.php?c=news&a=baogaodetail&id=3735&pid=5

community-level medical institutions, giving priority to the elderly, infants, pregnant women, people with chronic diseases and the disabled. It continued to establish and improve the medical consortium system and the tiered diagnosis and treatment mechanism, explored the implementation of tiered diagnosis and treatment of chronic diseases such as hypertension and diabetes under the medical consortium system, delegated the power of making definite diagnosis for some outpatient chronic diseases to community hospitals, and increased the reimbursement rate of medical insurance in community hospitals to guide residents to receive initial diagnosis at community-level medical institutions, thus achieving the purpose of tiered diagnosis and treatment. In 2016, Guangzhou introduced a new policy for outpatient chronic diseases, increasing the number of outpatient chronic diseases covered by the medical insurance to 20, and the limit of medicare reimbursement for employees from RMB150 per person per month to RMB200 per person per month with greatly simplified application procedures. In the first half of 2016 alone, the new policy benefited a total of 121,800 people. Among them, employees made 3,381,600 outpatient visits for chronic diseases, up by 15.92%, and the number of outpatient visits made by urban and rural residents also increased by 35.22% over the same period of the previous year. In the meantime, major public health services such as the screening of colorectal cancer, cervical cancer and breast cancer – the latter two for rural women were carried out in 2016 in Guangzhou. With continuous improvement of the basic medical service system, the implementation of the new policy and the promotion of major public health services projects, the level of medical service equalization was raised. According to a survey by Canton Public Opinion Research Center, respondents' satisfaction rate with medical services increased by 3 percentage points compared with that in 2015, and the proportion of satisfied citizens was 19 percentage points higher than that of the dissatisfied.

ii. The employment situation kept stable and the people's life was further improved

Employment is directly related to the survival and development of citizens and is an important part of people's livelihood. In 2016, Guangzhou's economic development faced complex domestic and international economic situations. In this context, Guangzhou, through deepening the reform in key areas, accelerated the construction of the Nansha New Area and the Pilot Free Trade Zone, enhanced the lead role of technological innovation, focused on the development of new business forms such as e-commerce, and started cross-border trade and e-commerce and other measures of expanding domestic demand, promoting investment, and stabilizing external demand.

Fixed-asset investment slowed down and stabilized. In 2016, the city made a total investment of RMB570.359 billion in fixed assets, with a year-on-year growth of 8.0%, exceeding that of Beijing and Shanghai. Foreign trade registered a steady growth. In 2016, the city's total import and export value reached RMB856.69 billion, with a year-on-year increase of 3.1%, higher than that of the nation (-0.9%) and that of the province (-0.8%). The consumption saw a steady rise, and the retail sales of consumer goods in the city for 2016 totaled RMB870.649 billion, up 9.0% over the previous year, with the growth rate ranking the first among the four Chinese first-tier cities. The "troika" that drove economic growth continued to exert force. In particular, positive progress was made in reform and innovation of key areas. The rapid development of major platforms such as the Nansha New Area and the Pilot Free Trade Zone has stimulated the development vitality and impetus of Guangzhou. According to statistics, in 2016, the number of newly registered domestic capital market entities in Guangzhou reached 242,100, an increase of 17.6%, and the registered capital stood at RMB770.255 billion, an increase of 42.5%. On average, 663 new registrations are made per day. The entrepreneurial atmosphere was soaring. In 2016, Guangzhou saw a net increase of 2,820 new technology enterprises, with an average of 7 births per day and the net increment ranking the second in China. A large number of pivotal enterprises including COSCO Shipping Bulk Co., Ltd., Cisco (China), and China Railway Tunnel Group are headquartered in Guangzhou. In 2016, the new industry in Guangzhou grew well, and new business forms (cross-border e-commerce) developed rapidly, and the investment in new fields continued to speed up. In 2016, by replacing the business tax with the value-added tax and reducing the medical, occupational injury and unemployment insurance rates, Guangzhou saved over RMB70 billion for enterprises, which motivated businesses to hire more, and eased the employment pressure on college graduates and people with employment difficulties to a certain extent. In 2016, Guangzhou promoted employment and reemployment of various forms by introducing a proactive employment policy, continuing to increase financial input, subsidizing college graduates who start their own business, promoting public-welfare job placements and skills training, etc. In 2016, Guangzhou registered 310,000 new employments and the urban unemployment rate of 2.4%. The employment prosperity index continually kept steady. The citizens' satisfaction rate with "resident employment" maintained a relatively high level for the past two years, which was above 30 percent (35%)[6].

---

[6] Canton Public Opinion Research Center: *Nearly half of Guangzhou citizens have a good sense of life*, http://www.c-por.org/index.php?c=news&a=baogaodetail&id=3742&pid=5

In 2016, the economy of Guangzhou operated steadily. The urban employment status was generally stable, which provided a strong guarantee for the growth of wage income. According to the *2016-2017 Report on Guangdong's Salary Survey* issued by South China Talent Market, the average monthly salary in Guangzhou reached RMB6,952[7]. The steady growth of income has provided a solid foundation for the continuous improvement of living standards. Stimulated by a series of policies of boosting domestic demand and consumption, against the background of moderate increase in the price index (a year-on-year growth of 2.7% in the year's urban consumer price index), the consumer market of Guangzhou saw a steady rebound. In 2016, the city's total retail sales of consumer goods registered RMB 870.649 billion, with a year-on-year increase of 9.0%, ranking the first among the four Chinese first-tier cities. The consumption structure of urban and rural residents has also been significantly improved and the consumption level has risen markedly, which is in line with the rapid growth of goods for luxury or developmental purposes (such as cars) and services (education), retail sales of above-designated-size daily necessities, cosmetics and Chinese and Western medicines increased by 22.9%, 16.6% and 12.9% respectively over the previous year; online consumption remained hot and above-designated-size online retail sales increased by 20.7%. Travel goods saw a good momentum of growth, with auto retail sales rising by 9.6%[8], which improved people's living standards continuously. According to a survey by Canton Public Opinion Research Center, 48% of the respondents were satisfied with the "living conditions" in 2016, up four percentage points from 2015, while only 10% were dissatisfied[9][10].

iii. The social security level was steadily improved, and residents' sense of gain was markedly enhanced

In recent years, Guangzhou has been adhering to people-oriented administration and the bottom-line thinking, giving top priority to meeting the needs of the people and improving their well-being. The public finance continues to lean significantly towards people's livelihood, the inclusive and shared social security system is constantly improved, the social security level steadily uplifted, and residents' sense of gain and happiness significantly enhanced.

---

[7] South China Talent Market, etc.: *Results of the pay survey in Guangdong for 2016-2017,* Dayoo.com, 16:55 November 16, 2016.

[8] Guangzhou Statistics Bureau: *Economic operation of Guangzhou in 2016,* see http://www.gdstats.gov.cn/

[9] Canton Public Opinion Research Center: *Nearly half of Guangzhou citizens have a good sense of life,* http://www.c-por.org/index.php?c=news&a=baogaodetail&id=3742&pid=5

-- The social security level in urban and rural areas was steadily improved, and residents' sense of gain was markedly enhanced. In 2016, Guangzhou's social security services continue to improve in all fronts. In terms of social assistance, after the unification of the urban and rural subsistence systems, the subsistence standard for urban-rural residents in 2016 was raised from RMB650 to RMB840. Throughout the year, a total of RMB410 million in subsistence allowance was granted to 48,000 urban and rural beneficiaries. After the regular adjustment to basic pension for urban and rural residents, the per capita monthly pension for corporate retirees increased from RMB3,200 to RMB3,316, with a per capita increase of RMB196.53/month, benefiting a total of 906,000 retirees. The per capita pension for urban and rural residents increased from RMB589/month to RMB624/month, benefiting about 400,000 urban and rural aged residents. As to medical insurance, while lowering the contribution rate for employees and freelancers, Guangzhou introduced a new policy for serious illness insurance: the reimbursement ceiling for employees was raised from RMB150,000 to RMB220,000. According to the hospitalization policy for employees, the overall payment rate of medical insurance was 85.3%. In accordance with the hospitalization policy for urban and rural residents with medical insurance, the payment rate was 60.48%. This has greatly reduced the medical burden on the insured. With the increase in urban and rural subsistence standard, medical aid and the relief for preferential groups have also risen. The maximum medical aid to serious diseases has been raised to RMB350,000 per person per year. In 2016, Guangzhou also introduced the public rental housing program, raised funds to build 28,000 indemnificatory apartments and provided 1,693 households with rental subsidies, easing the burden on fresh college graduates and households in need to some extent. The continuous increase of various subsidies and assistance allows the vast urban and rural residents to benefit from economic development and their sense of gain is significantly enhanced.

-- The application of information technology to medical insurance services and the implementation of the new policy alleviated the difficulty of getting medical services and the high cost of medical treatment. Guangzhou constantly tried to mitigate the problem with the access to medical services with the help of information technology. In 2016, Guangzhou released the WeChat official account of "Guangzhou Medicare", extending its counter service online. Citizens were provided with medical insurance services including location selection for outpatient services, online registration, policy consultation and online payment, so that they could stay at home to have relevant businesses handled. While continuing to upgrade the Pan-Pearl River Delta long-distance transaction, in 2016, Guangzhou launched full-scale IT-enabled inter-city direct clearing for medical expenses within the province. The insured could enjoy instant network settlement for remote medical treatment in 73 designated medical institutions in the province, which promoted the remote employment, remote elderly care and remote medical treatment of the insured in Guangzhou, and also alleviated the difficulties of getting medical services and reimbursement. In the meantime, in 2016, Guangzhou implemented for a new policy on outpatient chronic diseases that caused a heavy burden on residents due to the restriction of outpatient expense reimbursement, increasing the number of outpatient chronic diseases covered from 16 to 20 and the maximum monthly reimbursement to RMB200 per person per month for each disease. Meanwhile, Guangzhou made use of information technology to fully realize "one-stop" direct settlement of basic medical insurance, serious illness insurance, and medical assistance, so that the insured could conveniently and timely enjoy various medical benefits, effectively reducing the pressure of advance payment and the burden of medical expenses for urban and rural insured people.

iv. The system of integrated medical care and elderly care with Guangzhou characteristics began to take shape and the elderly-care industry was rising

By the end of 2015, the registered elderly population in Guangzhou had reached 1.475 million, accounting for 17.3% of the total holders of Guangzhou hukou. With the increasing of average life span, Guangzhou is faced with tremendous pressure of providing for the aged. Therefore, Guangzhou took full advantage of the national pilot reform of elderly care, and accelerated to refine policies and develop facilities for elderly care. Currently, the elderly-care system integrating medical services with Guangzhou characteristics and social participation began to take shape and the elderly-care industry is dawning.

-- The atmosphere of encouraging social forces to participate in old-age care services was created. Promoting the partnership among the government, the business and the general public in the delivery of services for the aged is an established path for Guangzhou to develop elderly-care services. In 2016, Guangzhou introduced the *Administrative Measures on Home-Based Elderly-Care Services in Guangzhou* and the *Action Plan for Strengthening Team Building for Elderly-Care Services in Guangzhou*. While continuing to build public elderly-care institutions and provide policy-oriented services for low-income old population, various measures to encourage and support social forces to participate in the construction of the elderly care system were launched one after another. By far, the city had built 149 home-based elderly service divisions, 24 comprehensive home-based elderly-care service centers, 1,460 elderly homes, 1,142 rural elderly activity sites, and 170 daycare organizations. In 2016, Guangzhou municipal government invested RMB92.59 million to start the pilot project of purchasing home-based elderly-care services: it purchased services for 13,000 old peoplein six groups who had no ability to work, no source of income, and no dependents; installed the "Ping An Tong" device for 41,000 households with elderly people over 80 years old for free; and delivered meal services for 363,000 elderly people in 106 neighborhoods and towns. In addition, through venture philanthropy with government investment and the engagement of enterprises and the society, in 2016, Guangzhou established 24 service projects for the elderly with an investment of about RMB4 million, carried out as many as 500 elderly service activities, directly serving nearly 15,000 people and indirectly serving 120,000 people.

-- Guangzhou sped up to build more nursing homes, seeing a rapid increase in the number of beds. In 2016, Guangzhou invested a total of RMB84.72 million to subsidize private elderly-care institutions. At present, the proportion of social capital investment in beds for the city's elderly-care institutions is near 70%. The construction of public elderly-care institutions is fully speeding up, focusing on the construction of "1+5" projects (the Guangzhou No.2 Nursing Home and the public elderly-care institutions in Tianhe, Huangpu, Huadu, Nansha, and Conghua districts), the expansion of "1+6" projects (the Guangzhou No.1 Nursing Home and the public elderly-care institutions in Yuexiu, Haizhu, Baiyun, Huangpu, Panyu, and Zengcheng districts), the geriatric rehabilitation hospital and other demonstration projects. In 2016, the number of beds in elderly-care institutions increased to 53,000, 40 per 1,000 elderly people, up 11% from 2015 (36), the highest among Chinese cities, meeting the goal set by the State Council (35-40 beds per thousand elderly people) five years in advance.

-- The elderly care system integrating medical care with Guangzhou characteristics started to take shape and the elderly-care industry was dawning. It is an established policy in Guangzhou to integrate health care with elderly care based on the physical and mental characteristics and needs of the elderly. For this purpose, Guangzhou introduced a variety of incentives to promote the integration. At present, there are 44 elderly-care institutions with internal medical service facilities in Guangzhou, and 23 of them are covered by the basic medical insurance. Various health service institutions, especially community-based ones, took the initiative to participate in community elderly-care services. In 2016, 103 medical institutions signed contracts to work with nursing homes. In the field of community old-age care, more than 98% of the city's community health service institutions proactively provided contractual services for community elderly-care institutions, daycare institutions, rural nursing homes and households with old people to promote the development of elderly care services integrated with medical care. After one year's efforts, the participatory old-age service system integrated with medical care has taken shape. Meanwhile, Guangzhou also leveraged market forces and introduced the world leading CCRC (Continuing Care Retirement Community) old-care model through policy support. Two large healthcare communities of "elderly care and health preservation + health management" with investment of RMB five billion by enterprises are under construction, of which, Yuekang Park in Luogang has been put into use. The elderly care services covering elderly education, elderly tourism, domestic services for the old, and the production and sale of old-age products and supplies are booming, and the old-age industry is at dawn.

v. The innovation in social governance continued to deepen and efforts continued to be intensified

In 2016, Guangzhou continued to transform its traditional governance pattern with platform thinking and explore in depth the construction of grassroots-level social governance system, actively developed various social organizations and continued to establish the governance framework and social mechanism suitable for the participation of diverse players, fully advanced the construction of the grid system, continued to deepen innovation in social governance with increasing efforts.

-- Vigorously developing various social organizations and promoting innovation in social governance. Social organizations with rich types, standardized operation and good cooperation with the government and the market have played an irreplaceable role in forming a perfect social governance system and improving the social governance manner. Therefore, Guangzhou has been trying to perfect the social governance system by developing various social organizations and integrating them into the overall design of social governance. Guangzhou not only promoted the development of social organizations by formulating laws and policies, but also cultivated various social organizations by means of social organization cultivation bases and government purchase of healthcare services. Through aiding ways of welfare lottery and public welfare funds, as of 2016, Guangzhou had established 39 cultivation base networks at such three levels – city, district (county-level city), and neighborhood (town) levels. All through the year, there were more than 1,200 social organizations moving into these cultivation bases, and quite a number of grassroots organizations had successfully transformed into formal organizations that were in conformity with existing norms and officially registered. Fueled by government purchase of services, private social service institutions developed rapidly. By September 2016, there had been 417 private social service institutions in Guangzhou, the most in the country. Thanks to government purchase of services and incubators, the number of registered social organizations in Guangzhou jumped to 6,845 (by September 2016), of which 2,608 were social groups, 4,214 were private non-enterprise units and 23 were non-public foundations. The development of social organizations in Guangzhou not only promoted social services, but also enhanced the social governance capacity at the community level.

-- With the improvement of grassroots governance capacity as the goal, a participatory grassroots governance framework was established. In 2016, Guangzhou continued to transform the traditional governance pattern with platform thinking, strengthened the community level governance platform and system construction, continued to introduce the legal consultant system to urban and rural communities, and introduced the community service system for Party representatives, deputies to the people's congress and CPPCC members. At the same time, Guangzhou vigorously developed and activated various community-based social organizations of public welfare, service and autonomy in urban and rural community level areas, and actively built various platforms and operational mechanisms suitable for community-based social organizations in serving community residents, meeting their needs and promoting community development. At present, a community-based social governance framework, involving various organizations, social workers and community elites, is taking shape.

In particular, since 2016, Guangzhou has continued its pilot project of constructing residents' consultative system in urban communities, with good results yielded. By setting up an autonomous consultative platform for community affairs with the engagement of multiple stakeholders such as the community residents committee, resident representatives, property management company and community police (such as in the form of "residents' discussion hall", etc.), it adopts the "one matter, one meeting" policy for hot issues including square management, pet management, parking management, elevator refitting for old buildings, and neighborhood disputes. It is implemented after the democratic consultation by all the parties in the community and is subject to the supervision of residents, which has overcome what's difficult to be fulfilled under existing community autonomy. By 2016, a total of 184 consultative platforms had been built in Guangzhou, which helped solve 6,779 above-mentioned hot issues, and install 410 elevators in old buildings. The participatory community governance framework has brought great changes to many communities. More than 55% of the communities are marked with harmony and the strong sense of belonging among residents.

-- Fully promoting the construction of the grid system, with full coverage of grid service management in urban communities. In 2016, Guangzhou fully promoted the construction of the grid service management system. By the end of the year, grid-based service management centers had covered 10 districts and 162 town/neighborhood-level communities, extending grid service management to all urban communities. By means of information technology, the information of people, places, objects, things, organizations, etc. within the grid was updated in real time in the database for management. Guangzhou had initially mastered the basic information of community residents and any change to it and realized seamless connection of communities and grids, which facilitated relevant management and services departments to conduct full-coverage management and services for affairs within the grid. In 2016, the grid-level case settlement rate in Guangzhou was above 96%. The grid management system has become an important means for Guangzhou to promote community services and management.

vi. Vigorously promoting the construction of "Safe Guangzhou" and maintaining social harmony an stability

In 2016, Guangzhou continued to strengthen the construction of a three-dimensional prevention and control system for public security, and promote the supervision of food and drug safety. The construction of "Safe Guangzhou" was advancing steadily, and the overall social situation was harmonious and stable.

-- Special rectification was carried out, and the construction of safe Guangzhou achieved remarkable results. In 2016, Guangzhou continued to promote the construction of a three-dimensional prevention and control system and investigated and rectified 26,600 illegally-leased apartments. The rectification of safety hazards in villages in the city and specialized remediation of market pipelines achieved substantial results. The comprehensive governance of public security was further advanced, the social order management was well-organized, and the construction of safe Guangzhou had yielded remarkable results, with continuous declining crime reports and rising satisfaction and sense of security of the masses. According to statistics of Guangzhou Municipal Public Security Bureau, by the end of November 2016, the criminal cases in Guangzhou continued to drop, down by 13.8% on a year-on-year basis. According to a survey by Canton Public Opinion Research Center,

94.5% of the respondents felt safe and 94.1% were satisfied with public security in 2016. In another survey by the Center, in 2016, 61% of the respondents were satisfied or relatively satisfied with the "social order" in Guangzhou, up 13% from 2015, while the proportion of the dissatisfied dropped to 11%[11].

-- A massive food safety campaign was launched and the situation of food and drug safety was getting better. In 2016, Guangzhou carried out the "Year of Food Safety" to strengthen the supervision of food and drugs, and continuously conducted special campaigns against counterfeit and shoddy goods. Through patrols, inspections, supervisions, spot checks and purpose-specific examinations, Guangzhou Food and Drug Administration supervised and spot-checked all the local food production enterprises and key business entities throughout the year, covering all the food varieties in a total of 28,400 batches of samples, making Guangzhou a national demonstration city for food quality. In 2016, there was no major food safety incident in Guangzhou, and the situation of food and drug safety was generally stable and maintained a good trend.

II. Challenges and Problems Faced by Guangzhou in Social Development in 2016

In 2016, the economic and social development in Guangzhou was generally better than expected, but many challenges existed in the external environment and the internal structure and quality. For example, systematic integration of the social security system and in-depth reform of the education and medical systems still had a long way to go, and there was still some gap from the citizens' demand for medical care, elderly care, education, housing and other issues that were vital to their interests. In particular, the soaring housing price and rent scared away many workers, would affect the optimization of population structure. The social development was still relatively lagging behind, and the community-level social governance was not keeping up with profound changes in the social structure, with poor awareness of participation. The consumption environment was to be improved, the general consumption experience was not that satisfying, especially the food & drug consumption, and the security of personal information remained a prominent concern. We must have a clear understanding of these problems, and properly solve them in the process of deepening the reform and accelerating the development.

In view of the social development in Guangzhou in 2016, the following issues deserve our special attention:

---

[11]Canton Public Opinion Research Center: *Guangzhou citizens' evaluation of social order is further improved*, http://www.c-por.org/index.php?c=news&a=baogaodetail&id=3747&pid=5

i. The main body of community governance was still underdeveloped and the community-level governance capacity was still weak

Guangzhou is a megalopolis with a 14 million permanent population. Urban communities are faced with growing disputes between residents, developers and property management companies while rural areas have a headache over the distribution of profits from land development or equity transfer etc.. These conflicts, if not properly handled, might easily trigger collective behaviors and escalate into public order cases and criminal cases, threatening social harmony and stability. Moreover, the community-level governance capability was still weak due to imperfect laws and regulations governing the autonomy by urban and rural residents and home owners, poor awareness of participation in community affairs, the underdeveloped main body of community governance and poor organization at the community level. The underdevelopment of main body of community governance was related to the inadequate development of community resident organizations. The weak community-level governance was due to the deficiency in policy, status recognition and organizational capability for community governance.

This was mainly manifested in the following aspects. Firstly, the legislation was of low level and the provisions on social organizations participating in community-level social governance were not clear. The relationship between the government and social organizations was not completely straightened out, and the regulations on social organizations' participating in community governance were unclear. In particular, Guangzhou is a city of immigrants, but it fails to define forms and methods for encouraging immigrants to engage in community governance through all kinds of community organizations. It's still difficult to establish social organizations targeting immigrants, or launch activities for them, or for them to participate. Secondly, social organizations lacked independence. At present, the resources of social organizations are mainly acquired through the government purchase, and few are from venture philanthropy projects and external foundations through bidding, as a result of which, social organizations are strongly dependent on government departments for resources. The lack of independence hindered their cooperation with the government. A considerable number of government departments often took social organizations as subordinate units, making it difficult for the latter to participate equally in local grassroots governance. Thirdly, social organizations faced objective restricts in participating in social governance. Due to the limited fund-raising channels, social organizations could hardly provide competitive salaries for their employees, resulting in their insufficient capacity of social governance. In addition, the internal governance structure of social organizations was not perfect and no attention was paid to the establishment of public credibility, which led to their woefully inadequate capability of community governance.

ii. The contradiction between the increasing demand for public services and the sluggish supply remained prominent

In recent years, Guangzhou has implemented the people-centered fiscal policy and been trying to increase the supply of public goods to improve people's livelihood, but with social and economic development and a growing population, the demand for public services especially high-quality ones has been growing rapidly. But currently, the supply of public services is inadequate, and the supply-demand contradiction featuring low quality of supply remains prominent. Taking pre-school education as an example, according to the prediction by Health and Family Planning Commission of Guangzhou Municipality, with the implementation of the two-child policy, the total number of registered births in Guangzhou in 2016 was near 120,000, while the total number of births by non-permanent population in Guangzhou was about 200,000. It will peak in 2018, with the births of registered population reaching about 140,000 and the births by non-Guangzhou permanent population reaching 230,000. The increase of births has raised higher requirements for preschool education facilities. However, since preschool education is not compulsory, it receives little input from government finance. Currently, the pre-school education fund of Guangzhou accounts for around 2% of the total education fund (compared to 5.9% in Shanghai), which leads to inadequate preschool education facilities for children, especially high-quality and non-profit ones. According to statistics, in 2015, the number of school enrollments in standardized kindergartens in Guangzhou was 389,092, accounting for 87.39% of the total number of students. In other words, nearly 13% of children received pre-school education in kindergartens that did not meet the basic conditions for school running. The enrollments in kindergartens with relatively complete educational facilities and of provincial and municipal Class-I standards occupied only 18.8% of the total number of students. Only 74% of the kindergartens were inclusive, subsidized by the government and charged fairly. Therefore, it has always been "difficult to enter public kindergartens, expensive to enroll in private kindergartens" in Guangzhou. Expensive high-quality preschool education has, to a certain extent, impeded the implementation of the two-child policy in Guangzhou and is adverse to the improvement of the population quality. Correspondingly, quality compulsory education resources are far from enough to meet the needs. According to statistics of Guangzhou Municipal Education Bureau, in 2014, the number of primary schools in Guangzhou that reached the standards for public standardized schools was 777, accounting for 65.10% of the total. In other words, only 65.10% of pupils in the city received compulsory education in public standardized schools. Among them, Yuexiu District boasted the highest proportion (96.3%), while in Baiyun, Huadu and Tianhe where the floating population is concentrated, the proportion of pupils receiving compulsory education in public standardized schools was 47.8%, 55.2% and 53.2% respectively. Moreover, the quality education resources in Guangzhou are geographically concentrated in the old urban quarter. The residence-based enrollment and fixed-point enrollment policy gave privilege to school estate in Yuexiu District, etc. Every year, the scope of admission and the allocation of enrollment quota are the biggest concern of parents. And the old, poorly-maintained and crowded apartments in the designated areas see their price surging year after year, arousing heated discussions in the society. How to balance the allocation of quality compulsory education resources for children of school age is a prominent issue faced by Guangzhou in the equalization of education.

iii. The aging society and its elderly care system were far from meeting economic and social development needs in Guangzhou

At present, the registered elderly population over 60 years old in Guangzhou has reached 1.264 million, exceeding 10% of the city's population. The average life expectancy of registered permanent residents in Guangzhou is 81.72 years. It is worth affirming that Guangzhou has been leading the country in cultivating the elderly care system, promoting the integration of medical treatment and old-age care, and boosting the construction of the elderly care system. Meanwhile, we should note the aging society and elderly care system still lags far behind economic and social development needs in Guangzhou. Firstly, there is a sharp contradiction between the ever-growing demand for elderly-care services and the inadequate old-age service facilities. In fact, the needs of the elderly population are stratified according to their age and health status. The young and middle old have healthcare and cultural needs and other needs, while the population of advanced age and the disabled old people need more assistance with their daily life. At present, among the elderly people with a Guangzhou hukou, about 240,000 are disabled or half-disabled and about 170,000 are of an advanced age. As a result of the one-child policy, a considerable number of advanced-age, disabled or half-disabled old people have the "rigid demand" for living in the nursing institutions. However, there is a serious shortage of public nursing institutions for low-income and needy elderly people. As a result of the sharp contradiction between the growing demand for institutional elderly-care services and the lagging service facilities, low-income elderly people often have to stay on the waiting list for years before they are accepted. Secondly, the huge demand of the young and middle old has not been fully met. With the improvement of living standards and medical treatment level, the elderly population of low and middle ages has great demands for physical health care, culture and entertainment, education and retirement life. However, many products and services available fail to meet their expectations. Taking the university for the aged as an example, it is an important facility for the elderly to realize self-fulfillment and meet their spiritual needs. However, there are only a small number of elderly universities in Guangzhou and the enrollment is insufficient. Although the programs they offer might not totally adapt to the needs of the elderly, the competition for the enrollment is still fierce. How to raise public awareness of the contribution by the old population and meet their various needs is a question the government, the society and enterprises should all well consider. This is a challenge, but it could also create opportunities for Guangzhou's economic development.

III. The Trend of Guangzhou's Social Development in 2017 and Suggestions

In the year 2017, Guangzhou will deepen the supply-side structural reform and promote the merger and restructuring of enterprises as well as market clearing. As to social   development, in 2017, Guangzhou will adhere to the principle of serving the people and giving priority to people's livelihood, give play to the support role of social policies, seek innovation in the social security system and upgrade social undertakings concerning people's livelihood. It will improve the urban and rural public security system, strengthen fine urban management, and promote reform and innovation in all aspects of social development. In addition, the city will focus on improving people's livelihood and innovating social governance, place more emphasis on doing practical things for people's livelihood, strive to improve the structure of social governance, and explore new ways for the coordinated development of economy, society, politics, culture and ecological progress.

Based on the work arrangement of Guangzhou, we believe that the social development in Guangzhou will show the following trends in 2017:

Firstly, the integration of urban and rural development will be accelerated and the allocation of public resources balanced. *TheOpinions of the CPC Central Committee and the State Council on Further Strengthening Urban Planning, Development and Management* introduced in February 2016 clearly emphasizes to "create convenient and accessible life circles and generate more benefits for people through joint contribution and sharing". In alleviating urban problems, the new development areas play an irreplaceable role. The urban subway in Guangzhou is undergoing vigorous development, and new subway lines are extending and the new development zones in the east may receive more attention. In new development areas and urban renewal, priority should be given to public service facilities for transportation, education, medical services, culture, sports and so on, so as to promote the balanced allocation of public resources. This shall be emphasized for new-new development areas including Huangpu, Nansha, Zengcheng. For example, Zengcheng proposes to stay oriented toward making up for deficiencies in social development, particularly focusing on the quality supply of education, medical and housing resources, expedite more balanced allocation of public resources, and intensify efforts to enhance the people's sense of happiness and gain. Therefore, it can be expected that in 2017, the urban-rural integration in Guangzhou will be further accelerated and the allocation of public resources balanced.

Secondly, the social security network and the public service system will continue to be improved. In 2017, the city will promote the innovation of the social security system and the coverage of social insurance to realize instant inter-city settlement of medical expenses within the province, and use the unemployment insurance to stabilize the employment situation. The coverage of basic public services for immigrants will be further expanded, and the compulsory education for their children will be fully popularized. In the meantime, in 2017, Guangzhou will further deepen the reform of the old-age service industry, carry out the national pilot project of combining medical services with elderly care and the first pilot long-term care insurance system, deepen the reform and innovation of home -based care services, promote the integration of medical services and elderly care, develop education for the aged, adapt the living environment to the needs of the elderly, launch the "Old-Age Health Action" and establish the meal service network. It can be estimated that the social security system in Guangzhou will see tremendous development in 2017, in particular in the elderly insurance and service system, and various needs of the elderly will be satisfied.

Thirdly, community governance will keep advancing and community-based social organizations will continue to develop. In 2017, Guangzhou will promote the democratic consultation and co-governance system at the community level, perfect the mediation mechanism for labor relation contradictions, help immigrants fit into the local society and promote collaborative innovation in social governance. The grid service management will be deepened, the construction of pilot community service complexes and pilot rural communities will be promoted, the strategy of "social worker +" will be innovated and implemented, and social workers will play an important role in community governance. According to the plan, an important starting point for community governance will be to promote the development of various types of community-based social organizations and give play to the role of platform governance. Therefore, it can be expected that in 2017, the fostering of various community-based social organizations in Guangzhou will speed up and the community social organizations will develop rapidly. All kinds of community organizations with the engagement of migrant workers will become an important platform for them to participate in community governance, integrate into Guangzhou, and perhaps contribute to the deepening of grid service management.

Fourthly, the level of public welfare will continue to rise, and the public safety concerns will be further emphasized and resolved. In 2017, Guangzhou will focus on improving the welfare conditions for the elderly, women and children, and actively promote the development of education, culture and health, and support the national fitness program. It will also continue to carry out the "Year of Food Safety" campaign, build into a national model city for food safety, and exercise the most rigorous whole-process supervision of food and drugs, to ensure food safety. Specifically, it promises to continue to do well in ten matters concerning people's livelihood, including increasing the supply of old-age services, maternal and infant facilities, housing, and basic education. Thus, in 2017, Guangzhou will input more resources in education, culture, healthcare, housing and other public welfare undertakings, to raise the public welfare level for urban and rural residents, and in particular, allow the elderly, women and children to benefit more from economic and social development.

Looking into 2017, we believe that improving people's livelihood remains the fundamental way to resolve social conflicts and problems in view of the current situation in Guangzhou, and lays the foundation for social harmony and stability and people's happiness and well-being. The key is to mobilize the market, the society and the government to work together in improving the basic living conditions and the social governance mechanism. In response to a number of issues in Guangzhou's social development in 2016, we put forward the following suggestions:

i. Develop the main body of community governance and improve the grassroots governance capacity

There are various objective conflicts of interests in urban and rural communities, and the key to mitigate them is to strengthen the main body of community governance, create participatory community governance models with joint consultation and cooperation, and enhance the grassroots governance capacity. First, Guangzhou should cultivate the main body of community governance. On account of limited resources, it's reasonable and legal for interest groups to appear while competing for resources , and the key is to cultivate the main body of community governance. Therefore, Guangzhou should vigorously develop various types of community organizations, and based on the local reality, support those engaged in charity aid, community services, culture & sports, community education, and community affairs. In areas where the floating population is concentrated, the focus is to engage them in community organizations, especially those dedicated to community affairs, and allow them to play a role in them, and resolve community-level conflicts as soon as possible. Second, Guangzhou should promote the establishment of a participatory and consultative mechanism involving all relevant stakeholders. In terms of policies, community-level social organizations should be allowed to participate in community governance, and the community council and other systems should be improved continuously. The government should continue to find out what the community residents need, rely on their wisdom, and consult them on policies and policy effects. All groups involved in community affairs and related public interest representatives shall be allowed to consult jointly, make mutual compromises and independent decisions, and supervise each other. To this end, it should refine laws and regulations on property management as soon as possible, boost the development of the home owners' committee, promote urban-rural self-governance by residents, and implement direct elections for village committees. It should also define the status and role of various organizations (especially community-based organizations of social workers and volunteers) and individuals (including the floating population) in participating in and supervising urban and rural community affairs, as well as measures to allow community residents without a Guangzhou hukou to participate in community affairs. Only in this way can urban and rural community residents effectively express their needs, integrate the interests of all stakeholders, and well protect their own interests. Third, Guangzhou should strengthen the capacity building of community organizations. On the basis of straightening out the relationship with the community residents committee and community-level social organizations, the government shall create favorable conditions for community-level social organizations to carry out activities independently. Differentiated guidance, regulatory requirements and priorities shall be imposed on different types of social organizations to help them improve the internal governance mechanism, build up credibility, create internal and external accountability mechanisms, and improve the management level.

ii. Continue to increase the supply of public services and promote balanced development of education

It is the responsibility of the government to provide public goods and services, including education, and improve the people's livelihood. Guangzhou has done a lot in education. In 2014, the city spentRMB22.904 billion on education, accounting for 16% of the annual local public expenditure. But preschool education is still to be further popularized and quality educational resources are insufficient. Guangzhou still has great space for improvement in promoting the balanced development of education. In view of this, the following suggestions are put forward:

Firstly, local legislation should be employed to increase the input in and popularize preschool education. Though the popularization rate of preschool education in Guangzhou rose to 74% in 2016, it's still far below the public's expectation. As an economically developed city, Guangzhou has the ability and obligation to increase the supply of educational resources to meet the public's needs, especially for preschool education. Considering the absence of relevant state laws and the difficulty of including preschool education into compulsory education, it is suggested that Guangzhou should, based on the respective size and criteria of preschool education for children with or without a Guangzhou hukou, conduct research and estimation, and define measures to finance preschool education through local legislation, so as to promote local governments to lean the expenditure structure towards preschool education, gradually raise the level of financial input, popularize preschool education, and allow all children alike to enjoy the fruits of economic development. Meanwhile, it should properly set standards on teacher training, professional title appraisal, tuition, etc. for public and private kindergartens, promote the uniform and standardized development of software and hardware facilities for inclusive preschool education, and make sure children receive proper education.

Secondly, Guangzhou should promote school district-based compulsory education, and solve the problem with equalized allocation of high quality compulsory education resources. Guangzhou no longer rates primary or secondary schools. The "provincial" and "municipal" key schools were in the history. The non-provincial key schools active in educational innovation are also recognized by the educational circle and parents. In fact, in September 2016, five primary and secondary schools in Guangzhou were incorporated into Pui Ching Education and Yucai Education Group, two educational groups which share high-quality educational resources among their member schools to promote the balanced development of education. Therefore, it is suggested that Guangzhou, on the basis of summing up the experience and lessons of existing educational groups, introduce applicable measures, continue to increase investment, encourage prestigious schools to help with the disadvantaged through partnership or trusteeship, promote school district-based compulsory education, and increase the supply of quality educational resources to meet the urgent needs of parents and students.

iii. Measures shall be taken to promote development of the silver industry in Guangzhou

In 2015, the registered elderly population over 60 years old in Guangzhou reached 1.475 million, accounting for 17.3% of the registered population, and that of elderly people over 65 years old reached 988,000, accounting for 11.6% of the registered population. In addition, in the floating population, there were nearly 200,000 people above 60 years old[12]. The old population is big and growing rapidly. Nationally, the number of old people above 60 years old in 2016 reached 212 million, of which 137 million were aged 65 and above. To provide for the huge old population, Guangzhou has been actively developing old-age services and exploring their integration with medical services, with some achievements made. However, all this is done based on the hypothesis that the elderly population is a burden on the society, and limited within the city. In fact, the elderly population not only poses an enormous challenge for Guangzhou's economic and social development, but also creates a major opportunity for the restructuring of its economy. Therefore, the following suggestions are put forward:

Firstly, Guangzhou should correct the bias against of the elderly population. Though no longer working and relying on the society for support, the old population still has certain spending power and it is a bias to be corrected that the senior population is a burden on the society. They are not a burden, but an asset for economic development. Therefore, Guangzhou needs to think out of box, leverage its strengths, foster a national vision, formulate as soon as possible the development plan for its elderly care services and industry with national significance, and take strong measures to promote the development of Guangzhou's silver industry.

Secondly, Guangzhou should define the old-age industry as an emerging industry. The elderly population is stratified according to health status and age, and elderly people of different ages and different health conditions have different product and service needs. Meeting their needs can promote economic development, so the elderly

---

[12] Guangzhou Committee on Aging: *Data summary of the elderly population in Guangzhou for 2015*, http://gzll.gzmz.gov.cn/gzsllgzwyhbgs/gzslnrkxz/201702/72b9bd61e2324912b0281100a90cd3b4.shtml

population is not an economic burden but a great asset for economic development. The development of products and services that meet the needs of the elderly can stimulate economic development in Guangzhou. Guangzhou has all the conditions ready to do this. For one thing, Guangzhou has a well-developed manufacturing industry with a sound market mechanism which can produce various products for the elderly. Meanwhile, Guangzhou has a thriving pharmaceutical industry, with mature traditional Chinese medicines and medical services, catering to the diverse health needs of the elderly. In addition, its culture and education businesses are well developed and can meet the needs of the low-age old population. Therefore, it is suggested that relevant departments and think tanks in Guangzhou take the lead, in cooperation with businesses, to formulate the development plan for the elderly industry that take into account both the local and national markets. The direction of the silver industry should be laid down based on the analysis of advantages, disadvantages, opportunities and challenges. Measures should be taken to grow the silver industry, boost domestic demand and stimulate economic growth.

Thirdly, Guangzhou should reasonably position the silver industry according to the actual situation. Guangzhou has a solid manufacturing base, developed medical and health institutions, and strong traditional Chinese medicine support from Guangzhou University of Chinese Medicine, etc. In particular, in terms of medical services, Guangzhou had 54 tertiary hospitals by the end of 2015, next only to Beijing and Shanghai. And nine of the Class-III Level-A hospitals are rated among China's top 100 hospitals, and 28 specialty departments including the cardiovascular and other old-age diseases in Guangdong People's Hospital and the First Affiliated Hospital of Sun Yat-sen University have entered the top 10 specialty departments in the country. Thus Guangzhou is fully capable of satisfying the needs of the elderly in a considerable number of areas. At the same time, Guangzhou has a developed exhibition and convention industry, is a national highland for social work, education and research, and is leading the country in providing social services for the elderly. Guangzhou should take all these advantages to find out its role in the old-age industry. Specifically, it is suggested that Guangzhou should be positioned to be the hub of elderly care business headquarters, the center for education, training and research on elderly services, the R&D center for high-tech elderly products, the exhibition, convention and marketing center for elderly-care supplies, and the medical service and rehabilitation center. The priority can be adjusted based on the demographic characteristics of the elderly.

Fourthly, policies and measures for developing the old-age industry shall be clarified.

It is suggested to set up a cross-department research group on policy for the development of Guangzhou's senior industry as soon as possible, integrate the government, research institutes and think tanks, and introduce policies and measures to encourage the development of the old-age industry and build Guangzhou into the hub of elderly care business headquarters, the center for education, training and research on elderly services, the R&D center for high-tech elderly products, the exhibition, convention and marketing center for elderly-care supplies, and the medical service and rehabilitation center. Upstream and downstream resources shall be integrated, and enterprises, medical and health institutions and various service organizations shall be encouraged to contribute to the rise of the silver industry in Guangzhou.

Reasons for Growing Doctor-Patient Conflicts and Countermeasures in Guangdong Province[1]

Tu Jiaying   Tu Chenglin[*]

Abstract: At present, medical disputes in Guangdong are becoming increasingly violent and arousing deeper public sentiment, which has brought negative impact on social stability. This paper analyzes main reasons for growing doctor-patient conflicts in Guangdong, with several countermeasures and suggestions put forward.

Keywords: Doctor-patient conflicts, collaborative governance, all regions

According to data released by Guangdong Medical Doctor Association and the People's Mediation Committee of Guangdong for Doctor-Patient Disputes, since 2014, the number of medical disputes in Guangdong has seen continuous decline, but the number of vicious medical disturbance and violence cases remains high. There are more than 500 cases each year, and 64.29% of medical staff having been abused, threatened, or experienced personal attack by patients or their families, far higher the national average level of 59.79% over the same period. The statistics on violence against medical staff released by *The Beijing News* in May 2016 also showed that among the 60 casesof violence against medical staff reported by the media from 2015 to May 2016, 12 were from Guangdong, making it the province with the highest frequency of violence against medical staff in China.

Medical disputes and doctor-patient conflicts are common phenomenon all over the world and not rare in European and American countries where the medical level is higher, thus requiring no special attention. But currently, medical disputes in Guangdong are becoming increasingly violent and arousing deeper public sentiment, so we have to be vigilant. Doctor-patient conflicts are getting off the track of the rule of law and evolving into fierce violent confrontation, which further triggers strong ethnic antagonism and social conflicts. This not only severely affects the normal

[1] This report is a research result of the National Social Science Fund's major program "Research on Safeguarding National Cultural Security from the Vision of Core Values" (14ZDA057) and the decision-consulting innovative team of Guangdong colleges and universities for comprehensive urban development of Guangzhou.
[*] Tu Jiaying, Desautels Faculty of Management, McGill University. Tu Chenglin, corresponding author, dean, professor and doctorate tutor of Guangzhou Development Research Institute, Guangzhou University.

medical order in Guangdong, but also has negative impacts on Guangdong's social environment and image, hence deserving further attention.

I. Reasons for the Growing Doctor-Patient Conflicts in Guangdong Province

The growing conflicts between doctors and patients in Guangdong are the result of multiple factors such as unreasonable allocation of medical resources, underdeveloped medical management system, the lack of doctor-patient-media trust, irrational medical treatment view of the public, non-professional engagement of public media, the spread of social impatience, weak law enforcement by public security organs, and low cost of private remedy.

i. The lack and uneven distribution of medical resources is the primary reason for frequent or growing doctor-patient conflicts

Seen from the perspectives of regions and attributes of medical institutions, in recent years, conflicts between doctors and patients in Guangdong have concentrated in the Pearl River Delta cities with abundant medical resources, such as Guangzhou, Shenzhen, Foshan and Huizhou. Medical disputes mainly occur at large and medium-sized public hospitalsat Grade-II and above,which adopt high-level medical technology. The abundance of medical resources and the rank of hospitals show an abnormal close positive correlation with the incidence of medical disturbances.

The root cause for this paradoxical phenomenon that violates the common rule is the imbalance of insufficient resources. Guangdong faces the problem that its per capita share of medical resources is below the national average and these limited medical resources are highly concentrated in the Pearl River Delta area and large and medium-sized public hospitals, while primary hospitals and private hospitals fail to perform the due function of diversion. As a result, large and medium-sized public hospitals in the Pearl River Delta area are overcrowded, making it particularly difficult for registration, diagnosis and treatment, payment, and fetching medicine. This leads to the outbreak of grievance and suspicion accumulated by patients or their families once the treatment effect does not meet their expectation. In particular, when a patient dies or is irreversibly injured, they will launch resentment-venting violent attacks on medical institutions and medical staff, which leads to vicious injuries and large-scale group and public sentiment incidents.

ii. Conciliatory law enforcement and improper handling by the law-enforcing departments directly lead to the growing doctor-patient conflicts

The analysis of the vicious conflicts between doctors and patients in Guangdong in recent three years which have caused great sensation in the society, for example, "pregnant pediatrician being beaten" in Changping Hospital of Dongguan in April 2016, the violence against medical staff in Baoan District People's Hospital of Shenzhen in October of the same year, shows that many incidents were originally some simple medical disputes, but they eventually escalated to incidents of public sentiment and violence against medical staff because of theimproper handling by local governments, public security organs and medical institutions, as well as their ambiguous and indecisive attitude toward disposal. At present, some primary-level public security organs in Guangdong do not regard themselves as law-executors but as peacemakers when handling medical disturbances and they dare not to enforce the law for fear of the intensification of conflicts. Instead, they like to give equal punishment to both sides to force them to accept mediation. Actually, such so-called conciliatory law enforcement is to connive at illegal acts. And those medical institutions in medical disturbance always try to stay away, pass the buck, dare not to bear responsibility, while thinking about how to patch up a quarrel and reconcile the parties concerned. Due to the lack of effective coordination between public security organs and medical institutions, the "zero tolerance" proposed by Health and Family Planning Commission of Guangdong Province has become an empty slogan. Seemingly, the overly conciliatory law enforcement by public security organs alleviates conflicts, but in fact, it knowingly allows medical disturbances and causes greater conflicts and even group and public sentiment events.

iii. The disorderly speculation by social media and the lack of mainstream media's guidance have pushed medical disputes into the public spotlight and extended the antagonism

Disorderly dissemination by online social media and netizens' irrational comments and dissatisfaction catharsis have further deteriorated the discordant relationship between doctors and patients and sown the seeds of mutual distrust and hatred for doctor-patient conflicts. Local mainstream media organizations fail to voice their opinions, guide the public with correct information, or help to release the antagonistic emotions between doctors and patients. Due to the lack of guidance by mainstream media organizers, adverse remarks spread wantonly, which caused growing distrust and disappointment of the public in Guangdong's medical system. The combination of the two undoubtedly causes the patients to tend to solve medical disputes through private power.

For example, for the May 7 Incident during which Dr. Chen Zhongwei was stabbed to death, according to the survey results of Kdnet (a data research center) and Jinan University@ Public Opinion Observation Room (an official account), 81.22% of netizens showed "negative emotions" while only 18.78% had "positive emotions". As for such an abnormal emotional reaction online, some mainstream media organizations in Guangdong collectively failed to voice their opinions and did not take a stand, which was rare. Except *Southern Metropolis Daily*, GZTV News, xkb.com.cn and so forth which briefed the incident, there was no full-length news report or guiding comments published. Although the photos of doctors and medical students' spontaneous mourning at the Hero Square with candles were released by *Southern Metropolis Daily* on WeChat Official Account which received over 100,000 clicks, they were deleted one hour later.

iv. The trust crisis and group impatience are the social psychological reasons behind the escalation of conflicts between doctors and patients

The growing doctor-patient conflicts also expose to a certain extent the serious lack of trust between doctors and patients, between medical institutions and media in our province, and this distrust is based on the current trust crisis of the whole society. This is also the primary social psychological reason for the intensified conflicts between doctors and patients and their deterioration in Guangdong. The distrust leads to many doctors' adopting defensive treatment for self-protection, which raises the cost of medical treatment of patients imperceptibly, and the dishonesty in the medical system also lead to patients' extremely low trust in medical staff. Thus, in the event of death, they will make their own conclusion that it was due to the improper treatment by the medical staff, and make violent attacks on medical institutions and medical staff, including abuse, sieving and smashing the establishment.

Another important social factor is the prevalence of impatience in our society and such impatience is prevalent among such three groups as medical staff, media and patients. The medical staff race against time in haste and have no patience to answer questions of patients. The media vie for the timeliness of news and start reporting without questioning the news source; if it turns out to be a mistake, "plot reversal" will get things over. Netizens will become irritated at the news of conflicts between doctors and patients and start verbal attacks arbitrarily and tend to have sympathy for the disadvantaged without learning about the truth. Patients are impatient in the medical treatment, waiting, dispute resolution and they are eager for medical effects and strain to seek medical services in large hospitals for whatever illness. When waiting for diagnosis, they always wish to be given priority to and hold that their own illness needs the most urgent care, which is the reason why the Emergency Department in Guangzhou is the place where the most severe doctor-patient conflicts occur.

II. Countermeasures to Solve the Growing Doctor-Patient Conflicts in Guangdong Province

i. Establish the concept of interdepartmental and multi-level collaborative management of conflicts between doctors and patients, and speed up the improvement of organizational and institutional guarantee mechanisms

In the short term, the urgent problem to be solved in management of doctor-patient conflicts in Guangdong is to curb the violent and public sentiment trend as soon as possible and set up relevant mechanisms to urge related parties to solve the conflicts according to law. In the long run, the problem of inadequate and unaffordable medical services should be solved to rebuild trust between doctors and patients, so as to fundamentally eliminate the causes for doctor-patient conflicts. However, practical experience at home and abroad has proved that the management of doctor-patient conflicts is a complex and long-term process that needs a strict and sound guarantee system, and cannot be done overnight with any campaign of severe measures. Moreover, the increasingly fierce conflicts between doctors and patients in Guangdong are beyond the disposal capacity of the medical system, and it is impossible for healthcare authorities and medical institutions alone to fundamentally solve the current increasingly sharp conflicts between doctors and patients.

It is necessary to introduce and adopt the concept of collaborative governance in building the institution and mechanism for solving conflicts between doctors and patients. It is suggested that the Steering Committee for Co-Governance of Doctor-Patient Conflicts be established under the provincial, municipal and county-level governments, with deputy provincial governor (mayor of city, head of county) as Director of the Committee, and the members consist of heads of healthcare, general administration, justice, public security, finance, publicity, civil affairs, insurance supervision, medical dispute mediation committee, industry associations, etc., with the permanent office set in the Health and Family Planning Commission. The Steering Committee shall mainly be responsible for system design, supervision and assessment, and to lead the participating units to jointly formulate governance planning and action plans. Meanwhile, at the provincial level, the *Measures for Collaborative Governance of Doctor-Patient Conflicts in Guangdong Province* shall be formulated speedily to clarify scope of responsibilities, target tasks and collaborative approaches of government agencies involved, with an accountability mechanism established.

ii. Construct a third-party conflict resolution mechanism with multi-agent coordination to further improve the institutional system of "third-party mediation and one insurance"

Firstly, it is necessary to further improve the third-party mediation mechanism in Guangdong and build smooth, reliable and optional complaint channels and mediation mechanism to gradually realize diversified and socialized development of third-party dispute resolution channels. In the urban area, based on the government-led medical dispute mediation committee, qualified public welfare organizations should be allowed to set up private medical dispute mediation institutions to operate with small profits, so as to provide patients with more options and build up trust. The government shall formulate corresponding entry and exit rules, conduct credit ratings and annual assessment on these medical dispute mediation agencies to ensure their standardized development. In rural areas, local celebrities and religious organizations should be encouraged to actively participate in the mediation of doctor-patient conflicts, and they should be included in the expert database of local medical dispute mediation committee. Secondly, we should accelerate the popularization and implementation of medical liability insurance and medical accident insurance in medical institutions and medical activities. The method of mandatory liability insurance for traffic accident can be adopted to require all medical institutions to purchase medical liability insurance. Provided it is not implemented, responsible persons of public hospitals will be subject to accountability; business licenses of private hospitals can be revoked. At the same time, patients are encouraged to purchase medical accident insurance for high-risk treatment, so as to ensure reasonable compensation even if it is not the fault of the hospital.

iii. Promote the building of "zero tolerance" and accountability mechanism in a coordinated way to safeguard normal medical order

First, local government and public security organs should have "zero tolerance" for occupational medical disturbance and violence against medical staff. In the case of medical disputes, local governments and public security organs should intervene promptly to ensure disputes are resolved under the legal framework. The public security organ shall crack down on occupational medical disturbance and violence against medical staff according to law immediately after its occurrence and resolutely curbs the social hostility with all their might. Local governments and public security organs should be held accountable for ineffective implementation of the "zero tolerance" system. Second, the government agencies in charge of healthcare and discipline inspection should have "zero tolerance" for medical institutions and medical workers that violate professional ethics. We should intensify the anti-corruption efforts in the medical industry and rebuild the trust of the public in the medical system. The medical staff that give extraordinary prescription at random or ask for red envelopes should be resolutely disqualified and blacklisted, so that any medical institution in the province will not employ them. Third, the publicity department should have "zero tolerance" for media organizations and news workers that disseminate false information on medical disputes and doctor-patient conflicts. The public media are forbidden from arbitrarily disseminating conclusive, biased and inflammatory news. The experience of Chengdu in handling fictitious news of the real estate industry should be drawn on, and media organizations and news workers that spread false information will be held fully accountable.

iv. Properly give play to the leading role of news media in public opinion, and promote the rebuilding of doctor-patient-media trust through a sound public opinion field

Nowadays, the public media profoundly affect or even control the standpoint and judgment of the public. Therefore, first of all, we should rationally make use of the media advantages of Guangdong and intensify the overall planning and dissemination of positive energy and warm stories in the medical industry, so as to reverse the current landscape of excessive exposure of medical disturbance and violence against medical staff. Secondly, governments at all levels should work out detailed plans for leading regular public opinions and managing crisis communication concerning doctor-patient conflicts, and formulate practical and feasible media publicity and control plans for official and civil public opinions. In the event of medical disturbance and violence against medical staff which arouse public opinions, local governments should timely release official information to curb the negative emotions on the Internet. The mainstream media should boldly follow up the whole incident with a high sense of responsibility and positively guide the online public opinions. Thirdly, in the age of mobile internet and social media, hospitals and medical workers should learn to voice their opinions through news media and microblog, WeChat and so on. They should enhance trust and dispel misconceptions in medical issues through scientific, professional and rational ways.

In the accident during which doctor Chen Zhongwei was killed, the Black Ribbon campaign launched by the medical staff on social media is a very good example.

v. Strengthen the training of communication skills for medical staff and ease conflicts between doctors and patients through humanistic care

According to statistics of Chinese Medical Doctor Association (CMDA), 90% of doctor-patient conflicts are caused by improper communication between the two sides. In particular, doctors' "undesirable words" often aggravate the conflicts. Therefore, the current situation that medical staff only focus on diseases and are indifferent to patients' inner feelings should be reversed promptly. And medical workers need to learn to properly talk with patients and enhance their communication skills. It is suggested that Guangdong Province should conduct a large-scale training on doctor-patient communication in large and medium-sized public hospitals to urge medical workers to acquire doctor-patient communication skills as soon as possible, with code of conduct for doctor-patient communication and exchanges formulated as quickly as possible. At the same time, all medical schools should attach importance to the development of students' communication skills, make communication skills a basic compulsory course for medical students, and offer rigorous training courses. The medical schools in the United States have listed the training of communication skills as one of the nine aspects needing to be enhanced for medical students in the 21st century. Courses on sociology and behavioristics for effective control of negative emotions, listening to patients and body language interpretation are introduced. All these deserve our studying.

vi. Practically evaluate the effects of relevant policies after intensive introduction and further strengthen research on countermeasures and policies

In recent years, Guangdong has introduced a series of policies on promoting the development of the medical industry and alleviating the conflict between doctors and patients. Although it needs a long time for the policies to take effect, we should effectively review, follow up and assess the implementation of the policies, promote the connection and continuous improvement of policies, and gradually improve the scientific and systematic basis of the medical policy system, so as to provide necessary policy guarantee for reducing the risk of doctor-patient conflicts. Especially for some policies with unsatisfactory effects, we need to strengthen market survey and policy research, identify the problems and clarify whether the system is defective or not properly implemented, and then improve it in a targeted manner.

Research on Guangzhou Residents' Evaluation of Living Environment

The research group of Guangzhou survey team of National Bureau of Statistics[1]

Abstract: In combination with questionnaire survey, this paper proposes a comprehensive evaluation system of living environment quality in Guangzhou to learn about residents' evaluation of the living environment in Guangzhou, analyzes aspects of the living environment that need to be improved, and puts forward policy suggestions for the building of livable Guangzhou.

Keywords: Living environment, comprehensive evaluation, livable

In recent years, Guangzhou has made remarkable achievements in urban construction and the living standard of residents has improved significantly. However, it still faces the contradiction between the living environment quality and the rising living demand of residents. This paper proposes a comprehensive evaluation index system for living environment to study the development and status of the living environment in Guangzhou, conducts survey of residents' satisfaction with the living environment, and calculates the degree of satisfaction with the living environment through a comprehensive evaluation scoring method. And on this basis, suggestions for improving the urban living environment and building Guangzhou into a livable place put forward.

I. Development and Changes of the Living Environment in Guangzhou

According to the comprehensive evaluation results of the development and changes of the living environment based on objective indicators, the index of living environment construction in Guangzhou maintained steady growth from 2005 to 2015 (hereinafter referred to as "the past ten years"), with an average annual growth rate of 14.4% (see Table 1).

---

[1] Members of the research group of Guangzhou survey team of National Bureau of Statistics include Yu Jiarong, Du Shujian, Li Rihong, Wen Yuantang, Pan Xu, and Qiao Yong. The text is attributed to Pan Xu and Wen Yuantang.

Table 1 Indexes of comprehensive evaluation of the development and changes of living environment

Index \ Year	Comprehensive evaluation index for the development and changes of living environment	Of which			
		Living environment index	Residential environment index	Ecological environment index	Infrastructure construction and public service environment index
2005	0.2046	0.0241	0.0981	0.0052	0.0773
2006	0.2677	0.0307	0.0951	0.0258	0.1163
2007	0.3665	0.0381	0.1014	0.0638	0.1634
2008	0.4052	0.0567	0.1424	0.0441	0.1623
2009	0.4587	0.0730	0.1013	0.0667	0.2180
2010	0.4498	0.0579	0.0722	0.0843	0.2357
2011	0.5534	0.0483	0.1127	0.1228	0.2699
2012	0.6098	0.0679	0.1205	0.1178	0.3040
2013	0.5964	0.0806	0.0851	0.1196	0.3114
2014	0.6567	0.0957	0.1067	0.1293	0.3263
2015	0.7878	0.1083	0.1495	0.1394	0.3886
Average annual growth rate	14.4%	16.2%	4.3%	38.8%	17.5%

i. The quality of ecological environment was greatly improved

In 2015, the number of days with excellent air quality in Guangzhou reached 312 days; the overall qualified rate of water supply was 99.99%; the year-end urban forestation area reached 153,000 hectares. Compared with 2005, the air, water quality and urban ecological environment had been significantly improved. In the past ten years, the index of eco-environment construction rose by 38.8% annually on average (see Table 1), with the fastest growth rate among the four types of environment indexes.

ii. The development of infrastructure and public service environment was accelerated, with hardware and software improved simultaneously

In the past ten years, Guangzhou has vigorously promoted the development of social undertakings, with an average annual increase of 17.5% in the infrastructure and public services environment index (see Table 1).

1. Transportation infrastructure developed rapidly

Firstly, the carrying capacity of the city's transportation continued to grow. At the end of 2015, buses (including electric vehicles) and taxis in Guangzhou increased by 71.3% and 30.4% respectively compared with 2005. The total length of metro lines put into operation increased by 231 kilometers over 2005. Secondly, the transportation capacity outside the city was further enhanced. The number of passengers carried by civil aviation of Guangzhou in 2015 was 1.1 times that of 2005. More than 10 railways for intercity bullet trains and high-speed trains were put into operation successively, making it possible to reach the surrounding cities within a few hours.

2. The level of public services including culture and education was constantly improved

Firstly, the cultural industry made continuous progress. By the end of 2015, there had been 161 cultural centers and 15 public libraries in Guangzhou, providing an enriching intellectual and cultural life for citizens. Secondly, the fitness activities flourished among the public, and the citizens actively participated in various fitness activities. In 2015, 2,300 fitness-for-all activities at the city, district and sub district levels and other sports contests were carried out, and a total of 8.555 million people participating in the fitness-for-all activities. Thirdly, education continued to develop and the educational expenditure in 2015 was 6.1 times that of 2005. Fourthly, the medical and healthcare level was constantly raised. At the end of 2015, the numbers of beds and health personnel in Guangzhou increased by 71.8% and 97.4% respectively from those in 2005.

3. The social security system was gradually improved

Firstly, the scope of social security had been expanding and the number of people covered by basic insurance increased significantly. By 2015, the numbers of people covered by basic pension insurance and basic medical insurance in Guangzhou were 5.7 times and 5.0 times those of 2005 respectively. Secondly, social security for low-income groups has kept improving. In 2015, the subsistence allowances in urban areas were 2.7 times that of 2005.

iii. The economy developed well, which provided strong material support for the improvement of living environment

In the past ten years, Guangzhou's economic growth brought along stable employment and provided a solid material foundation, with an average annual increase of 16.2% in the index of living environment construction (see Table 1). From 2006 to 2015, the GDP of Guangzhou increased at an average annual rate of 11.8%, and the registered urban unemployment rate stayed below 2.5%. The rapid economic growth and stable employment laid a solid foundation for the growth of residents' income and consumption. The per capita disposable income and expenditure for consumption of urban residents in Guangzhou saw an average annual increase of 10.6% and 9.1%

respectively from 2006 to 2015. The prices maintained a moderate upward trend, and the consumer price index (CPI) of Guangzhou saw an average annual increase of 2.7% between 2006 and 2015.

iv. Living conditions were increasingly improved and the quality of living environment was upgraded continually

In the past ten years, the housing supply and security in Guangzhou had been increasingly enhanced, the supporting facilities were improved continuously, and the index of residential environment construction increased by 4.3% annually on average (see Table 1). Firstly, the support for the improvement of housing conditions was guaranteed and the total investment in housing construction in Guangzhou in 2015 was 3.7 times that of 2005. Secondly, basic housing of some low-income groups was guaranteed. In 2015, the expenditure on housing support reached RMB7.98 billion.

From the perspective of supporting residential facilities, in 2015, the qualified rate of drinking water in Guangzhou was 100%, the gas popularization rate reached 99.8%, and the decontamination rate of domestic waste was 95.2%. All indicators achieved significantly better results than those for 2005. The community service function was further enhanced, with the number of urban community service facilities in 2015 increased by 332 compared with that in 2005.

II. Evaluation on Guangzhou Residents' Degree of Satisfaction with the Living Environment

The results of comprehensive evaluation of the living environment satisfaction degree through the survey show that the total score of living environment was 73.5 points, indicating that the development of living environment of Guangzhou in the past ten years had been recognized by residents. From the evaluation scores of the four elements that constitute the living environment, the score of infrastructure and public service environment was the highest, which was 76.6 points, and the living environment had the lowest score, which was 65.4 points (see Table 2). The rankings were consistent with those of environmental indexes in the comprehensive evaluation of the development and changes of the living environment for 2015, which indicated that residents' satisfaction with the living environment was highly correlated with the development of the living environment. Therefore, to increase residents' satisfaction with the living environment, importance must be attached to improving the quality of the living environment.

Table 2 Index scores for comprehensive evaluation of residents' satisfaction with the living environment

Index	Residents' overall satisfaction degree with living environment	Of which			
		Living environment	Residential environment	Ecological environment	Infrastructure construction and public service environment
Score of comprchcnsive evaluation index	73.5	65.4	68.1	73.8	76.6

i. The residents were satisfied with the living environment on the whole

The survey shows that the residents are relatively satisfied with the living environment, and the comprehensive evaluation index scored 73.5 points. According to the proportions of residents with different satisfaction degrees, 62.9% of respondents are very satisfied or relatively satisfied with the current living environment in Guangzhou (see Figure 1).

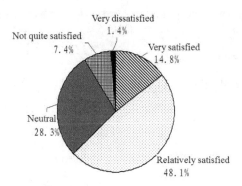

Figure 1: Proportions of evaluation on residents' degree of satisfaction with the living environment

ii. As for infrastructure and public service environment, residents were most satisfied with convenient transportation and most dissatisfied with road congestion and food safety issues

The score of comprehensive evaluation on residents' satisfaction with infrastructure and public service environment, which is 76.6 points, ranks first among the scores of the four elements of environment. Among them, residents are most satisfied with the convenience of transportation, with a degree of 90.4%, and the comprehensive evaluation index scores 86.3 points. Convenient transportation facilitates residents' shopping, and the degree of respondents' satisfaction with shopping convenience reaches 88.6%, with the comprehensive evaluation index of 84.8 points. The social security environment is also recognized by residents, and the comprehensive evaluation index of satisfaction with social security scores 80.1 points. The scores of residents' comprehensive evaluation on indicators such as the service quality of service counters, the quality of primary and secondary school education, the government's law-based administration, cultural and recreational facilities, recreational activities and consumer environment are all above 75.0 points, with the satisfaction degree above 70%.

The comprehensive evaluation index of traffic congestion has the lowest score, which is 61.5 points, and the satisfaction degree is only 32.6%. The survey of traffic congestion also indicates that up to 19.6% of the respondents think it is more congested than in the past. In addition, residents' comprehensive evaluation of food safety is also very low compared with other comprehensive evaluation indexes, which scores 65.3 points and the dissatisfaction degree reaches 16.4%.

Table 3 Comprehensive evaluation score and proportions of satisfaction degrees of the infrastructure and public service environment index

Index	Score of comprehensive evaluation index	Proportions of satisfaction degrees (unit: %)				
		Very satisfied	Relatively satisfied	Neutral	Not quite satisfied	Very dissatisfied
Public transport convenience	86.3	43.4	47.0	7.8	1.4	0.4
Smooth road	61.5	4.8	27.8	42.6	19.8	5.0
Shopping convenience	84.8	37.2	51.4	9.8	1.6	0.0
Guarantee for water, electricity and gas supply	85.4	35.0	57.0	7.8	0.2	0.0
Medical service	74.3	11.1	53.7	31.0	4.0	0.2
Medical security	74.7	11.2	56.0	28.3	3.8	0.7

Index	Score of comprehensive evaluation index	Proportions of satisfaction degrees (unit: %)				
		Very satisfied	Relatively satisfied	Neutral	Not quite satisfied	Very dissatisfied
Medical service	72.6	11.2	47.1	35.4	6.3	0.0
Medical security	72.6	9.1	52.4	32.0	5.3	1.2
Quality of primary and middle school education	79.5	18.5	62.1	17.9	1.3	0.2
Policies of primary and middle school education	75.4	15.0	54.2	24.6	4.8	1.4
Recreational facilities	78.0	15.7	61.1	21.0	2.0	0.2
Recreational activities	77.0	17.0	53.0	28.1	1.8	0.1
Consumption environment	76.2	12.1	60.6	24.0	2.6	0.7
Food safety	65.3	4.4	37.2	42.0	13.3	3.1
Social security	80.1	24.0	56.0	17.2	2.0	0.8
Service quality of subdistrict and neighborhood organizations and service counters	79.9	23.7	55.3	18.3	2.0	0.7
Law-based administration	78.3	15.9	62.3	19.8	1.4	0.6

iii. As for the ecological environment index, residents were highly satisfied with the forestation, but the degree of satisfaction with the cleanness of rivers, waterways and the air quality needs improving

The comprehensive evaluation index of ecological environment satisfaction degree scored 73.8 points, and residents' satisfaction degree was 63.5%. In particular, residents were most satisfied with a forestation, with a satisfaction degree of 82.0%, and the comprehensive evaluation index scored 80.7 points. The degree of satisfaction with the cleanness of rivers and waterways was only 39.6% and the comprehensive evaluation index scored 64.8 points. The degree of satisfaction with the air quality was 53.6% and the comprehensive evaluation index got 70.7 points, which reflects that there remained a gap from citizens' expectations about the cleanness of rivers, waterways and the air quality.

Table 4 Comprehensive evaluation score and proportions of satisfaction degrees of the ecological environment index

Index	Score of comprehensive evaluation index	Proportions of satisfaction degrees (unit: %)				
		Very satisfied	Relatively satisfied	Neutral	Not quite satisfied	Very dissatisfied
Air quality	70.7	12.0	41.6	35.6	9.6	1.2
Cleanness of rivers and waterways	64.8	5.1	34.5	42.6	14.9	2.9
Forestation	80.7	23.2	58.8	16.2	1.8	0.0
Tap water quality	76.2	17.2	53.0	24.2	5.0	0.6
City environment	76.3	13.4	58.4	24.8	3.0	0.4

iv. Residents' satisfaction degree with the living environment needs to be improved, and the key is to alleviate housing prices' impact on economy and residents' life

The comprehensive evaluation index of residents' satisfaction with the living environment got 68.1 points. 17.5% of the respondents were dissatisfied with the living environment because of the high housing price, while only 14.5% of the respondents were satisfied. According to the survey on residents' psychological affordability of housing price, only 6.4% of the respondents could accept the price of RMB25,000/ m² and above. There was a big gap between the price accepted by respondents and the actual price. However, we should notice although the housing price of Guangzhou was raising steadily, both the absolute value and the increasing rate ranked behind those of other first-tier cities in the country, which was a significant result of Guangzhou's effective regulation of the limited market.

Table 5 Comprehensive evaluation score and proportions of satisfaction degrees of the living environment index

Index	Index score of comprehensiv e evaluative	Proportions of satisfaction degrees (unit: %)				
		Very satisfie d	Relativel y satisfied	Neutra l	Not quite satisfie d	Very dissatisfie d
Residence situation	74.0	15.0	46.8	32.2	5.2	0.8
Community' s public facilities	74.0	14.4	48.6	30.0	6.4	0.6
Community' s integrated environment	73.7	12.2	53.8	25.4	7.6	1.0
Housing price	50.6	0.4	14.1	37.0	35.0	13.5

v. As for the index of the living environment, residents were relatively satisfied with the employment environment, but not very satisfied with the income and price

The comprehensive evaluation index of residents' satisfaction with the living environment scored only 65.4 points, and 16.1% of respondents were dissatisfied with the living environment. Specifically, the index of residents' comprehensive evaluation of income got the lowest score, which totaled 60.6 points. The index of comprehensive evaluation of the price level was also not high, which was 62.8 points. The numbers of respondents who were dissatisfied and satisfied with the income and price were both large. As sensitivity to price changes was greatly affected by the income level, such different survey results reflected the relatively wide income gap between the respondents.

Residents show proper recognition of the employment environment, with the comprehensive evaluation index scoring 72.0 points, and the satisfaction degree of employment environment was 55.9%.

Table 6 Comprehensive evaluation score and proportions of satisfaction degrees of the living environment index

Index	Score of comprehensiv e evaluation index	Proportions of satisfaction degrees (unit: %)				
		Very satisfie d	Relativel y satisfied	Neutra l	Not quite satisfie d	Very dissatisfie d
Price	62.8	2.2	33.8	42.6	18.6	2.8
Income status	60.6	2.4	27.4	43.3	24.4	2.5
Personal development prospects	66.2	3.9	34.0	51.8	9.7	0.6
Employment environment	72.0	9.9	46.0	38.5	5.4	0.2

III. Suggestions for Improving Urban Living Environment

On the whole, Guangzhou's living environment is being improved, but the internal development was imbalanced. Specifically, residents made higher evaluation of ecological environment, infrastructure and public service environment for public use than that of living environment and residential environment for individual use. The suggestions are as follows:

i. Efforts should be made to solve the three major problems of low traffic management level, disorderly parking, and frequent road construction to smooth the traffic

According to survey, the respondents think that the traffic congestion in Guangzhou was mainly caused by low level of traffic management, random parking and frequent road construction in addition to the objective factor of too many cars. To address this, firstly, we should improve the traffic management level, draw on experience of advanced cities, and work out appropriate policies and measures for traffic congestion control based on the actual situation of Guangzhou. Secondly, the publicity of transportation laws, regulations and courteous behaviors should be enhanced to raise public awareness of transportation rules and safety, and anyone violating traffic laws and regulations should be punished. Thirdly, government agencies of public utilities, planning, and traffic management, etc. should enhance communication and collaboration to minimize man-made traffic congestion.

ii. While improving food safety, we should focus on resolving the cognitive differences in food safety risks

In recent years, the passing rate in Guangzhou Food and Drug Administration's quarterly sampling inspection of food reached up to 99.0%, with the lowest at 95.6%, but residents' evaluation was not high, which reflected the cognitive differences in food safety. It is suggested that the food safety authority, while improving food safety, should vigorously enhance the communication on food safety risks, changing from isolated publicity and education to proactive communication with the public, from publicizing data to enhancing food safety services, thus resolving cognitive differences. At the same time, close attention should be paid to the public opinions on food safety and encourage the public to participate in the fight against fake and inferior foods.

iii. Consolidate and strengthen the improvement of rivers and waterways, and Improve urban water environment

Firstly, efforts should be made to continuously strengthen and improve the water control mechanism in cooperation with cities in the upper reaches of the Pearl River, raise the investment for improving the Pearl River system to the level for provincial major projects, and create a synergistic effect in the harness of urban water environment with a higher vision and platform. Secondly, we should lay emphasis on classified disposal of industrial and residential sewage, strictly implement the goal of industrial wastewater reduction, strengthen the treatment capacity of household wastewater, and strive to achieve wastewater treatment before it flows into the river. Thirdly, we should continue to adjust and optimize the manufacturing industry, eliminate backward production capacity, develop emerging industries with low energy consumption, and reduce wastewater discharge from the source.

iv. Stabilize the expectation for housing price and create better physical space for living and entrepreneurship

First, we should fully understand the scarcity of land resources, properly raise the standard of floor area ratio, increase the compactness of cities through vertical spatial development, and clearly convey the expectation of steady rise in housing prices to the market. Secondly, we should vigorously curb speculative demand, and clearly deliver to the market the expectation of preventing precipitous rise of housing prices. Thirdly, we should calculate and study the city's carrying capacity of population, so as to avoid overgrowth of residence demand while replenishing sufficient demographic dividend for economic development. Fourthly, we should strengthen the establishment of public service facilities and the building of the living circle in the non-central urban area, and divert the population from central urban area to non-central area, alleviating the overgrowing housing price expectation in the central urban area. Fifthly, we should stabilize prices in the housing rental market, strengthen the construction of low-cost rental housing, guarantee the basic housing needs of residents, and convey to the market the determination of stabilizing housing prices.

v. Ensure the balance between supply and demand, and prevent violent price

fluctuations

Firstly, we should start with strengthening the supply of agricultural and sideline products and reducing their circulation cost to curb excessive rise of food prices. Secondly, we should strengthen the inspection and supervision of changes of the market price and crack down on hoarding and speculation, price gouging and other illegal behaviors. Thirdly, we ought to ensure the price stability of resource products and public services. Price adjustment should not only exert the leverage effect of price, but also ease the impact on people's livelihood.

vi. Smooth the mobility of social stratum with fair opportunity, and reduce the gap between the rich and the poor by "expanding the middle-income group and raising the income of the lower-income group"

Firstly, we should stabilize and ensure the employment for residents, especially those with low and middle-level income, and reduce the impact of the economic downturn on low and middle-income residents, laying the foundation for raising the overall income level of residents. Secondly, we should encourage and guide low and middle-income people to enhance their working skills through continuing education, employment training and other measures, so as to improve their income-earning ability fundamentally. Thirdly, we should speed up the income distribution reform and further give preference to the low and middle-income group to gradually narrow the income gap between low and middle-income earners and high-income earners.

Analysis of Guangzhou's Cultural Development in 2016 and Prospects for 2017*

Guangzhou Development Research Institute Research Team,
Guangzhou University**

Abstract: In 2016, Guangzhou made significant progress in cultural development. Public cultural services are improved and the structure of cultural industries is optimized. Cultural heritage is better protected and local cultural forms are further promoted. More festival events, conferences, and exhibitions have been held and etiquette and ethical standards of citizens improved. In 2017, we will undertake extensive public awareness activities and provide strong support for hosting the Fortune Global Forum; integrate public cultural resources to enhance the efficiency of cultural services; leverage new media to strengthen the production of cultural contents; help young people to better understand and identify with the culture of Guangzhou and increase their sense of belonging; and accelerate the reform of the cultural system to build a modern market –oriented cultural system.

Keywords: Guangzhou, cultural heritage protection, local culture, public cultural service system

I. Overview of Cultural Development in Guangzhou in 2016

i. Improve the system of public cultural services to provide quality services

1. Advance the development of public service system through plans and policies

In December 2016, Guangzhou released *theOpinions on Accelerating the Establishment of a Modern Public Cultural Service System in Guangzhou*. It proposed to focus on community-level development and take reform and innovation as the driving force. It made clear a series of goals including the standardized provision of basic public cultural services in a digital, equitable, and socialized manner. According to the document, 1,500 square metersof indoor public cultural facilities need to be made available for every 10,000 people. The city should basically put in place eight urban cultural centers and strengthen the building of libraries. In August 2016, Guangzhou enacted *the Special Plan for the Distribution*

* This report is the joint outcome of studies by Guangzhou Development Research Institute of Guangzhou University, a Key Research Institute of Humanities and Social Sciences in Universities of Guangdong Province and the Collaborative Innovation and Development Center for "Guangzhou Studies" of Guangdong Provincial Department of Education, the Guangzhou Urban Integrated Development Decision-making Consulting Team under the Innovation Team Program for Guangdong Regular Institutions of Higher Learning, and Guangdong Provincial Philosophy and Social Science Project (GD15CMK02).

** Team leader:Tu Chenglin; members: Huang Xu, Tan Yuanfang, Zhou Lingxiao, Lv Huimin, Wang Wenjiao, Ding Yanhua, and Wen Zhaohui. The report is written by Huang Xu, Associate Professor and Ph.D. at Guangzhou Development Research Institute of Guangzhou University.

of Public Sports Facilities and Functional Areas of the Sports Industry, putting forward the goal of more than doubling the city's fitness area in the next 4 years. In addition, the city is currently carrying out on-site studies to facilitate the development of a *Working Plan on Museum Legislation in Guangzhou*. The formulation and enactment of these policies and plans have effectively promoted the improvement of the cultural service system.

2. Strengthen the construction of cultural infrastructure and improve both the cultural service facilities and technology

At present, Guangzhou is vigorously promoting the construction of large cultural infrastructure. Along the axis the city proudly presents Guangzhou Museum, Guangzhou Science Museum, and Guangzhou Art Museum. Guangzhou Cultural Center, located on the north of Haizhu Lake in Haizhu District, is a perfect example of natural beauty and architectural elegance which showcases the unique features of Guangzhou's Lingnan culture.

In addition to the construction of cultural facilities, Guangzhou has started to digitalize its cultural infrastructure in recent years. The city has made use of modern information technologies and Internet technologies to build digital service platforms, like digital museums for cultural heritage. It has used modern techniques to optimize the spatial layout and functional distribution of cultural facilities in order to improve public access to quality services and better meet the cultural needs of citizens.

3. Provide diverse cultural services during festivals

A major feature of the delivery of public cultural services in Guangzhou is its diverse festival activities. For example, authorities in charge of cultural affairs of the city will organize various public cultural events during the Spring Festival so as to engage citizens and enrich their cultural life. According to incomplete statistics, this year more than 300 cultural events were organized by the city's cultural authorities during the Spring Festival, including over 150 performances, more than 70 exhibitions and over 100 popular cultural activities, such as folk performances, group singing and dancing, lantern shows, story-telling competitions, and salons.

ii. Promote innovative development of cultural industries and optimize industrial structure

First, the city has encouraged the development of new media and promoted its integration with traditional media. Guangzhou-based traditional media used to take the lead in the country. However, new media has produced profound impact on traditional media in recent years, greatly affecting its growth momentum. How to integrate with new media and regain growth and vitality remains an important development topic for traditional media.In order to promote the integration of traditional media and new media, Guangzhou enacted the *Action Plan for Facilitating Integrated Development of Traditional Media and New Media in Guangzhou* in 2016 and earmarked RMB50 million for the integration of traditional media and new media. This document helps Guangzhou-based traditional media to better reflect on Internet thinking while following the rules of news communication and the development trends of new media. It enables traditional media and new media to draw on each other's complementary advantages and achieve common development. It advocates practices that facilitate in-depth integration of their channels, platforms, contents, operations and management, and lays a solid foundation for a well-integrated and multi-dimensional modern communication system and an influential and reliable new media conglomerate with communicative strength. Thanks to its efforts, a multi-layered integrated development pattern is now basically taking shape. The system, based on the traditional media, consists of "a major newspaper (a major TV station) + a series of newspapers and magazines (channels) + new media cluster". In recent years, Guangzhou Daily and Guangzhou Broadcasting Network have launched several mobile news applications, such as the Central Editorial Office, Guangzhou Reference, Guangzhou Government Media Center, Central Kitchen Editing Platform, and Guangzhou News Network in Your Hand, which all prove to be masterpieces of the integrated development of traditional media and new media. In January 2016, Guangzhou TV set up a media integration laboratory and assigned TV program G4 and its entire staff to support its development. Now the laboratory has become an important incubator for media integration. Other integration projects are also witnessing steady progress. These include the media integration project of Guangzhou Daily Data and Digit Institute and the Micro Community and e-Pass project, the Subway + Channel Integrated Media project, the South Reviews Media Think Tank project, and the Silk Road Post Integrated Media project, all initiated by Guangzhou Daily Group media. Meanwhile, Guangzhou Daily is running over 30 WeChat media platforms, such as *Healthy Life, Eat in Canton,* and *Study Guides,* etc. According to the *2016 China Media Integrated Communication Index Report* released by People's Daily Online, Guangzhou Daily ranked fourth among all press media in terms of strength in integrated communication and first among all local media.[1]

Second, the city has made great efforts to promote the development of animation, games, and copyright industries. It has issued the *Opinions on Accelerating the Development of the Animation and Games Industries* and promoted the implementation of the *Opinions of Accelerating the Development of Cultural Industries in Guangzhou, Action Plan of Guangzhou for Promoting the Integrated Development of Cultural, Creative, and Design Services and Relevant Industries (2016-2020)* and *Opinions on Promoting the Integration of Culture and Science and*

---

[1] http://www.ycwb.com/. http://news.163.com/16/1215/21/C8BTV4VB00014AEE.html, visited on February 25, 2017.

Technology in Guangzhou, etc. These documents are aimed to speed up the integration of cultural and other relevant industries and extend the cultural industrial chain. In addition, Guangzhou has actively promoted the development of a national copyright trade base in Yuexiu District which focuses on copyright protection and trading so as to build an industrial chain ecosystem that integrates a copyright industrial park, copyright protection, services, trade and finance.

Last, the city has leveraged culture and tourism strength to develop the cultural tourism industry. In order to accelerate the development and utilization of urban cultural tourism resources, Guangzhou has utilized funds from the government and the public and private sectors. For instance, the *Guangzhou Urban Renewal Measures*, which took effect on January 1, 2016, encourages "micro-renovation" of partial demolition and renovation of the old town so as to fully exploit its potential resources and advantages. In this way, history becomes a live album of city memories and industrial development is supported by rediscovered historic and cultural brands. The entire old district is full of vigor and vitality. Other government-initiated programs that involve the use of social capital include the City of Flowers Tourism Project and the "Riverside Economic, Innovative, and Landscape Belts" initiative.

In 2016, the added value of Guangzhou's cultural industry was approximately RMB104.3 billion, accounting for about 5.3% of the local GDP.

iii. Improve ethical standards of citizens and social etiquette of the city

In 2016, Guangzhou devoted its efforts to building a national civilized city, raising intellectual and moral standards of citizens, and enhancing social etiquette and civility. It has made significant progress in improving online behaviors of citizens, advancing the civility of individuals and the city as a whole providing effective mental and moral support for the development of a major national central city.

1. Strengthen top-level design and overall deployment

In 2016, Guangzhou issued *the Outline of the Thirteenth Five-year Plan* to Improve Public Etiquette and Ethical Standards of Guangzhou, detailing plans for the next five years. Other policies enacted this year included the Outline of the *Reading-for-All Plan (2016-2020)*, *the Assessment System of Civilized Urban Communities in Guangzhou*, and *the Assessment System of Civilized Rural Communities in Guangzhou*, etc., all contributing to the improvement of the city's civility. Moreover, etiquette and moral standards were introduced as an important index in corporate performance assessment. Detailed procedures were defined to rate and rank agencies and organizations according to their attitude and monitoring efforts.

2. Establish a Long-term Mechanism to Advance Reading-for-All programs

In 2016, Guangzhou developed a five-year plan and a ten-year outline to promote Reading-for-All programs. It also issued the *Regulations on Public Libraries in Guangzhou* and the *Development Plan of A City of Libraries in Guangzhou*. A four-tier reading network is basically in place. At present, the city has 5,300 reading venues of various kinds, providing a total of 27.926 million books. These well guarantee the operation of Reading-for-All programs.

Citizens of Guangzhou had access to a wide variety of reading-related activities in 2016, such as the City of Ram Book Fair, the Fragrance of Books Reading Month, the 2016 Southern City Book Festival, the 13th Reading Star Competition, and the "Growing up with Books: Ten-year Youth Reading Initiative", etc., all with increasing brand effect. Moreover, the "Reading Plus 7"[2] program was further developed. All these activities have contributed to create a better reading environment in Guangzhou and witnessed more citizens turning into readers.

3. Initial progress in digital libraries

An important measure of advancing "Internet + Culture" is to develop digital libraries and help the public enjoy the convenience of digital reading. In April 2016, Guangzhou formally launched its digital library with sections such as Resources, Services, and Activities to Interactions and Themes. A Social media version, a mobile version, and a multi-lingual version were provided alongside. Guangzhou citizens aged above 14 can register and enjoy the massive digital resources by scanning the QR Code. Citizens may also have free access to a number of classic audio books by scanning the QR Code of *"bookting.cn"*. These initiatives have successfully met the requirements of different readers.

4. Help citizens foster an appreciation of fine culture through cultural competitions

In 2016, Guangzhou organized various competitions to help its citizens foster an appreciation of fine culture. These included the 3rd Guangzhou Chorus Festival and the 12th "One Hundred Songs for China" Singing Contest, the 5th Clean Governance Book Review Contest (July 2016), and the Guangzhou Amateur Dancing Competition and Joint Performance (December 2016), et. These competitions advanced the overall development of citizens and enjoyed wide participation and positive social influence. According to statistics, about 480 large-scale fitness-for-all events and competitions were staged throughout the year in Guangzhou, an increase of 6.7% over the same period of the previous year; more than 6.5 million people participated in these activities, an increase of 8.3%.

iv. Attach importance to protecting and carrying forward cultural heritage and score new progress in heritage protection

Guangzhou has attached great importance to protecting and carrying forward cultural heritage in recent years. 2016 was no exception, and remarkable progress was made at an even faster pace.

1. Ensure institutional improvement through restructuring measures

In March 2016, Guangzhou set up a new Bureau of Cultural Heritage as the

---

[2] Short for "Reading in the Countryside, Communities, Households, Schools, Government Bodies, Companies, and Military Campuses".

competent authority for protecting and carrying forward heritage, in accordance with the *Notice on the Mandates, Organization, and Staffing of Guangzhou Municipal Bureau of Culture, Radio, TV, Film, Press and Publication*, which was released in September 2015. Actually, the Bureau of Cultural Heritage and the Municipal Bureau of Culture, Radio, TV, Film, Press and Publication were one organization with two names. Therefore, no additional resources were required. When the agency exercised its function in heritage and museum management, it would use the name of the Bureau of Cultural Heritage. The Bureau has four divisions, namely, the Planning Division, the Heritage Protection and Archeology Division, the Museum Division, and the Heritage Security Division.

In the government agency reform in 2009, the Bureau of Culture, the Bureau of Press and Publications, and the Bureau of Radio, TV, and Film were merged into the Bureau of Culture, Radio, TV, Film, Press, and Publication, which also took charge of cultural heritage protection, among many other functions. This time, the Bureau of Cultural Heritage was made a separate entity. Though not an overhaul of organizational structure, it showed the importance the city attached to heritage conservation. Guangzhou had gradually realized the important role that local heritage played in its development as the capital city of Guangdong Province, a renowned national historical and cultural city, a major central city, a center of international business and trade, and an integrated transport hub. The decision was made at a strategic moment as cultural development became a priority for both the country and the province. It was also a major measure taken by the city to keep up with the new national plan of conserving historical and cultural heritage.

2. Expand research institutions and ensure adequate funding

In 2014, the Guangzhou Municipal Center of Cultural Heritage and Archeology was renamed the Guangzhou Municipal Institute of Cultural Heritage and Archeology, in order to expand the research force and support research efforts. The new institute was assigned 100 full-time positions and during the recent three years, nearly 30 employees had been recruited. The research team was greatly expanded. For capacity building purposes, the Institute organized a professional training session in Zengcheng in 2016. A total of 60 people, including all the staff on the payroll and some contract workers, attended the session.

In 2016, Guangzhou reviewed all the conservation units in charge of municipal-level intangible cultural heritage and determined that 22 units would share a total subsidy of RMB1.55 million. The units were responsible for training, promotional events on campus, archives discovery and restoration, teaching materials preparation, and research and study, etc. The subsidy would provide the financial support for the protection and conservation of cultural heritage in the city.

3. Attach importance to carrying forward the culture

Apart from heritage protection, carrying forward the culture is another important aspect of work related to cultural heritage. Protection is the means while carrying forward the culture is the final purpose. Carrying forward the culture has, therefore, remained a priority for Guangzhou in recent years. The city has made full use of festivals and school campuses to promote the local culture. Every year, festival events featuring unique local culture are organized in every district, such as the Canton Temple Fair in Yuexiu District and the Boluo Birthday Celebration in Huangpu District, etc. The rich variety of cultural events brings local culture closer to the public and allows them to be culturally nurtured. People find it easier to identify with traditional culture and the society finds such events nourishing. As a proactive measure to bring intangible cultural heritage to campus, Guangzhou and Guangzhou Light Industry Polytechnic College has jointly organized the Lingnan Cultural Heritage Festival since 2016.

In terms of promoting local cultural through regular courses, Guangzhou Cultural Center has set up the Intangible Cultural Heritage School, which offers three programs a year, respectively in spring, autumn, and summer vacation. Every program is open to about 200 students. Inheritors of intangible cultural heritage are invited to be mentors. The School now has a mature teaching model, a fixed venue, and an institutionalized operating mechanism. It enjoys some fame and continues to contribute to public good. In 2016, the city announced 33 municipal bases for passing on intangible cultural heritage for 2015-2017. On the list were institutions of higher education and research, such as the School of Sociology and Anthropology of Sun Yat-Sen University, and some cultural centers, etc. So far, Guangzhou has identified 96 representative projects and 151 representative inheritors of intangible cultural heritage.

v. Expand the influence of Guangzhou culture through enhanced communication

In 2016, Guangzhou launched a series of cultural activities to promote the local culture.

1. Local promotion and communication

Events were organized to promote the unique culture of the city. For instance, the Guangzhou Maritime Silk Road Cultural Season kicked off in March 2016. The festival consisted of 53 events organized under seven themes, namely, the "Two Thousand Years of Sailing: the City of Guangzhou and the Maritime Silk Road" exhibition and academic series, the "One Day through Guangzhou and the Maritime Silk Road" travelling series, the "City of Ram School" lecture series, the "Guangzhou Opens a Book" public reading series, the "City of Ram Youth School" lecture series, and the "Canton Capital New Talk" humanity lecture series, etc. The festival was a grand cultural event for the past year. In the districts, various cultural activities were launched and public cultural brands were formed, such as the Guangzhou Folk Culture Festival and Huangpu Millennial Birthday Celebration held in Huangpu District, the Canton Temple Fair in Yuexiu District, the Panguwang Birthday Celebration in Huadu District, the Old Guangzhou Folk Arts Festival, and the Pearl River Delta South Cantonese Opera Concert in Haizhu District. Each district had its own cultural brand and collectively provided important platforms to promote the city's culture.

2. National promotion and communication

In the past year, Guangzhou has made new progress in promoting local culture to the national audience. After three years planning and producing, *Crossing the Maritime Silk Road*, an eight-episode documentary which focused on Guangzhou's extensive involvement in the maritime Silk Road historically and culturally, was broadcast on China Central Television International Channel and was well received by the public. The first season of another documentary, *Memories of Canton*, was first broadcast on China Central Television Science and Education Channel on December 11 and 12, 2016, which for the first time presented the whole picture of canton culture to the national audience.

3. International promotion and communication of Guangzhou's cultural image

The Guangzhou International Cantonese Opera Festival is a good example of how Guangzhou cultural image is promoted internationally. The festival was first held in 1990 and last year was the sixth time it was held in Guangzhou. Years of efforts have contributed to its fame both at home and abroad. Approximately 10, 000 artists and enthusiasts from 143 Cantonese Opera theaters (troupes) in 20 countries and regions attended the 6th Festival. As an international cultural exchange event with unique local characteristics, the 2016 Festival focused on promoting Lingnan culture and on carrying forward and further developing Cantonese Opera for the sake of the people. It made positive contributions to expand the performance market of Cantonese Opera and promoted the international exchanges among artists.

Another important measure to enhance the influence of Guangzhou culture is promoting its modern art works. In 2016, Guangzhou hosted Xu Hongfei's International Sculpture Exhibition Tour, the Red Thread Woman Commemoration and a series of other cultural activities, which helped bring traditional and modern Guangzhou culture to the world stage. These events not only allowed the city to show its ancient charm, but also provided platforms for its modern vigor.

4. Government's use of new media tools as an important way to promote Guangzhou culture

According to the *2016 People's Daily Governance Index and Weibo Influence Report* released by People's Daily Online in January 2017, Guangzhou took a leading position among the cities and ranked the sixth in terms of the influence of its official Weibo accounts. On the Top 50 list of the most influential government-run Weibo accounts, two were from Guangzhou. The Weibo account @Guangzhou Release, with 4.55 million followers[3], ranked the thirty-second while @Guangzhou Public Security ranked the fourteenth. In their specific category, @Guangzhou Release

---

[3]Data as of April 11, 2017.

ranked the fifth on the Top 20 Party and government news release Weibo accounts and @Guangzhou Public Security ranked the eighth on the Top 20 public security Weibo accounts. @Guangzhou Weather came out third on the Top 20 weather forecast Weibo accounts and @Guangzhou Subway took the fourth position on the Top 20 public transportation Weibo accounts[4].

These government-run Weibo and WeChat accounts have become important platforms to promote the image of Guangzhou. For example, @Guangzhou Release once led a discussion titled "Talking about Guangzhou Tenderly", where netizens joined to share their observations of the scenery, the people, and the food in Guangzhou. The discussion had significantly boosted the cultural image of the city. As of April 11, 2017, the discussion had received 1233 responses and registered 22.475 million readings. The Guangzhou government plays an important role in leveraging Weibo and other social media forms to promote the local culture.

vi. Growing influence of a wonderful array of festivals, conferences and exhibitions

Guangzhou hosts a number of major festivals each year. In 2016 the city hosted Guangzhou Art Festival, the 2016 China (Guangzhou) International Documentary Film Festival, Guangzhou International Art Fair, the 2016 China (Guangzhou) International Performing Arts Fair, the 9th China International Cartoon and Animation Festival, the 21st Guangzhou International Art Fair, the 6th China International Copyright Expo, and other large-scale events. These festivals have become Guangzhou's cultural business cards, demonstrating the charm of the city and its culture. This year's festivals have the following characteristics:

1. Learn from the past and expand the influence of festival events

It is both necessary and imperative for Guangzhou to learn from the major festival events that have been held in the city over the years. In recent years, reflection on the organization of major festival events has been put on the agenda. For example, a documentary was produced in 2015, which went through the twelve-year (2003-2014) development course of China (Guangzhou) International Documentary Film Festival. In 2016, the book *Road and Encounter: Twelve Years of China (Guangzhou) International Documentary Film Festival* was published, featuring the same theme. In the same year, the city started building Guangzhou Documentary Research Center. Another TV documentary *Echo of the Era: Review of the Golden Bell Awards* looked back on the creation of the awards and its development path.

2. Tell the stories of China and of Guangzhou to the international audience

Festival events hosted by Guangzhou in recent years all focused on telling China's and Guangzhou's stories well. Aimed to promote our unique national and local culture and improve our international image, these events strived to significantly increase our cultural soft power and international influence. For example, a special

---

[4]*2016 People's Daily Governance Index and Weibo Influence Report.*

item was added to the agenda of China (Guangzhou) International Documentary Film Festival, namely, the "Chinese Story" International Co-Production Proposal Conference. Focusing on three aspects of such co-production projects, i.e. content, funding, and promotion, the Conference aimed to promote the adoption of the model by more film companies in a more standardized manner. 27 proposals were received, which would bring Chinese stories to the world audience through signed contracts or annual reports in the future.

3. Promote cultural festivals through the Internet

With the advent of the Internet era, the integration of the Internet and culture has become a global trend. Festivals held in Guangzhou were no exception. The 2016 China (Guangzhou) International Performing Arts Fair took the lead to set up CPAA Trading Platform, the first "Internet + Performing Arts" B2B Trading Platform in China. This online platform integrated the functions of exhibition, trading, and information sharing, etc. and focused on critical theme planning, creative guidance, personnel training, and database construction. It vigorously implemented such development strategies as "Culture + Science and Technology", "Culture + Finance", and "Culture + Network". Guangzhou International Cultural Industries Fair, on the other hand, paid special attention to the interpretation of "Internet +" policies and the demonstration of model projects and new technologies, etc. It provided a platform for cultural fair practitioners, those with private companies, and the general public to better understand copyright trading policies, industrial integration policies, and relevant project development strategies against the backdrop of an Internet + cultural heritage era.

4. Facilitate public access and increase public participation

International as they are, cultural exhibitions and events need to register the needs of the local community, encourage public participation, and bring true benefits to local people. While hosting cultural events, Guangzhou pays special attention to engaging its citizens. A common practice is to stage events that can truly benefit the people. How to encourage more people to become sources of creation rather than mere audience? How to realize in-depth public participation? Guangzhou made some attempts in 2016. For example, the College Student Documentary Film Contest was held during China (Guangzhou) International Documentary Film Festival. As an important part of the festival, the contest provided a platform for Chinese college students to participate in a world-class contest and find a way to realize their dreams.

II. Major Issues and Challenges for the Development of Guangzhou Culture

i. Existing public cultural resources are not fully utilized

In recent years, Guangzhou has vigorously promoted the construction of public cultural service facilities with remarkable achievements. However, some inadequacy is observed in terms of fully discovering and utilizing existing public cultural service and resources. Increasing high-quality supply and improving the allocation of available resources will help the city maximize the use of public cultural service resources. It will not only contribute to the modernization of public cultural service facilities, but also improve cooperation, facilitate the sharing of cultural resources, reduce costs, increase output and allow existing cultural resources to be used most efficiently. Therefore, it should become a priority for the city in upcoming years.

As the capital city of Guangdong Province, Guangzhou has better cultural resources than other cities in the same province. For example, it has the largest number of colleges and universities with their own libraries and sports venues. Some colleges and universities even have access to unique cultural resources. For example, Xinghai Conservatory of Music and Guangzhou Academy of Fine Arts are respectively blessed with rich music and arts resources. Moreover, Guangzhou has the best museums, libraries, cultural centers, and other cultural infrastructure works in the province. In other words, Guangzhou is abundant in quality cultural resources. However, existing cultural resources are not well fully discovered and utilized at present. For example, the public have no access to playgrounds in primary and secondary schools. Even students can only use their school playground during school hours. Although there are ten colleges and universities in Guangzhou University City, most colleges and universities only allow their teachers and students to use their libraries (with a few exceptions where alumni are also allowed). There are so many obstacles that it is almost impossible to borrow books from a neighboring university. For public libraries and museums, their educational function is yet to be discovered, with so many resources never touched upon or seldom used.

ii. The production capacity is disproportionately low considering the continuously growing consumption in the cultural field.

In recent years, cultural spending has continued to grow in Guangzhou. Statistics show that both the per capita cultural consumption and per household cultural consumption have observed a rise in recent years. In 2016, Guangdong Province registered 187 million visits to the cinema, an increase of 12.58% over the same period of last year. That would mean 1.75 visits per person, if we take the statistics by the end of 2014 which suggested that the province had a resident population of 107 million. When it came to Shenzhen and Guangzhou, the figures were even higher. The citizens of the two cities respectively made 3.64 and 2.34 visits to the movies per person, keeping abreast with European and North American cities.[5] Guangzhou enjoys a robust book consumption market as well. According to *Ten Years of Reading: Dangdang National Book Consumption Report* released by *dangdang.com*, a Chinese e-commercial book company, in April 2016, Beijing, Guangdong, and Shanghai firmly established themselves as the top three provinces (municipalities) in terms of book consumption between 2006 and 2015. Guangzhou proudly took the first position on the top 50 cities.

Although Guangzhou maintains a strong momentum in cultural consumption, its cultural productivity fails to match it. Statistics show that of the 394 films released in

---

[5] http://news.163.com/17/0109/21/CAC9MG3800014AEE.html

Guangzhou in 2015, only 3 were produced by local companies. In the publishing industry, newspaper sales are plunging and the media hub, a pride of the city, is seriously challenged.

ii. Guangzhou needs to further expand its international cultural influence

Despite the importance that the city attaches to bringing its culture abroad and the significant efforts that it has made to accelerate the process, there remains a considerable gap between Guangzhou and other global cities in terms of their cultural influence and international position.

Historically, as the center of Canton culture and Lingnan culture, Guangzhou culture used to have quite a strong influence in Europe, America and Southeast Asia,. In the Song Dynasty and the Yuan Dynasty, Canton, especially Guangzhou, was the center of China's overseas trade. In the Song Dynasty, the place witnessed commercial and political interactions with more than 50 countries. That figure increased to 140 in the Yuan Dynasty, when Guangzhou became known as the Southern Treasury Granary for Emperors and External Treasury House for Emperors. In the Ming Dynasty and the Qing Dynasty, China basically cut itself off from the outside world, but from time to time Guangzhou was used as the only port for foreign trade, which further consolidated the city's prominent position in China. Some scholars believe that because of the development of canton-centered marine trade, the first global economic system was well established before the 13th century. The system consisted of countries and regions around the Indian Ocean with orient as the center. Canton, as a result, became one of the most prominent world cultural brands for maritime transport and trade.

Canton culture used to have an important position in China. Its influence reached the peak in the 1980s and 1990s, when Cantonese songs and TV series were extremely popular among the national audience. Canton culture used to have a great influence in the world as well, with Cantonese being a widely used language among overseas Chinese. However, the influence of Canton culture has declined in recent years. Domestically, it is reflected in the way the Cantonese people are portrayed in the annual national Spring Festival Gala. While they were regarded as the most fashionable at the beginning of the country's reform and opening up, the Cantonese are typically considered to be vulgar upstarts nowadays. The cultural image of Canton further suffers as the criticism of their cuisine and other cultural forms amounts. Internationally, Guangzhou is no longer the only connection to the outside world as other places become more and more engaged in foreign trade. Consequently, Canton culture is no longer the dominant cultural form among overseas Chinese. As time passes by, overseas Chinese are becoming less attached to the culture of their origin. That also explains the diminishing influence of Canton culture.

Besides objective reasons, the decline of influence is also related to the city's failure to properly promote its culture in the past. It has not attached enough importance to communicating with the outside world, its promotional efforts are not sufficiently effective, there lacks overall planning and coordination among different media forms, the methods could be improved to leverage overall strength, and the system could be further strengthened. Therefore, Guangzhou should devote concerted efforts to improving its cultural promotion capacity. It should pay special attention to enhancing the influence of its culture as it continues to develop the economy, which will ultimately contribute to its international image.

III. Prospects for Guangzhou Culture in 2017 and Policy Recommendations

i. Prospects

1. The protection of cultural heritage will become a priority for cultural workers

In recent years, China has attached great importance to carrying forward and developing historical and cultural traditions. Such traditions are sometimes passed on from mouth to mouth, and sometimes crystallized in historical relics as our collective memories. Therefore, the discovery and protection of historical and cultural heritages plays a crucial part in carrying forward our traditions. In addition, such heritages provide ideal materials for cultivating patriotism and core socialist values and therefore, play an important role in ideological and political education.

In recent years, China has systematically stepped up its protection of cultural heritages. It has developed a clearer picture of existing cultural heritages and increased its financial input for their conservation. For example, the first national survey of movable cultural heritage was started in April 2013 and basically concluded at the end of 2016. After the survey, 14 categories of heritage information will be entered into a database, including heritage name, date, status, and place of origin.

In addition, China has also substantially increased its funding for cultural heritage conservation. Since the 18th CPC National Congress, government funding for cultural heritage has increased by more than 40% year on year. The funds are especially used to cover a wider range of heritage and support conservation efforts in Tibet, Xinjiang, and other border areas with mainly ethnic minority populations and poor areas.[6]

In recent years, Guangzhou has continued to make the protection of cultural heritage a priority and adopted a series of institutional, financial, and training measures. However, how to properly protect and utilize cultural heritage remains an important issue for Guangzhou as it strives to become a world famous cultural city. In the upcoming year, the city will have to continue its efforts in this area. It will have to properly utilize cultural heritage for educational purposes, especially the cultivation of patriotism and core socialist values and the education of traditional culture. It needs to make creative use of existing cultural heritage, such as launching pilot digitalization projects and establishing smart museums, etc.

---

[6]President Xi Jinping Ordered Authorities to Promote Proper and Moderate Utilization of Cultural Heritage: Bring Cultural Heritage to Life.http://news.sina.com.cn/c/2015-01-09/124131380524.shtml

2. The public cultural service system will find new opportunities and the service efficiency will continue to improve.

The need for public cultural services is an important driving force for building a public cultural service system. With its per capita GDP already exceeding RMB50, 000, China is turning into a middle-income country. Statistics of the National Social Survey shows that at present middle-income families make up 37.4% of the country's population.[7]As the old saying goes, "when the granaries are full, men appreciate rites and obligations; when food and clothing are enough, men have a sense of honour and shame." A relatively large and rich middle-income group will not only become an important force for promoting cultural consumption and developing cultural industries, but also show a greater willingness to advance the great prosperity and development of Chinese culture and to participate in the provision of public cultural services. At present,meeting the ever-increasing cultural needs has become a priority in social development.

Building a public cultural service system has always been an important issue for the Party and the State. The Third Plenary Session of the 18th Central Committee of the CPC proposed that we should establish a coordination mechanism for building a public cultural services system, make an overall plan for building a network of service facilities, and try to provide standard and equal access to basic public cultural services. In early 2015, the CPC Central Committee General Office and the State Council General Office issued the *Opinions on Speeding up the Building of a Modern Public Cultural Service System* and together with an implementation notice. In 2016, the National People's Congress Standing Committee adopted the Public Cultural Service Guarantee Law, providing legal confirmation and guarantee for public cultural services.

Guided by state policies and respond to the development of the times, Guangzhou attaches great importance to building a public cultural service system. A full-coverage network of service facilities is in place, which provides high-quality cultural services through diversified forms. Besides the government, market and the private sector are also actively involved in the development of the public cultural service system, in a bid to provide standard services that are equally accessible. However, there is still room for improvement, especially in terms of service quality and management. In December 2016, Guangzhou issued the *Opinions on Accelerating the Construction of a Modern Public Cultural Service System in Guangzhou*. The deadline for finishing the task is set in 2020, which means a very tight schedule and a very heavy workload. How to ensure that cultural facilities are properly built and utilized? How to achieve better protection, management, and utilization of cultural facilities and heritage in Guangzhou? How to set up a cloud platform for the city's public cultural services? How to strengthen community-level

---

[7]Chinese Academy of Social Sciences: China's middle-income families make up 37.4% of the country's population, http://business.sohu.com/20161221/n476494330.shtml, visited on February 25, 2017.

networks of public cultural facilities and improve digital services? These are all questions that Guangzhou needs to consider in real earnest if it wants to make breakthroughs in 2017.

3. Economic development will witness more integration of culture with tourism, science, technology, and finance.

Nowadays, culture has become an important part of a country's overall strength. Culture not only helps create a good image of a country, but also promotes economic development. It has become a common practice to boost economic growth through cultural activities. How can culture contribute to economic growth? Economic development in recent years has been accompanied by closer integration of culture with tourism, science, technology, and finance.

The development of new media forms and the Internet technology has made it feasible and even urgent to integrate culture with science and technology. Through technological measures, local historical and cultural resources can be long conserved, faithfully restored, and vividly presented to a large modern audience. That explained why the 18th Party Congress proposed to "promote integration of culture with science and technology, develop new forms of cultural operations, and make cultural operations larger in size and more specialized". The integration of culture with tourism actually means maximizing the effect of cultural resources through the development of the tourism industry to ultimately advance economic growth. It can be realized through the proper use of local historical and cultural resources in the development of cultural tourism products. The integration of culture and finance calls for more robust financial platforms that provide funding for cultural development. All these types of integration serve the same purpose of leveraging existing advantages to promote both cultural and economic development. *The Film Industry Promotion Law of the People's Republic of China*, enacted in 2016, is a concrete embodiment of the policy of integrating culture with tourism, science, technology, and finance.

In recent years, Guangdong Province has accelerated the integration of culture with tourism, science, technology, and finance. In 2016, the province took the lead in establishing two funds, namely, the Guangdong Southern Media Integrated Development Fund and the Guangdong New Media Industry Fund. Both funds attracted an investment of over 10 billion yuan. The Southern Finance Omnimedia Corporation (S.F.C) was established in Guangdong, focusing on the three services of media, data, and trading. In an agreement signed with Guangdong Province, Shanghai Pudong Development Bank promised to offer a credit line of no less than RMB50 billion for Guangdong-based cultural companies during the Thirteenth Five-year Plan period. Plus funds from other sources, investment and financing may exceed RMB100 billion, a new breakthrough in the province's cultural financing landscape.

Guangzhou has also started the integration of culture with tourism, science, technology, and finance. The renovation and upgrading of the Beijing Road cultural center was a typical example where new approaches were applied for better integration. In the future, Guangzhou should continue to promote the integration of culture with tourism, science, technology and finance so as to advance the great prosperity and development of its culture and economy.

4. Cultural reform will be accelerated and the relationship between the government and the market will be handled properly

The reform of the cultural management system has been on top of the agenda of the Party and the state in recent years. The 18th CPC National Congress put forward the strategic plan for deepening the overall reform. *The Decision of the CCCPC on Some Major Issues Concerning Comprehensively Deepening the Reform*, passed at The Third Plenary Session of the 18th Central Committee of the CPC, also set the goal of deepening the reform of cultural systems and mechanisms.

With many management system reforms taking place in the city, Guangzhou is in the vanguard of piloting the cultural system reform. Since the end of 2008, the cultural system reform has been carried out in full swing, focusing on the transformation of for-profit cultural institutions into business enterprises, the separation of production from publishing and production from broadcasting, the acquisitions of cultural enterprises and adoption of shareholding systems, and the restructuring of performing art troupes, etc. In the 2009 Big Department System Reform, the Bureau of Culture, the Bureau of Press and Publications, and the Bureau of Radio, TV, and Film were merged into a big bureau, with two names, i.e. the Bureau of Culture, Radio, TV, Film, Press, and Publication and the Bureau of Copyright. It was formally named Guangzhou Municipal Bureau of Culture, Radio, TV, Film, Press, and Publication (Copyright Bureau) in 2013. Another name, the Bureau of Cultural heritage, was added in 2016. These reforms have created some positive outcomes. Benefiting from the separation of operation from communication, *Guangzhou Daily* is able to score impressive economic benefits while maintaining its position as a major new organ for the Party and the state. The Big Department System Reform has streamlined government functions and improved administrative efficiency. However, there are still some problems. Some cultural enterprises find it difficult to survive in market competitions. The number of cultural enterprises above designated size is still low. The cultural market is not mature yet. The reform of performing troupes has not evolved as expected. How to let the market play its role? How to create a robust marketplace? How to further expand and empower cultural industries and cultural undertakings? These are all important issues faced by Guangzhou.

5. Take Fortune Global Forum as an opportunity to upgrade the image and influence of the city

China's efforts in recent years to better connect to the outside world and improve its communication capacity are mainly due to two reasons. On the one hand, with the improvement of China's comprehensive national strength, international influence and the ability to participate in international affairs, it is imperative for China to build its own discourse system and boost its voice in the international community; to tell its stories well and spread its voice well; and to build its international image and improve its cultural soft power. On the other hand, it is urgent for China to safeguard its self-interest globally, since it faces increasing external frictions, especially on issues related to ideology and cultural security, etc. The more prominent such frictions are, the more important it becomes for China to spread socialist values through online and offline platforms and win the fight for public opinions. Fully aware of the new development, the CPC Central Committee with Comrade Xi Jinping as general secretary places great importance on communication with the outside world. It is believed that China should develop a global vision and an institutional framework that suits the needs for more extensive international involvement. With innovative concepts, content, platforms, approaches, and methods, China should strive to tell its stories well, amplify its voice on the international stage, and increase its international discourse power so as to better serve the Party and the country.

As the pioneer in reform and opening up, Guangzhou is a window of external publicity. That makes it important to improve its communication capacity and enhance its outreach efforts. To become an important center for international exchanges, Guangzhou should treasure the precious opportunity of hosting the Fortune Global Forum in 2017 by making full use of high-end international communication platforms and coordinating internal and external outreaching efforts. It should strive to tell well stories not only about China but also about Guangzhou. It should attempt to amplify the voice not only of China but also of Guangzhou. It should upgrade the influence and image not only of China but also of Guangzhou.

ii. Policy recommendations

1. Make full use of hosting the Fortune Global Forum to upgrade the city's communication and outreach efforts and improve its international influence

Guangzhou should coordinate internal and external outreaching efforts to prepare for the 2017 Fortune Global Forum, a precious opportunity to promote its urban cultural image. Guangzhou should leverage different media forms such as the Internet, new media, television, and radio and local, national, and international media resources to promote the Forum from different aspects.

First, Guangzhou should launch promotional videos about the city on a global scale to maximize the effect. It should draw upon the influence of the Cantonese language and culture and encourage overseas Cantonese to spread the cultural image of Guangzhou through seminars and performances of Cantonese operas.

Second, the city should integrate its convention and exhibition resources to spread its fame. Canton Fair, China (Guangzhou) International Documentary Film Festival, and other large-scale international events are all ideal platforms to promote the Fortune Global Forum and its host city Guangzhou.

Third, the city should strengthen its partnership with the media. Through such events as "Guangzhou in the Eyes of Major Chinese Language Media abroad" or "Guangzhou in the eyes of International Mainstream Media", it may invite high-end media companies from both home and abroad to visit Guangzhou and tell stories about Guangzhou.

Fourth, the city should integrate traditional and new media resources in China to launch special stories, columns, or even editions about Guangzhou. It can even strive to create a media matrix for promoting Guangzhou. Wechat, for example, can be used as a platform to launch promotional advertisements and videos featuring the Fortune Global Forum and Guangzhou at large.

Fifth, local university resources can be utilized to promote the image of Guangzhou. The city may work with colleges and universities to stage their own Fortune Forum, which will support the overall outreach efforts. Guangzhou studies and the compilation of *Guangzhou Encyclopedia* provide ideal platforms as well. The city may support institutions to carry out relevant studies, engage in specialized research projects, publish treatises and books, and organize forums.

2. Integrate public cultural resources and improve the efficiency of cultural service

In order to better integrate its public cultural resources, the city can start from the following aspects.

First, local library resources should be further integrated. The public should be able to access not only provincial, municipal, and district public libraries but also libraries of Guangzhou-based colleges and universities. Starting with municipal colleges and universities, local citizens with a valid identity card should be allowed to enter these libraries and borrow books after completing certain procedures. There is no reason why Guangzhou, a pioneering city in reform, cannot ensure public access to college libraries while many cities in underdeveloped regions have already done so. In Baotou, seven colleges have joined the Library Alliance and opened their libraries to the public. In Chongqing, the public now enjoy the same privilege as the alumni of Chongqing University as they are allowed to borrow as many as 20 books from the university library.

Second, the city needs to ensure public access to sports facilities in schools and universities. Like libraries, these facilities should be considered public assets rather than belonging to a specific school or university. Therefore, they should be used by the public. As a measure to promote the fitness-for-all initiative, the city should strive to make these facilities, like school playground and stadium, accessible to the public in holidays.

Third, the integration of cultural resources in Guangzhou University City should be accelerated. The University City was designed, at the very beginning, to facilitate the sharing of educational and cultural resources among students through the interconnectivity between universities and their libraries. It was intended to maximize the utilization of resources and achieve intensive growth. However, these goals are yet to be realized. The city should better integrate the cultural resources of the University City and strive to make all resources accessible to students from other universities and the public. It should also pay attention to integrating the tourism resources of the University City, especially with its natural and human landscapes and adjacent tourist attractions so as to make the University City a popular destination for Guangzhou's residents and tourists.

3. Leverage new media to produce more and better contents

The advent of new media has contributed to the unprecedented prosperity of cyber culture. The development of cyber culture is not only related to the development of a country's culture, but also its economy. It not only reflects a country's cultural influence, but also affects its cyber security. That makes it essential for a country to strive to produce more and better cultural content. According to a report recently released by Statista, a foreign statistics portal, on the global digital publishing industry, the size of the global digital publishing market reached USD15.3 billion in 2016, or 18.2% of the global digital media market. 79.7% of the global digital publishing market was dominated by the United States, China and Europe, with their combined revenue reaching USD12.2 billion. The market is expected to register a relatively steady compound annual growth rate at 7.1% between 2016 and 2021. With revenue of USD10.8 billion, or 71.1% of the entire digital publishing industry, the e-book sector was the unquestionable core sector in all regions.[8]

Guangzhou should make full use of this opportunity to develop its cyber culture. With its strength in traditional media, the city should make every effort to advance the integration with new media. It should offer more training programs, create a more favorable environment for personal growth, and provide support for the production of cultural content. Second, it should properly use WeChat's public accounts and other new media platforms to produce competitive content. Third, it should further explore its strength in cartoon and animation production and provide support for the development of relevant industries and enterprises.

4. Help young people better understand and identify with Guangzhou culture so as to improve their sense of belonging

The young people, as leaders of tomorrow, play an important role in carrying forward and developing the culture. Educating young people in local culture will enhance their identity and pride. These are necessary conditions for future inheritors. Guangzhou should strengthen its education of the young people in the local culture from the following three aspects.

First, the city should make sure that more courses on local culture are provided for the young people. Teaching materials on local history and culture should be prepared as supplement to standard textbooks. Students should be required to spend a certain period of time in museums every semester or school year and their attendance shall

---

[8]www.statista.com, visited on February 28, 2017.

constitute part of the assessment of their practical abilities. Extracurricular activities featuring unique local cultural forms should be organized to help young people develop concrete experience and better identify with the city.

Second, the city should make sure that the young people are offered more opportunities to experience intangible cultural heritage in person. Concrete efforts should be made to bring intangible cultural heritage to school, to classrooms, and into textbooks. Inheritors should be required to spend certain hours educating the public.

Third, the city should properly handle the relationship between regional culture and ethnical culture and enhance people's identification with the latter through the advancement of the former. The two forms of culture should be better integrated and consolidated. Thanks to their inclusiveness and inherent connection, the education of the young people can draw upon both cultural forms.

5. Speed up the reform of the cultural system and establish a modern cultural market system

First, efforts should be made to accelerate legislation so that there is always a law to follow. At present, there are not many laws that regulate culture related issues in our country. Some existing laws do not apply to culture. For example, the *Law on the State-owned Assets of Enterprises* which applies to state-owned enterprises fails to cover state-owned cultural assets. Therefore, it is very necessary to enact laws and regulations that strengthen the management and supervision of cultural assets. Such laws and regulations must be strictly observed and rigorously enforced.

Second, the city should properly handle the relationship between the government and the market and let the market play the fundamental role. All assets, be it state-owned or private, must be utilized according to market rules. The Party and the government should clearly define the mandates and responsibilities of designated authorities for culture management and asset managements and separate government agencies from private companies. Institutional arrangements should be made to improve decision-making and operation, maintain and increase the value of cultural assets, investigate accountabilities, and exercise supervision. The ultimate aim is to promote the sound development of state-owned cultural enterprises and increase their market performance and competitiveness. Considering the unique ideological feature of culture, the government should continue to provide sound guidance and strict supervision over the content while letting the market play its role.

Third, differentiated approaches should be adopted to promote the reform of performing troupes. Every situation has its uniqueness and there is no "one size fits all" pattern. For Cantonese Opera theaters and other troupes that are entrusted to pass on traditional local culture, financial support should be provided to ensure their mission can be accomplished. For song and dance ensembles, ballet theatres, and other popular arts troupes, the market should be allowed to play a decisive role while the government mainly functions as supervisor.

The Status of Intangible Cultural Heritage Protection in 2016 in Guangzhou and Policy Recommendations*

Lyu Huimin**

Abstract: In 2016, the work on intangible cultural heritage in Guangzhou was carried forward steadily. Specifically, it cultivated Canton embroidery the symbolic intangible cultural heritage of Guangzhou, conducted in-depth academic research, held training programs , actively participated in local international exhibitions and attached great importance to copyright protection for intangible cultural heritage. But there were also problems. For example, Guangzhou failed to properly integrate "commercial operation" and "base support", paid insufficient attention to the inheritance of intangible cultural heritage in rural areas, and did a poor job in inheriting folk-culture intangible cultural heritage. The research group suggests integrating "commercial operation" and "base support", inheriting intangible heritage culture in the vast rural areas and doing a better job in inheriting intangible cultural heritage of folk literature and traditional drama.

Key words: intangible cultural heritage, inheritance, in-depth

In 2016, Guangzhou endeavored to implement the thinking of building a cultural power put forward by the central government and emphasized the protection of intangible cultural heritage (hereinafter referred to as "ICH") and the upgrading of Guangzhou's cultural soft power to build a strong cultural city. In May, Guangzhou held the working conference on ICH to deploy the work of ICH for the coming year. While routine ICH work was proceeding steadily, conscious efforts were made to take it further.

I. Progress in ICH Protection in Guangzhou in 2016

i. ICH projects: Dual-drive by the government and the market to cultivate the landmark ICH project for Guangzhou

* This research report representsthe research results of Guangzhou Development Research Institute, Guangzhou University – a key research base of humanities and social sciences in colleges and universities of Guangdong Province, "Guangzhou Study" Collaborative Innovation and Development Center, Department of Education of Guangzhou Province, and Guangzhou Decision Advisory Team for Comprehensive City Development - the team innovation project of Guangdong ordinary institutions of higher learning; research results of the project of Guangzhou education science planning - "Research on Campus Inheritance of Intangible Cultural Heritage in Guangzhou" (project number: 1201534170); research results of Guangzhou 13th Five-Year Plan project in philosophy and social sciences - Research on "Guangzhou Model" for Remote Inheritance of Intangible Cultural Heritage (project approval No.: 2017GZYB02).

** Lyu Huimin, Ph.D., associate researcher of Social Policy Research Office, Guangzhou Development Research Institute, Guangzhou University.

In 2016, among the many ICH projects, Guangzhou listed ivory carving, jade carving, wood carving, Canton enamel, Canton embroidery, Cantonese opera, puppet show, Cantonese tunes, wooden-fish narration and chanting, and Cantonese legends as key protection projects. In particular, Canton embroidery was developed into a landmark ICH project of Guangzhou through the City of Embroidery - Canton Intangible Cultural Heritage Creativity Competition.

The well-planned Canton Embroidery Style contest was dedicated to the promotion of Canton embroidery, driven by both the government and the market. On the one hand, led by the government, it employed public platforms for the dissemination of knowledge and mobilized various social forces to contribute to it. On the other hand, the market-oriented contest valued the practicability and modernity of entries, helped improve the industrial chain of Canton embroidery, and introduced the traditional crafts into every aspect of modern life[9].

ii. ICH research: Two local records were published and academic activities on ICH were actively conducted

In 2016, two books on the ICH in Guangzhou were published, namely, *Records of Guangzhou Intangible Cultural Heritage* and *Development Report on Guangzhou Intangible Cultural Heritage Protection (2016)*.

Meanwhile, Guangzhou was also actively engaged in ICH academic activities, showing three characteristics. Firstly, multiple academic conferences were held, such as the Seminar on Intangible Cultural Heritage Protection and Innovation (sponsored by Guangzhou), Seminar on Intangible Cultural Heritage Protection (sponsored by Guangzhou), Seminar on the Protection of Intangible Heritage Intellectual Property (sponsored by Guangzhou), Intangible Cultural Heritage Story - Cultural Center and National Folk Culture Protection Forum (undertaken by Guangzhou). Secondly, these conferences involved a wide range of regions. For example, the Intangible Cultural Heritage Story - Cultural Center and National Folk Culture Protection Forum was sponsored by China Public Cultural Centers Association (CPCCA), undertaken by Guangzhou Cultural Center, and the co-organizers were Fujian Provincial Gallery of Art and Ningbo Cultural Center, with the attendance of more than 200 colleagues from cultural centers all over the country. Thirdly, these conferences continued to receive strong academic support from the Intangible Cultural Heritage Research Center of Sun Yat-sen University.

---

[9]Wu Bing'an, The Way to Revitalize Traditional Crafts Is to Introduce Them to Every Aspect of Modern Life, China Folklore Network, http://www.chinesefolklore.org.cn/web/index.php?NewsID=15326, December 15, 2016.

iii. ICH training: Organizing ICH training programs

In 2016, Guangzhou Academy of Fine Arts commissioned the School of Arts and Humanities to set up a popular training program on Canton enamel firing craft, and Guangzhou University commissioned the School of Fine Arts & Design to set up a training program for inheritors of Hami embroidery of Xinjiang, making it the first university in Guangdong Province to carry out trans-provincial ICH training programs. The above ICH training programs further promoted ICH inheritance in colleges and universities, allowing more inheritors to enter the campus and increasing college students' understanding of ICH. What's more, the Hami embroidery training program was conducive to promoting cultural exchanges between Guangzhou and ethnic minority areas.

iv. ICH display: Participating in local international conventions and exhibitions to expand the influence of Guangzhou's ICH

In December 2016, Guangzhou International Art Fair was held with the Intangible Cultural Heritage Center set up to increase the international visibility of local ICH resources. This fair showed two major features.

First, the introduction of the ICH into daily life. On the theme of "intangible cultural heritage in living space", the exhibition hall was built into a living space of Lingnan residential houses and made all kinds of ICH items part of it. In addition, the exhibition allowed citizens to draw Canton enamel on paper cups and take them home. It also invited viewers to drink tea and taste little chicken pie at Cantonese tea tables to make citizens feel that ICH is part of their daily life.

Second, on-site interaction with visitors. This exhibition invited inheritors to give on-site display and interactive experience. For example, the viewers could try copper forging and olive-stone carving by themselves.

v. Copyright of ICH: Emphasizing the copyright protection of ICH

In 2016, Guangzhou took the opportunity of Canton embroidery competition to place emphasis on the protection of ICH copyright, with a number of lectures under the title of "Copyright Protection and Risk Prevention of Art Design" held before and during the contest.

On August 27, the Seminar on Intellectual Property Protection of Intangible Cultural Heritage was held in the Intangible Cultural Heritage Protection Center in Guangzhou. In December, the competition organizing committee, in cooperation with Yuancang Intellectual Property Register Center, listed competition entries that agreed to trade the copyrights on CREATORSIPR, as a way to protect the property rights of Canton embroidery.

Among the above ICH activities, there were many lectures on knowledge popularization, higher-level research activities, theoretical education and concrete copyright trading practices.

vi. Routine ICH-related activities: The fifth batch of municipal-level ICH inheritors announced

In April 2016, Guangzhou Administration of Culture, Radio, Film, Television, Press and Publication announced the fifth batch of representative ICH inheritors at Guangzhou municipal level, covering a total of 33 people in nine categories of ICH projects. Up to then, there had been a total of 161 ICH inheritors at the municipal level in Guangzhou.

Table 1: Classified statistics of Guangzhou municipal ICH inheritors

	Folk literature	Traditional music	Traditional dance	Traditional drama	Chinese folk art forms	Traditional sports, and acrobatics	Traditional fine arts	Traditional skills and crafts	Traditional medicine	Folk customt
The 5th batch	1	4	3	1	0	4	6	9	2	3
total	1	25	18	15	7	6	36	35	11	7

For the above table, there are three main features in this list of inheritors:

First, it consolidates Guangzhou's advantage in traditional art and traditional skills. Among the fifth batch of ICH inheritors at the municipal level, there are 15 inheritors of traditional fine arts and traditional skills and crafts, accounting for 45.5% of the total in this review, showing an absolute advantage.

Second, there is an increase in the number of inheritors of traditional sports, entertainment and acrobatics. There were only two such inheritors among the past four batches of, while the fifth batch alone has approved four such inheritors, which shows that great importance had been attached to it.

Third, the older-generation inheritors are respected. Of the inheritors recognized from the first to the fourth batch, the average age is getting younger. But in this batch, one of the sports inheritors is an 88-year old man. It reflects the respect for the older generation in ICH protection.

II. Main Problems with ICH Protection in Guangzhou in 2016

i. "Commercial operation" and "base support" of ICH failed to be integrated properly

ICH protection in China is a top-down movement. The research group believes that the smooth development of ICH protection needs four indispensable elements: government support, inheritance in the non-public sector, commercial operation, and base support. In 2016, Guangzhou attached great importance to governmental support and inheritance in the non-public sector in the protection of ICH, but ignored commercial operation and base support which could complement and reinforce each other ICH inheritance.

Viewing from the development of ICH in 2016, commercial operations of ICH were scattered across the city and ICH products were decentralized, making it difficult to form a constellation effect of circulation, exchange and consumption of ICH products. Too many fragmented ICH exhibition bases make it difficult to build a landmark base of greater influence. In addition, what needs to be carefully considered is how to combine commercial operations with base support.

ii. ICH display and inheritance were mainly carried out in urban areas, but those in rural areas needed further attention

Rural Guangzhou has a vast territory, has accumulated a wealth of ICH resources throughout the history and is home to most of the ICH resources in Guangzhou. At present, there are two major problems in the ICH protection and inheritance in Guangzhou countryside.

Firstly, the demonstration of ICH is mainly in urban areas and rare in the countryside. In 2016, all the ICH activities in Guangzhou, including the grand Canton embroidery contest, ICH training programs and international exhibitions, were all carried out in the urban area and failed to reach the rural area.

Second, Guangzhou rural tourism failed to make full use of local ICH resources. Currently, Guangzhou's rural tourism mainly focuses on the development of rustic scenery and agritainment. However, the development of cultural heritage is inadequate, and in particular ICH has not been fully incorporated into the rural tourism system.

iii. Inheritance of folk-literature ICH is relatively weak and little progress is made in the inheritance of traditional drama

China's ICH projects are divided into ten categories, and folk literature belongs to the first major category. There are 7 municipal-level folk literature projects in Guangzhou (including the extended list), accounting for 5.6% of the total (125). There is only one inheritor for folk-literature ICH among the fifth batch of municipal-level ICH inheritors in 2016, accounting for 0.6% of the total (161). (See Table 2)

On the one hand, in terms of quantity, the proportion of folk literature inheritors, in particular, that of representative inheritors of folk literature is small. On the other hand, there are few inheritance activities for folk literature such as exhibitions, lectures and academic activities in Guangzhou.

Table 2: Classified statistics of representative ICH projects and inheritors in Guangzhou

	Folk literature	Traditional music	Traditional dance	Traditional drama	Chinese folk art forms	Traditional sports, entertainment and acrobatics	Traditional fine arts	Traditional skills and crafts	Traditional medicine	Folk custom	t
Number of projects	7	7	13	2	3	7	16	30	9	31	1
Percentage in the total number of projects	5.6%	5.6%	10.4%	1.6%	2.4%	5.6%	12.8%	24%	7.2%	25.6%	1
Number of inheritors	1	25	18	15	7	6	36	35	11	7	1
Percentage in the total number of inheritors	0.6%	15.5%	26.7%	36.0%	4.3%	3.7%	22.3%	21.7%	6.8%	4.3%	1

In recent years, the inheritance of drama has received more and more attention and Guangzhou is also committed to the promotion of drama on campus. Nowadays, there are mainly two ways of drama inheritance on campus: one is via classroom education, the other is through extracurricular activities. It is hard for the former to guarantee the effect of inheritance, because drama is a professional performance art too difficult for ordinary teachers to teach. The latter has a better teaching effect, but could reach only a few students, which makes it difficult to guarantee the effect of inheritance.

III. Countermeasure Proposals for ICH Protection in Guangzhou

i. Form ICH display bases with one principal base and multiple supporting bases and combine "commercial operation" with "base support"

As commercial operation and base support are important factors affecting the inheritance of ICH, the research group recommends:

(1) Forming an ICH display base system with Guangzhou Intangible Cultural Heritage Expo Park as the principal base, folk-custom museums and the ICH hall at the newly built Guangzhou Cultural Center as supporting bases. In order to expand the influence of ICH exhibition, the research group proposes to build Guangzhou ICH expo park into a landmark ICH exhibition base to display all ICH projects at the municipal level and above in Guangzhou in various ways. Other ICH bases should give play to their respective strength and display certain categories of ICH projects that suit them. For example, Guangzhou Folk Museum may display the ICH of folk custom, Chen Clan Ancestral Hall may exhibit traditional fine arts and traditional craftsmanship, and the ICH hall at newly built Guangzhou Cultural Center may be dedicated to ICH of distinct local features. This base system will lead to the boom of ICH inheritance in Guangzhou.

(2) Trading ICH products and property rights in Guangzhou ICH Expo Park. The expo park can not only display ICH projects, but also trade ICH products, commercializing each and every tradable ICH product, and showing the advantages of Guangzhou as a commercial capital.

ii. Contribute to countryside construction in Guangzhou and inherit the ICH culture in the vast countryside

Considering the inferior position of ICH inheritance in rural Guangzhou, the research group suggests combining ICH inheritance with countryside construction. Specifically, efforts can be made in the following aspects in 2017:

(1) Surveying the 10 Rural Tourism Demonstration Sites and 8 Beautiful Villages released by the Tourism Administration of Guangzhou in 2016 to dig out their ICH resources of distinct local features;

(2) Organizing local intellectuals, experts and scholars to fully interpret traditional cultural connotations of these representative ICH resources and their relevance to the contemporary society;

(3) Employing public platforms to promote these ICH resources and raise public

awareness;

(4) Designing travel routes and luring more tourists to these ICH resources.

iii. Take advantage of Guangzhou's animation industry to produce animation works based on folk literature

The inheritance of folk literature in Guangzhou is relatively weak. Yet folk-literature is the starting point of China's ICH movement and the No.1 category of China's top ten ICH projects, which is very important. In the omni-media era, ICH heritance and display must comprehensively make use of text, picture, sound, light, and electricity. [10]The research group believes that Guangzhou can take advantage of its advanced animation industry to produce animation films and TV programs based onits folk literature.

Guangzhou boasts a prospering animation industry. On the one hand, it is home to well-known animation companies such as Guangdong Alpha Animation and Culture Co., Ltd. and Guangzhou Comic fans Co., Ltd. On the other hand, Guangzhou has produced national animation sensations such as the *Pleasant Goat and Big Big Wolf.* Thus Guangzhou can absolutely bring folk literature to the screen and create animation films and TV programs with local characteristics to boost ICH inheritance and influence

iv. Launch the ICH awareness campaign on campus to cultivate teenager inheritors for ICH of performing arts, especially of traditional drama

In view of the state's emphasis on the inheritance of traditional Chinese operas and the problems with the inheritance of traditional-drama ICH in Guangzhou, research group suggests cultivating young inheritors of traditional drama through ICH awareness activities on campus in 2017 and creating theatergoing opportunities for teenagers. The Intangible Cultural Heritage Protection Center in Guangzhou contact local theaters to develop a popular repertoire acceptable to and suitable for the young audience, and contact schools to stage performances.

---

[10] See Ning Feng, Hou Jingjuan, Research on the Propagation Strategy of Intangible Cultural Heritage in the Omni-Media Era, *Journal of Nanchang Normal University* (Social Science), February 2016.

Research on Measures to Improve the International Influence of "Guangzhou Award"[*]

Tu Chenglin, Yang Yubin, Tan Yuanfang[**]

Abstract: The "Guangzhou Award" plays an important role in enhancing the international influence of Guangzhou and promoting the city's external exchange, but is still far from the expected effect. This paper puts forward specific suggestions on improving the international influence of "Guangzhou Award" as soon as possible, including building a scientific evaluation system, conducting case studies, promoting the study results, and developing a review team and think tanks, etc.

Keywords: Guangzhou Award, international influence, suggestions

I. The Value of "Guangzhou Award" for Guangzhou

Guangzhou International Award for Urban Innovation ("Guangzhou Award") is not only an important means to enhance the organizer's international reputation, but also a powerful support for Guangzhou to reach the commanding height of urban development in the future. Only by bearing that in mind can we give full play to its multiple values and promote the great-leap-forward development of Guangzhou.

i. Build a platform for innovation and exchange among international cities

For the world's participating city representatives, "Guangzhou Award" not only provides a display platform, but also creates an opportunity for global cities to exchange experience with each other. Taking the 1st "Guangzhou Award" as an example, the organizer Guangzhou Municipal Government deliberately arranged two activities, "Interview with Mayors" and "Case Exchange Meeting", to promote city administrators' interaction and exchange on urban innovation. By exchanging experience with each other, cities can plan better, not only in terms of the city

[*] This research report is a fruit of the collaboration between Guangzhou Development Research Institute of Guangzhou University - a provincial key research base for humanities and social sciences, "Guangzhou Studies" Collaborative Innovation and Development Center under Guangdong Provincial Development of Education, and the decision-making consultancy and innovation team for integrated development of Guangzhou - a provincial university innovation team of Guangdong.

[**] Tu Chenglin, head, research fellow and doctoral supervisor of Guangzhou Development Research Institute of Guangzhou University; Yang Yubin, assistant research fellow and Ph.D. of the Institute; Tan Yuanfang, deputy head, professor and Ph.D. of the Institute.

appearance, but also in aspects of urban governance and services, to ensure more scientific, convenient, transparent and popular policy making and implementation.

ii. New form of urban diplomacy

The urban diplomacy is both inter-governmental and non-governmental, involving a great diversity of players and activities in international contacts. The "Guangzhou Award" is a permanent international award established with the help of the World Organization of United Cities and Local Governments (UCLG) and is a rare sustainable brand in city-level diplomacy and public diplomacy. Through it, traditional local foreign affairs work is evolving into innovative urban diplomacy. As Yang Jiechi, former Foreign Minister of China, said: "The Guangzhou Award goes beyond the conflicts and disagreements caused by ideological and institutional differences and enriches the form of foreign exchange and cooperation".

iii. Show the rest of the world the image and development achievements of Guangzhou

The biennial Guangzhou Award is another important opportunity for Guangzhou to show its image and charm to the outside world following the 2010 Asian Games. To maximize the effect, recent administrations of the city have done a thorough job in hosting the Award event, allowing foreign guests to appreciate Guangzhou's economic and social development and the unique Lingnan culture from multiple perspectives and impressing them with Guangzhou's urban development.

iv. Provide experience for Guangzhou's city development

At present, Guangzhou is devoted to the creative, scientific development into a super-city, and is striving to explore a low-carbon, economical, intelligent and efficient new path towards urbanization focusing on people's wellbeing. An important vehicle for urban innovation practice, the Guangzhou Award gathers experts and distinguished guests to share their insights and winner cities and projects to share their experience, which will help break the "ceiling" in the innovative urban development of Guangzhou and elevate the city to a new level as a whole.

II. Assessment on Current Status of the International Influence of "Guangzhou Award"

The past three editions of the "Guangzhou Award" have built up great international influence. Among them, the 3rd edition held in 2016 registered the entries of 301 projects in 171 cities from 59 countries and regions, a significant increase from previous editions. This fully illustrated the overseas influence of the "Guangzhou

Award"

But we should see that there is still room for improvement. The Award not only fails to meet the expected goal set by Guangzhou Municipal Government, but also lags far behind other international influential urban awards or forums. First, despite the increasing entrants, the proportion of voluntary entrants is still not high. Because of the award's limited influence, Guangzhou still needs to mobilize the entrants, some of which apply for the award as a favor for the city. Second, only a few entrants are from major western developed countries and world powers while mostly are from third-world countries or are small- and medium-sized cities from developed countries. This shows that the "Guangzhou Award" is far from international in the real sense, and that it has little for Guangzhou, a megacity, to draw from participating small- and medium-sized cities and their innovation in urban development and management. Thirdly, the field investigation and in-depth study of entrants are not enough, and as a result, some projects which haven't been carried out or haven't produced effects are granted with the award, damaging the authority and value of the award. Fourthly, at present, there are obvious deficiencies in the evaluation system of urban innovation, case study, and coordination of academic resources, which are more administrative actions taken by the government. Due to the failure to mobilize sufficient academic resources at home and abroad, the Guangzhou Award has missed the premium opportunity to establish its say, authority and influence to a certain degree. Fifthly, the Guangzhou Award is spending more and more from edition to edition, raising the suspicion over that   some entrants are taking "free lunch" or "free riding", and making it difficult for the award to generate both social and economic benefits in the short term. Sixthly, except for the foreign affairs department, the security department, the cultural and communication departments and the media circle, other government departments, district governments, neighborhoods, public institutions and social organizations are not that enthusiastic about the nomination or awarding of the event. They simply regard themselves as onlookers. And the event is even less known to ordinary citizens. Without the inter-departmental collaboration and full support of the general public, it will be difficult to build the "Guangzhou Award" into an international event in the real sense.

III. Suggestions on Improving the International Influence of "Guangzhou Award"

i. Develop a scientific evaluation system as soon as possible to enhance the credibility and international influence of "Guangzhou Award"

To enhance the credibility and international influence of "Guangzhou Award", we must first of all formulate a scientific evaluation index system while bearing the following things in mind. The first is to distinguish the objects for evaluation. We should determine which object to evaluation, the city, the project, the government or the enterprise, and then establish the index system accordingly. The second is to consider the diversity of urban types. Domestic and foreign cities vary greatly in population size, economic status and management mode. The evaluation system needs to reflect the gap and comparability between mega-cities and small and-medium-sized cities, cities in developed and underdeveloped countries. The third is to accommodate the diversity of urban innovation projects. Some projects are about urban planning and regional development, some about public administration and social services, some about ecological environment and smart city, and others about housing and transportation. We need to develop a convention to compare these different innovations projects. The fourth is to verify the authenticity of application materials. Reasonable, scientific and feasible application means and research methods should be established to conduct objective assessment of application projects and field investigation on the implementation of projects, so as to exclude projects which haven't been implemented and experimental projects from the final review and safeguard the authority of "Guangzhou Award". Fifthly, attention should be paid to the reliability of innovation projects. Nominated or award-winning projects must be innovative and universal, whose experience and practice can be promoted in other cities, especially Guangzhou, so as to fuel the innovation-driven urban development in the rest of the world.

ii. Strengthen case study for the "Guangzhou Award" and vigorously promote innovation in Guangzhou's urban management

Firstly, we should strengthen the preliminary research. We should know the trend, dynamic of international urban innovation and successful cases of innovation, so that we will have clear criteria for solicitation and review. The second is to increase efforts in pre-review investigation. We may consider sending a number of investigation teams, led by senior government officials and renowned experts of Guangzhou, to carry out field investigations and research on some entrant projects. The organizing committee can also entrust the expert committee in the project country to do the investigation. The third is to increase efforts in project reports, exchange and research. At present, the review of projects and the presentation by the nominated city are hasty, resulting in insufficient knowledge, exchange, and study of projects; therefore, it is necessary to increase the input of time, money and manpower in such aspects. The fourth is to strengthen the follow-up study. Experts and scholars from universities and research institutions should be commissioned to review the application materials and conduct follow-up research on excellent cases, so as to summarize the reference value of specific cities and projects.

iii. Strengthen the capacity building of the review team and make it more international, more widely representative and more authoritative

In order to gain international influence, "Guangzhou Award" must, first of all, have public credibility. In addition to formulating a scientific evaluation index system, an international, representative and authoritative review committee should be established. Therefore, relevant departments of Guangzhou should promptly set up an expert team of a considerable size for the "Guangzhou Award", i.e., "International Expert Database for Urban Innovation Consultation". First, the expert team should be extensive. It should include top experts at home and abroad, the academia, political figures, and representatives of other walks of society to show the professional and geographical coverage of the award. Second, the expert team should be professional. Experts in the expert database should be specialized in such fields as natural science, social sciences and humanities, who cooperate with each other to provide intellectual support and sustainable impetus for the evaluation of the award. Third, the expert committee should be randomly selected. The expert database is to provide professional and technical support for the review of "Guangzhou Award" and to ensure its credibility and authority. In order to prevent nominated cities from "lobbying" and "canvassing", it should ensure that the number of experts in the expert database is 8 to 10 times that required for each edition, and the review experts for each edition shall be determined by drawing lots and their position is not permanent.

iv. Strengthen capacity building of think tanks, and develop research platforms through the partnership among government departments, universities and research institutions

Firstly, an international urban innovation think tank platform should be established with joint efforts. To become a sustainable international award with extensive attention, "Guangzhou Award" must have in-depth theoretical research and profound knowledge reserve. To achieve this, it is suggested that relevant departments set up an international urban innovation think tank platform with universities and research institutes from inside and outside the city. We should not only conduct in-depth research on international urban innovation and strengthen case study through regular cooperation and commissioned research tasks, but also prepare research reports, book series, and papers and improve the existing data bank to raise the theoretical level of local urban innovation research. The second is to invite bidders for research projects. Currently, the academic research and media reports on the "Guangzhou Award" are mostly superficial and lack systematic and in-depth research process and data accumulation. If this trend continues, it will be adverse to the international influence of "Guangzhou Award". Hence we suggest in-depth theoretical research and countermeasure research on issues related to "Guangzhou Award". We may consider appropriating a certain amount of funds every year to set up a number of long-term follow-up or emergency counseling research projects, and commission them to domestic and foreign universities and research institutes through bidding annually, which can attract wide attention from the academic circle and the society and accumulate rich research results through long-term and systematic research. The third is to hold symposiums dedicated to the "Guangzhou Award". At present, several forums take place alongside the evaluation and awarding of the "Guangzhou Award", but are reduced to mere formalities by the limited duration and research efforts. Measures should be taken to tackle this problem. Universities and research institutes undertaking the "Guangzhou Award" research projects can be commissioned to hold seminars on certain topics. Or comprehensive seminars can be held in cooperation with the social science planning department and the publicity department to strengthen theoretical research through award evaluation, expert review.

v. Introduce social resources to strengthen and Guangzhou Institute for Urban Innovation

First, Guangzhou should continue to exert the government's role as the primary promoter. The Foreign Affairs Office of Guangzhou Municipal Government has played a leading role in setting up the Guangzhou Institute for Urban Innovation (GIUI) and should continue to play the lead role in the future. It should not only give full authority to GIUI to carry out all ongoing work but also sincerely support GIUI to act independently from governmental institutions, thus getting rid of the embarrassing status of "secondary government" and "the dependent". It should be an independent social organization delivering government-commissioned services. Second, an open platform with social resources should be in place. As a social organization, GIUI should, on the one hand, jump out of its small circle and absorb all kinds of social resources with an open mind to jointly contribute to the "Guangzhou Award"; on the other hand, GIUI should focus its development on recruiting group members, especially universities, research institutes and other social organizations to participate in its decision-making and daily operation, so as to expand its current circle and diversify its composition. Third, it should give active play to its professional functions. It is suggested to set up a number of special committees in accordance with the classification of entrants for in-depth background research on them. At the same time, academic exchange between the special committees is encouraged, so as to give play to the advisory function of GIUI.

vi. Make the Guangzhou Award a carnival for the whole city instead of a one-man show for the government

First, the city government should be more open-minded about the "Guangzhou Award", instead of limiting it to the sphere of Guangzhou or Guangzhou's foreign affairs department, and refusing the help from other cities or departments. It ought to make it clear that "Guangzhou Award" is an international event which needs the actual participation of different cities and international organizations. It is also necessary to clarify that "Guangzhou Award" is not only a duty of Guangzhou's foreign affairs department, but also requires the collaboration and contribution from all other departments and offices in Guangzhou. Second, social resources should be introduced to the planning and holding of the "Guangzhou Award". "Guangzhou Award" should not be regarded as a government action. In fact, it is more than that. We ought to learn from western countries in holding international awards and take the initiative to invite universities, research institutes and social organizations to participate in the planning and project undertaking of the award. By so doing, we can leverage social resources and save government at the same time. Third, more publicity channels should be explored to step up publicity efforts. On one hand, it is necessary to publicize widely through various channels to raise the public awareness of, support and participation for the "Guangzhou Award". On the other, foreign troupes should be invited to stage shows, and the float parade and urban innovation competition be staged to engage and entertain the general public, turning the "Guangzhou Award" into a carnival for the whole city to build up its influence at home and abroad.

Analysis of Guangzhou's Urban Development in 2016 and Prospects for 2017[1]

Research group of Guangzhou Development Research Institute, Guangzhou University;[2]

Abstract: The report analyzes the overall situation of Guangzhou's urban development in 2016, summarizes the main achievements in the fields of urban planning, development, transportation and land, focuses on the challenges and problems encountered in 2016, and finally predicts and puts forward suggestions on Guangzhou's urban development in 2017.

Keywords: Urban development, network city, situation analysis, Guangzhou

I. Analysis of the Overall Situation of Urban Development in Guangzhou in 2016

The year of 2016 saw the launch of Guangzhou's 13th Five-Year Plan. This year, the city comprehensively followed the instructions of the 5th and 6th plenary sessions of the 18th CPC Central Committee and national and provincial conference on urban development. While adapting to the new normal of economic development, Guangzhou continued to pursue innovative, coordinated, open, green and shared development, respected and followed the pattern of urban development, and adhered to the sustainable development strategy featuring coordinated economic, population, social, resource and environmental development. To improve the quality of new-type urbanization, the government employed scientific mindset, advanced philosophy and expertise to plan, develop and administer the city, modernized the city governance system and capacity. To enhance the city's overall strength and achieve sustainable development, it adopted the innovation-driven development strategy on all fronts. To consolidate and elevate its status as a national central city, Guangzhou kept

---

[1] This research report is a fruit of the collaboration between Guangzhou Development Research Institute of Guangzhou University - a provincial key research base for humanities and social sciences, "Guangzhou Studies" Collaborative Innovation and Development Center under Guangdong Provincial Development of Education, and the decision-making consultancy and innovation team for integrated development of Guangzhou - a provincial university innovation team of Guangdong.

[2] Head of the research group: Tu Chenglin, researcher, doctoral supervisor, and head of Guangzhou Development Research Institute of Guangzhou University. Members: Yao Huasong, associate research fellow and Ph.D. of the Institute; Zhou Lingxiao, deputy head, associate professor and Ph.D. of the Institute; Liang Ningxin, associate research fellow and Ph.D. of the Institute; Lyu Huimin, associate research fellow and Ph.D. of the Institute. Author: Yao Huasong.

strengthening its comprehensive functions and building its regional and international influence. Positioned itself to be a national central city, an international trade center and a comprehensive transportation hub, Guangzhou took the initiative to undertake projects under the Belt and Road Initiative, issued Opinions on Strengthening Urban Planning, Development, and Administration, accelerated to build itself into a network city and an international hub for shipping, aviation and technological innovation, and formed a multi-point coordinated development pattern featuring the economic, innovation and landscape belts along the Pearl River. By coordinating urban-rural planning, development and administration, it built a good momentum for accelerating progress in urban planning, development, transportation and renewal.

i. Infrastructure construction for the seaport, airport, rail port and information port was sped up and the development of three strategic hubs went on well.

"Accelerating to build Guangzhou into a hub-type network city" was the keynote of Guangzhou's urban development in 2016 and the effect was best illustrated by infrastructure construction and investment. In 2016, Guangzhou's key infrastructure investment increased significantly. From January to November, the infrastructure investment was RMB128.5 billion, an increase of 21.7% over the same period last year. In particular, 53 projects related to the development of three strategic hubs secured a combined investment of RMB39.2 billion, accounting for 118% of the yearly target. The combined investment in the 35 provincial key infrastructure projects reached RMB52.8 billion, 134% of their yearly target. Guangzhou sped up infrastructure construction for the seaport, airport, rail port and information port and generated encouraging results. In 2016, Baiyun Airport ranked the 3rd among Chinese airports with the passenger throughput of nearly 59 million; Guangzhou Port ranked the 3rd in China with the cargo throughput of 544 million tons and the container throughput of 18.75 million standard containers; the international tourist throughput grew up 19.3%.In 2016, four more railways traveled through Guangzhou including the Nanning-Guangzhou Railway and the Guizhou-Guangdong Railway. By the end of 2016, Guangzhou's total expressway mileage hit 972 kilometers and subway mileage 308 kilometers consisting of 10 in-service subway lines (sections).

In 2016, Guangzhou did a great job in building the international shipping, aviation and technological innovation hubs. As to shipping, the city actively pushed ahead 21 projects for the building of the international shipping hub, completed and put the Phase III project of Nansha Port into operation, built 24 dry ports and representative offices, opened eight more international sister ports and 11 international liner routes, launched the Pearl River Freight Rate Index and ranked the 3rd in China for the size of its cruise tour market. As to aviation, Guangzhou launched eight projects for the building of the international aviation hub, opened and resumed 27 international air routes, completed the construction of the main body of Terminal 2, landed the provincial headquarters of China Eastern Airlines, and completed the construction of the aircraft hangar of ST Aerospace.

For the building of the international hub of technological innovation, the city government of Guangzhou formulated and promulgated Administrative Measures for High-tech Business Incubators, Measures on Leaning Government Services towards the 100 Model Enterprises in Innovation, Measures on the Commercialization of Research Findings, Opinions on Accelerating the Pooling of Industry Leaders, and four supporting policies (collectively known as the "1+4" policies for human resources) to optimize the policy environment in favor of technological innovation. In 2016, Guangzhou's government input into science and technology (S&T) amounted to RMB11.287 billion, taking up 5.81% of the municipal government expenditure. The growing government investment in S&T and business initiative to innovate injected great vitality into the city's technological innovation, leading to improvements in both quantity and quality. In 2016, Guangzhou handled a total of 99,070 patent applications, up by 56.52% from the previous year, including 31,850 invention patent applications, up by 58.7%.

ii. Guangzhou achieved breakthrough in the building of the comprehensive transportation hub

In 2016, Guangzhou was named a national model city in comprehensive transportation services. Its program to build into an international hub of comprehensive transportation has been included into the national 13th Five-Year Plan, meaning that mobilize national, provincial and municipal resources would be mobilized to facilitate the program. The master plan on the railway hub passed the review by China Railway. In addition, Guangzhou launched the main-body construction of three national railway projects, six inter-city rail projects, 11 subway projects and eight expressway projects; the new Guangzhou Bridge, the expanded Guangzhou-Qingyuan Expressway, the Phase II project of Subway Line 6 and the Phase I project of Subway Line 7 were open to traffic; the construction was sped up for the road and bridge engineering project of Liuhua Lake Tunnel and the remodeling of Huangpu East Road. In that year, Guangzhou completed the preparatory work for a number of major road and bridge engineering projects including the Chebei Road – Xinjiao West Road Tunnel and the eastern extension of Riverside Boulevard, and coordinated to advance the preparation for key transportation projects to kick off in

2017 including the Ruyifang radial road system project. In 2016, Guangzhou completed or basically completed 10 highway projects, including the Kaichuang Street Overpass on Guangzhou-Shenzhen Highway, remodeling of Yixin Road, and the entry/exit project of Daguan Road on Guangzhou-Shenzhen Expressway; and completed the remodeling of the Kangwang Road Tunnel beneath Liuhua Lake and Huangpu East Road (the Huangpu Avenue feeder – Huakeng Road section), the expansion of Guangzhou Bridge, and the construction of roads near the Xiaoping welfare housing program. The combined mileage of bridges and roads built in 2016 totaled 16 kilometers.

iii. Guangzhou made active efforts in building the underground utility tunnel system and a sponge city

In April 2016, Guangzhou was named a national pilot city for the development of the underground utility tunnel system with the highest overall score. In the absence of a municipal policy governing the underground tunnel system, Guangzhou laid down concrete specifications regarding related planning, construction, administrative law enforcement, maintenance, administration and technical requirements. It was also active in exploring the public-private partnership (PPP) mode and accumulated helpful experience in social capital operation. In 2016, three pilot projects, namely, the Guangzhou Downtown – Huadu Class I Highway, Subway Line 11, and Tianhe Intelligence Business District, kicked off. The city finished the field survey of 38,009km underground tunnel system in the downtown, promoted the joint collection and sharing of related data, and submitted the Municipal Administrative Measures on the Underground Utility Tunnel System for review. It also issued Regulations on Accelerating the Development of the Grid, built eight substations and a total of 285km of transmission lines of 110kV and above, and gradually improved fire stations and wheelchair accessibility. Because of its topography and climate, Guangzhou has been vulnerable to floods, typhoons, storm surges and rainstorms since ancient times and its streets are often flooded. In response, Guangzhou proposed to build itself into a sponge city, in an attempt to tackle issues with the water ecology, water resources, water environment, water safety and water culture brought by intense urbanization. In 2016, it did a great job in preparing for the nomination of a pilot sponge city. To fix the chronic water logging problem amid rapid urbanization, the city government proposed to preserve the existing mountain and water resources, promote the river chief system, and build the city into a scenic sponge city based on existing ecological corridors and infrastructure. To this end, it designated 35 development zones, 131 drainage zones and 176 development units.

iv. Guangzhou continued to advance urban renewal.

According to the Opinions on Strengthening Urban Planning, Construction and Administration, Guangzhou will continue to advance differentiated urban renewal for spatial optimization, social and economic development, cultural inheritance and living environment improvement. In particular in Liwan and other old districts, the city government shall gradually replace the undifferentiated demolition and reconstruction with mini-reconstruction and made the latter as important as the former for urban renewal. In 2016, Guangzhou adopted the policy of sweeping reconstruction in key functional zones and mini-reconstruction in the rest of the city. Unlike undifferentiated demolition and reconstruction, the mini-reconstruction mode values cultural inheritance, revamps historical buildings, follows advance planning, introduces proper industries without damaging historical and cultural heritage, gives cultural heritage and historical buildings new purposes, and eventually injects new life to local neighborhoods. In 2016, the city government delegated the power of examining and approving 26 key urban renewal projects to local governments, and issued the Plan on Mini-Reconstruction of Old Neighborhoods in Guangzhou, aimed at improving the living environment in these neighborhoods.[3] A total of 26 pilot projects were launched in 2016. They were distributed in 11 districts of Guangzhou and fell into the following four categories: rural specialty towns, villages for sweeping demolition and reconstruction, village industrial parks and neighborhoods for mini-reconstruction. Taking Liwan District, an old district of Guangzhou, for example. In June 2016, it issued the Three-Year Action Plan for Mini-Reconstruction of Old Neighborhoods in Liwan District (2016-2018), determining to complete the mini-reconstruction of 126 neighborhoods in the district in three years. The core mechanism behind it is the Steering Committee on Neighborhood Development which comprises representatives of local residents, is administered and governed by local residents, conducts polls on neighborhood revamping, and applies to the government for funding based on "actual needs." This practice breaks away from the traditional undifferentiated reconstruction mode. Besides, it also trusts local residents with the follow-up work of property management, such as the maintenance of septic tanks and sewage pipelines.

---

[3] Administrative powers over urban renewal to be delegated to lower-level governments include: verifying the basic data of key projects, checking the building is built legally, examining the main body for reconstruction and the land use plan (the area and scope of self-financed renovation, financed lots, and government-purchased land), checking the price of financed land, verifying the total volume of the resettlement project, checking the reconstruction cost, examining and approving the land preparation plan and the qualifications of the land purchaser, examining and approving the phase-specific construction plan, recognizing villagers' voting results, and examining and approving the implementation plan.

v. Guangzhou tightened control over the real estate market.

In 2016, the city government of Guangzhou did a remarkable job in the oversight of the real estate market. On one hand, it managed to maintain the healthy, stable development of the real estate market. Shortly after the central government gave relevant instructions, Guangzhou issued Opinions on Promoting the Stable, Healthy Development of the Real Estate Market, in an attempt to prevent the violent fluctuation of the housing price. It actively promoted the supply-side structural reform and reduced the housing stock. In 2016, it took 6.5 months and 15.7 months to sell the first-hand residential and commercial properties, respectively, on average in Guangzhou, 3.7 months and 3.2 months less than the previous year, beating the yearly target. Meanwhile, it tightened market regulation, accelerated the development of the rental housing market, guided public opinions and stabilized the market expectation. In 2016, a total of 140 million square meters of first-hand residential properties were sold across Guangzhou, up by 30% from the previous year, at the average price of RMB16,700/m2, up by 9.9%; 12.7 million square meters of second-hand residential properties were sold, up by 70%, at the average price of RMB15,500/m2, up by 17%.In August and December, Guangzhou's experience in real estate market control was promoted by the central leadership and the Ministry of Housing and Urban-Rural Development, respectively. On the other hand, centering on the improvement of people's livelihood, Guangzhou took concrete actions to enhance the housing welfare for its citizens. In 2016, Guangzhou raised funds for the construction of 25,830 government-subsidized apartments, completed 7,441 of them, issued the rental subsidy to 1,693 households, and beat the yearly target set by the provincial government. Throughout the year, it received 10,335 applications for public rental housing, and provided 10,406 such apartments to local low-income households and migrant workers, greatly easing the housing problem for the disadvantaged.

vi. Guangzhou continued to improve the urban and rural environment and develop demonstration towns and villages

In 2016, Guangzhou scored encouraging progress in creating a clean, tidy, safe and orderly city environment. First, the air quality was better. The average concentration of PM2.5, PM10, SO2, NO2, and the 95th percentile of CO was 36 mg/m3, 56 mg/m3, 12 mg/m3, 46 mg/m3 and 1.3 mg/m3, down by 7.7%, 5.1%, 2.1%, 7.7%, and 7.1% from the previous year, respectively; the 90th percentile of O3 was 155 mg/m3, up by 6.9%.The air quality met the national standard in 84.7% of the days throughout the year, a year-on-year decrease of 0.8 percentage point. The improvement in air quality was attributed to the city's tighter control over industrial pollution and vehicle exhaust.

Secondly, the water quality was stabilized on the whole. Throughout the year, 100% of the rivers and centralized sources of drinking water across the city met the national standard for water quality; the proportion of water sections not suitable for usage any more (below Class V) was 15.4%; that of good surface water quality (Class III or above) was 53.8%; and 100% of the converging sections of cross-city rivers (estuaries) met the national standard for water quality. In 2016, Guangzhou shut down 292 small companies that had caused serious water pollution, and launched crackdowns in 10 major polluting industries including papermaking, electroplating and printing & dyeing as well as highly polluting industrial clusters. By the end of 2016, it had investigated a total of 3,493 industrial companies in 490 villages (neighborhoods) and demanded 2,423 of them to make rectifications, of which 2,176 actively followed, with the rectification rate of 89.8%.

As to the improvement of the urban environment, Guangzhou concentrated its efforts in Jinshazhou, Tongdewei and Luochongwei and all the key projects went on smoothly. The Tongde Hospital was expected to finish in 2017, Luochongwei started the preparation for 11 reconstruction projects, and Jinshazhou saw continuous progress in the Xunfeng Substation project and the Xunfeng Hill Park Phase II project. Besides, after three years of hard work, the city had basically completed the task of revamping 269 urban villages, greatly improving the living environment and public security for local residents, and contributing to the formation of a clean, tidy, safe and orderly city environment.

As to the improvement of the rural environment, Guangzhou launched a three-year action plan on building a beautiful countryside. It opened a public account on WeChat to raise public awareness of specialty towns and villages. The city government worked with villages in planning 470 infrastructure and public service projects. So far, 89 pilot projects for the building of a beautiful countryside have passed the acceptance check, and the latest phase of the road lamp installation project in rural areas has been going on smoothly. Meanwhile, Guangzhou actively promoted the development of central towns, especially demonstration towns. Among them, Taiping Town was named a national demonstration town in new-type urbanization, Paitan recommended for the first batch of national specialty towns, and Aotou named both a national demonstration town in new-type urbanization and a national pilot administrative town.

II. Challenges and Problems Facing Urban Development in Guangzhou in 2016

In 2016, the overall situation of urban development in Guangzhou was better than expected, but there were still challenges regarding the external environment and internal structural optimization and quality improvement.

While we examined the urban and social development in Guangzhou last year, the following issues stood out and caught our attention.

i.   Urban infrastructure failed to meet the demands of local citizens

The latest master plan on urban development has made it a key task for years to come to build Guangzhou into a hub-type network city. In recent years, Guangzhou has done a lot of work in urban infrastructure, with remarkable progress in subway, BRT, regular bus, water bus and Ruyue Bus programs. But its urban infrastructure still falls short of the vision of building a hub-type network city and fails to meet the growing demands of citizens. To address this issue, improvements shall be made in the following outstanding aspects.

First, transport infrastructure. Generally speaking, transport is convenient within downtown Guangzhou, but not so easy from the central area to the peripheral area such as Conghua, Zengcheng, Panyu, Huangpu, and Nansha. For one reason, traditional means of transport such as the public bus system have only a limited supply of vehicles and fail to meet the huge demand of commuting between the central and peripheral areas. For another, there lack sufficient expressways connecting urban and rural areas, or suburban areas, and traffic jams are common. For example, it takes only 30 to 40 minutes to drive from the downtown Guangzhou to the industrial park in Qingyuan, but more than one hour to northern districts of Huadu and Baiyun in Guangzhou.

Second, infrastructure concerning people's livelihood. As a comprehensive central city in South China, Guangzhou tops Guangdong in terms of educational and medical facilities, but they are overly concentrated in the central area, reducing the suburban area to a much inferior position in both quantity and quality. Guangzhou has been trying to develop a sub-center to ease the pressure on the old quarter, but fails to build sufficient schools, hospitals, sports facilities and other infrastructure closely associated to people's livelihood in the peripheral area, challenging the spillover of its urban functions. In industrial agglomeration zones such as Huangpu, Luogang and Nansha, the desired integrated industrial and urban development hasn't materialized and the number of schools, hospitals and sports facilities, all major vehicles of urban functions, falls far short of the demands of local residents.

Third, supporting municipal works. Guangzhou's municipal works are generally poor: some are old and worn out and some are to be built. On the whole, in central, peripheral and suburban areas, the planning and development of municipal works such as the underground utility tunnel system, sewage and waste treatment facilities, oil and gas stations, and markets is backward and fails to meet the needs for daily life and production.

ii. Urban renewal fails to meet people's need for a beautiful urban environment

With the intensifying scarcity of land resources, it's the inevitable choice of Guangzhou to expand into the peripheral area and improve the quality of existing facilities in the central area. In this context, sweeping demolition and reconstruction in the old quarter becomes equally important as the development of new neighborhoods in the peripheral area, and urban renewal is pressing. In certain sense, the progress and effect of urban renewal has become a key measurement of the transformation of the city. Guangzhou put into effect Measures on Urban Renewal from January 2016 and has passed the Plan on the Mini-Reconstruction of Old Neighborhoods in Guangzhou, in an attempt to explore the mini-reconstruction mode, phase it in old neighborhoods with outdated facilities and poor living conditions, and make it an equally important means of urban renewal as sweeping demolition and reconstruction.

The mini-reconstruction mode aims to eliminate threats to housing safety, improve the living environment and facilities, and replace and upgrade public service facilities such as roads, electricity, gas, and water supply, sewage treatment, fire protection, environmental sanitation and communications. But mini-reconstruction is still a novelty and has many obstacles to overcome.

First, so far mini-reconstruction efforts have focused more on community-level maintenance and improvement of the physical environment through property management, but less on the building of the soft environment including the sense of belonging, the community spirit and community cohesion, etc. Table 1 shows the content of mini-reconstruction in Bantang, Liwan District, and Guangzhou. In Xicun Neighborhood of Liwan, a public poll by the Steering Committee on Neighborhood Development collected concrete concerns about bumpy roads, burst tubes in septic tanks, low tap water pressure, and the lack of fire-fighting water. Likewise in Bantang Village of Liwan, the mini-reconstruction efforts were directed to the building of kindergartens, community service centers, public toilets, farmers' markets and parking spaces. Both of them neglect the spiritual bonding of local residents by organizing certain activities. In other words, the current mini-reconstruction efforts are too practical to care about the formation of the community spirit. The author has no intention to argue whether to build a clean, tidy, safe and orderly physical urban environment is sensible and scientific or not, but he does believe that the sense of community, vitality and charm of a city or a neighborhood is a higher goal worth fighting for.

Table 1 Content of Mini-Reconstruction in Bantang, Liwan District, Guangzhou[4]

Item	Content
Cultural inheritance	To designate one cultural heritage site under provincial protection, two under district protection, 15 recommended cultural heritage sites, and 57 traditional historical buildings
More service facilities	To build one community service center, one kindergarten, one service center for the elderly, one farmers' market and public toilets
More public activity space	To increase 17,000m2 public green space
More parking space	To build 30 parking spaces for tourist coaches

Secondly, the projects and money for mini-reconstruction are not equally distributed, but overly concentrated in Liwan and other old districts. To the author's notice, the city government of Guangzhou provides financial support for neighborhood mini-reconstruction. According to the Urban Renewal Projects and Funding Scheme of Guangzhou in 2016, out of the RMB198.8 million budget, RMB188 million was divided by 38 mini-reconstruction projects, most of which were in Liwan, with the combined government investment of RMB114 million. From Figure 1 we can see that Liwan and Yuexiu together hosted 48.3% of all mini-reconstruction projects, leaving other districts far behind. The research group believes that mini-reconstruction should not be limited to Liwan and other old districts, and newly-developed districts including Nansha also have strong demand for mini-reconstruction to address issues such as the missing sense of community due to the massive scale of neighborhoods and the inconvenient interaction among residents caused by poorly designed infrastructure.

---

[4] Source: Zhan Ting. Examination and Approval Powers Delegated to Lower-level Governments for 26 Key Projects. *Southern Metropolis Daily*. December 6, 2016.

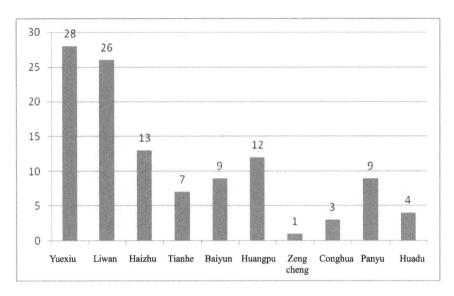

Figure 1 Distribution of Urban Renewal Projects in Guangzhou

Thirdly, the funding source for mini-reconstruction projects lacks diversity. In 2017, the city government of Guangzhou plans to earmark RMB600 million to mini-reconstruction projects, in particular public-interest projects, and the receiving districts shall each match the city fund at the 1:1 ratio. In other words, the city government and the district government are the two primary sources of funding for mini-reconstruction projects. That is not enough, but private and social capital hasn't been allowed to enter this area.

iii. Rural development is inferior in quality on the whole.

In an age of post-urbanization and counter-urbanization, rural development and coordinated urban-rural development have become a public consensus, and the Beautiful Countryside Campaign has remained a priority project for the city government of Guangzhou in recent years. Spurred by government-led pairing for poverty reduction, government fund allocation, project landing and investment attraction, against the backdrop of suburbanization and counter-urbanization, the nostalgia economy, agritainment, outings and rural tours have been flourishing in recent years. Thanks to that, Conghua, Zengcheng, Huadu and Panyu, all located in rural Guangzhou, have developed rapidly, farmers' income has increased too, the urban-rural interaction has been strengthened, and villages have witnessed significant improvement in their roads, transport facilities, schools, hospitals, public health, natural environment and comprehensive services. But there are also some structural problems. Limited by backward planning, the absence of relevant regulations and rules, and the overall low educational level of villagers, rural development in Guangzhou, especially that in some remote towns and villages, is inferior in quality and still far from the true meaning of "beautiful countryside".

First, there lacks a master plan, the development is extensive and illegal use of land is rampant. Driven by the huge profits from land requisition compensation and land development, illegal use of land is common in many rural areas in Guangzhou. With the absence of laws on rural development planning and procedures for the planning, approval and acceptance check of rural houses built by villagers, it's common for villagers to build houses at will, resulting in a lot of idle homesteads and houses and the ownership of multiple houses by single households. Without doubt, this phenomenon goes against Guangzhou's advocate for building into an intensive city and for intensive land utilization.

Secondly, rural specialty resources are to be better developed. Rural areas such as Conghua, Zengcheng, Panyu and Huadu boast many scenic spots, protected cultural heritage sites, forest parks, historical sites, and the association with many historical figures and events. But these precious vehicles for cultural development are scarcely developed or utilized; even if they are, their cultural connotation is often neglected due to vulgar taste. As a result, the resources are not well used to develop these places into specialty towns. There is still a long way ahead to build up the cultural brand of rural areas and improve the physical rural environment.

Thirdly, rural economic development excessively relies on the form of agritainment which is operated by rural households separately without planning or resource coordination. Patrons of such business know that many owners don't have any planning, design or seek for expert advice for their agritainment facilities. Most of them feed the customers in their own house and park the customers' cars or coaches' right at the front yard, displaying features of the unsophisticated roadside economy. There are also worries and doubts over the food quality, road safety, interior decoration, business model, and the health permit of service providers and the owner's business license.

iv. There is a big gap between Nansha's current status and its positioning as the sub-center of Guangzhou

According to the official statement, Nansha is positioned to be a strategic hub for the implementation of the Belt and Road Initiative, the pilot zone for gathering high-end factors in the Pearl River Delta, and the sub-center of Guangzhou by proceeding from the city's reality, serving the international market, and leveraging its advantages as a national new area, a pilot free trade area and a national demonstration area for indigenous innovation. Old districts like Yuexiu and Liwan and traditional industrial and business districts such as Tianhe and Huangpu all face the challenges for improving the quality and efficiency of existing facilities and resources and optimizing the development effect. In comparison, Nansha, a newly-developed area, is likely to be the bigger driving force for future economic development of Guangzhou for years to come. But given its weak foundation, Nansha needs to address the following issues in order to truly live up to the name of sub-center.

First, the population in Nansha is too small to produce the regional production scale and agglomeration effect or fully stimulate the consumption demand. By the end of 2016, the permanent population of Nansha was about 680,000, of whom 90% were absorbed from Panyu after the adjustment of administrative divisions. The main reason for Nansha's lack of appeal to newcomers is that its original industrial system was dominated by the heavy industry while the newly-developed industries are too sophisticated and high-end, such as shipping services, financial services, and high-end equipment manufacturing, leaving little market space for comprehensive and general commercial and trade services, medical services, senior care, community services and the informal sector. The local economy is taken up mostly by high-output, high-tech, intelligent industries with a long business cycle, which, however, are weak in boosting the development of other industries or improving the local livelihood. And the jobs they offer are limited. Besides, Nansha is located in the suburb, with a short supply of service facilities and poorly integrated urban and rural development. The pendulum lifestyle is common among local workforce - commuting to work in Nansha in the morning and back to downtown Guangzhou at night. As a result, the workers have little sense of belonging here and most of them regard Nansha merely as a place for work.

Secondly, Nansha's development is too extensive and should be more intensive and refined. To our notice, Nansha's roads are spacious and clearly oriented towards the use of motor vehicles. But their greenery is limited and density low, with very few lanes reserved for pedestrians and cyclists, which is bad for the gathering of population and intensive social and economic activities and bad for the formation of the sense of belonging and emotional attachment to the district. As far as intensive urban development is concerned, the GDP of Singapore, an internationalized metropolis, is 16 times that of Nansha's, its population more than eight times, but the construction area only about twice that of Nansha. It means that Nansha still has much room to increase its industrial and population capacity per unit area.

Thirdly, Nansha needs to strengthen its transport infrastructure to better play the role of regional transport hub. At present, Nansha is mainly connected to downtown Guangzhou by subway lines, expressways and express bus lines. But any of the above means of transportation will take more than 60 minutes. For local residents, Nansha feels more like "another city" than "suburban Guangzhou". Besides, transit traffic takes up about 53% of the total traffic in Nansha. The substitution rate of public transport is very low. Subway Line 4 covers only a small population and is difficult to transfer to other means of transportation. Local travel is realized primarily by car, motorcycle or electric bicycle.

Fourthly, since Nansha was designated as a free trade area, the land and housing price has been surging and numerous residential buildings have mushroomed everywhere. But most of the buyers are speculators, holiday takers or retirees, reducing Nansha into their enclave. In addition, consumers from Dongchong and Dagang tend to spend in Panyu and the old quarter of Guangzhou, and local consumption is sluggish. In other words, except for property investment, the spending in other aspects of life and production is seriously lagging behind, which is very bad for the formation and development of the living center in Nansha, or the sub-center of Guangzhou.

III. The Trend of Urban Development in Guangzhou in 2017 and Policy Recommendations

In 2017, Guangzhou will comprehensively implement the instructions made by the 5th and 6th plenary sessions of the 18th CPC Central Committee and the Central Work Conference on Urban Development, quicken the pace of growing into a national central city and a hub-type network city, vigorously implement the innovation-driven development strategy and the "hub+" strategy, strive to build the international shipping center, logistics center and trade center and modern financial service system, develop infrastructure that matches its capacity of global resource allocation, and expand the city's absorption capacity and influence. Based on relevant work arrangements by Guangzhou, we believe that the city will display the following development trend in 2017.

i. The basic status

Guangzhou will strongly advance projects for the development of three strategic hubs. Following the guideline laid by the provincial Party Committee and the provincial government of Guangdong to "make infrastructure construction the top priority of economic work", Guangzhou will continue to fiercely push ahead its key infrastructure projects in 2017.In 2017, Guangzhou will schedule 258 key projects with the annual combined investment of RMB122.5 billion. It plans to launch 34 infrastructure projects, including 19 by the end of May, and 15 by the end of October, with a combined investment of RMB173.3 billion, of which RMB14.5 billion will be secured by the end of 2017.The construction of the southern section of Airport Expressway No.2, the Phase II Resettlement Area for the construction of the No.3 Runway of Baiyun International Airport, Subway Line 18 & 22, and the central container station of Guangzhou Railway will kick off in 2017.Guangzhou will also step up efforts to develop the international shipping hub, speed up key projects including the deep-water channel expansion of Guangzhou Port, the construction of the international cruise terminal, Phase IV project of Nansha Port, and Nansha Port railway, etc., improve the multimodal transportation system, open at least 10 international routes, and boost the development of shipping finance, port logistics, and ship transaction, etc. For the development of the international aviation hub, Guangzhou will speed up the expansion of Baiyun Airport and the construction of the air service base at the airport, advance the construction of Nansha Business Airport, accelerate 11 highway projects including Airport Expressway No.2, prepare for the construction of the Runway No.4 & No.5, resettlement zone and T3 building of Baiyun Airport, open more than 10 international routes, start to select the site for the second airport, and obtain approval for the status of demonstration zone in airport economy.

Guangzhou's integrated transportation network will be improved. In 2017, Guangzhou will promote the integrated development of land, sea and air transport, and grow into an international comprehensive transport hub and a national demonstration city in the integrated transport system. While advancing three national railway projects, six inter-city rail projects, 12 subway projects, eight expressway projects and 10 national (provincial) artery projects, it will build or expand nine passenger transport hubs and five freight transport hubs, try to start the construction of Tangxi Station, Guangzhou-Shantou Expressway, Guangzhou-Foshan-Jiangmen-Zhuhai inter-city rail, central container station, Pazhou line of Guangzhou-Dongguan Inter-City Rail, and Subway Line 18 and 22, and try to finish the Phase I of Subway Line 9, Phase I of Guangzhou-Qingyuan Inter-City Rail, and the Phoenix Hill Tunnel and open them to traffic. Meanwhile, it will further adjust a number of bus routes and stations, optimize the construction and management of charging posts and parking lots, develop distributed energy networks, reform the taxi industry, regulate the car-hailing business, actively develop the slow traffic system, and form a "hub+community+industry" mode for rail transport development.

Nansha will embark on the fast lane of development. As the central government calls for the development of the Guangdong-Hong Kong-Macao Greater Bay Area, Nansha, a core and strategic platform for Guangzhou to contribute to the national scheme, should establish its presence in the Greater Bay Area as soon as possible, and make full use of the advantages brought by the development of the Greater Bay Area and the free trade area. By so doing, it will surely strengthen its urban functions as the subcenter of Guangzhou and embark on the fast lane of development. In 2017, Guangzhou will strive to improve the transport infrastructure of Nansha, plan to build an expressway network, build four high-quality functional zones, namely, Haigang, Jiaomen River Central Area, Mingzhu Bay Takeoff Area, and Nansha Bay, actively develop new-energy vehicle, high-end equipment manufacturing, shipping service and specialty finance industries, expand exchange centers for nonferrous metals, iron & steel, grains, and plastic stools, and strive to develop a national demonstration base for cross-border e-commerce.

The housing price will be stabilized. In the course of urbanization and urban renewal, the housing price in Guangzhou has outgrown that in Beijing, Shanghai and Shenzhen, but Guangzhou's second-hand property market is the most mature and its rental housing market is prospering. The housing price of Guangzhou is thus more determined by second-hand property sales than by first-hand property sales. Besides, the city government of Guangzhou has done a terrific job in curbing the housing price. Taking all the above into consideration, we believe the city's housing price will be comparatively reasonable.

ii. Policy recommendations for promoting urban development in Guangzhou

The following policy recommendations are proposed in light of problems Guangzhou encountered in 2016, the instructions of the 3rd and 4th plenary sessions of the 18th CPC Central Committee and Guangzhou's guidelines and goals for the implementation of the new-type urbanization strategy.

1. To continue increasing efforts in infrastructure construction and accelerate the formation of hub-type network city

Specific measures to promote infrastructure construction are listed as below.

First, speeding up the construction of urban transport infrastructure. Based on the survey of residents' trips, the present bus system should optimized, and the frequency of bus trips should be increased during rush hours for the convenience of passengers. The construction of expressways connecting the urban and suburban areas should be accelerated to enhance transport connectivity. Especially, the government should put the construction of expressways connecting central Guangzhou to such outlying areas as Conghua, Zengcheng, Panyu, Huangpu and Nansha on the agenda and keep improving the urban transport network. The government should be more efficient in land acquisition, demolition and examination & approval of land use, speed up major transport infrastructure projects such as the construction of the second airport, high-speed railways, subway lines and expressways, and continue to consolidate Guangzhou's status as the regional transport hub in South China.

Strengthening infrastructure concerning people's livelihood. It is suggested that municipal education, medical and health care, sports, gardening & greening authorities take the lead to carry out an all-round assessment of the planning in their respective field, re-plan and re-design infrastructure concerning people's livelihood for the equalization of public services and integrated urban-rural development, and consult with finance, land resources departments and the development and reform commission to improve the overall service capacity of infrastructure in Guangzhou. They are also recommended to follow the unified deployment of the municipal Party Committee and the municipal government, and pair up with their counterpart in suburban areas so as to channel high-quality resources from the central to the peripheral area and benefit more residents with the infrastructure.

Strengthening supporting municipal works. It is suggested to strengthen supporting municipal works in the central urban area, and repair and upgrade relevant facilities especially in the course of urban renewal. At the same time, in the planning and construction of peripheral new areas, the sub-center and suburban areas, the government should ensure a sufficient supply of the underground integrated utility tunnel system, sewage and waste treatment facilities, oil & gas stations, markets and utility lines, and meet the needs of both production and living instead of meeting the production needs of at the expense of living conditions as it did before.

2. To pay more attention to social planning, space equality and diversified financing in the urban renewal process, and upgrade the urban renewal level on the whole

For the development of super cities like Guangzhou, urban renewal in the central area is really important in addition to the development of new areas in the peripheral area. Despite obstacles such as historical disputes, fragmented and complicated land ownership, the sky-high compensation for land acquisition and demolition, and function swap, urban renewal, if properly managed, will without doubt greatly boost urban development. For example, it can restore the once lost sense of community as a remedy for the spiritual void of atomization and fragmentation associated with modernization and industrialization.

Mini-reconstruction was advanced rapidly in 2016 as one of the biggest highlights of urban renewal, but also faced problems such as uneven development of the physical and soft environments, space inequality and financial shortage. In response, the following measures are suggested for the better effect of urban renewal and the building of the sense of community.

In addition to physical planning, it's imperative to strengthen social planning of mini-reconstruction projects. They are not about increasing the supply of service facilities such as farmers' markets, public toilets and service centers for the elderly, but should seek to enhance the sense of belonging and the sense of community by organizing community activities and improving the neighborhood environment. Urbanization is just about space, but also people. The ultimate goal is to improve the overall qualities of community residents, foster the awareness of citizenship, and cultivate the ability to spot and solve problems with the community or the society. To this end, we suggest, first of all, increasing public space such as tea houses, ponds, pavilions or mini-squares, where residents can exchange and interact with each other, learn from each other and tap their potentials. By so doing, we can enhance the sense of community and the community cohesion among residents.

The city should coordinate the distribution of mini-reconstruction projects and funds. The Urban Renewal Projects and Funding Scheme of Guangzhou for 2017 released at the end of 2016 includes 111 municipal-level projects covering 14.14 square kilometers and 22 district-level projects of 65.41 square kilometers. It is noteworthy that the number of municipal-level projects in 2017 more than doubles that in 2016, with a significant increase in micro-reconstruction projects. As mentioned above, the distribution of projects and money in the Scheme leans towards the old quarter, with 48.3% of the projects concentrated in Liwan and Yuexiu districts. In the future, more work should be done to enhance space equality and increase mini-reconstruction efforts in new urban areas and suburban areas, instead of leaning the resources towards the old quarter.

Actively absorbing private and social capital to diversify the funding source for mini-reconstruction. Urban renewal in historical neighborhoods might be troubled with the complex ownership structure and the long return cycle in the short term, but for long-term benefits, we should mobilize social forces to contribute to it. In the future, the funding source should consist of municipal and district-level government finance plus social and private capital. Mini-reconstruction investment might take 20 or even 30 years to yield returns, so developers of such projects are not after short-term returns, but long-term returns such as creating jobs, fulfilling corporate social responsibilities and building up the corporate reputation and image.

3. To strengthen coordinated planning of rural areas and build specialty platforms and specialty towns

Drawing experience from Jiangsu and Zhejiang and proceeding from Guangzhou's rural reality, we believe the city should focus on building rural development platforms with distinct characteristics and specialty towns based on existing resources. To this end, the following suggestions are proposed.

Guangzhou should earnestly follow the Measures on the Implementation of the Rural Development Planning Permit System, utilize idle homesteads and residences, curb the ownership of multiple residences by single households, and tighten control over the examination and approval of home building by farmers. It must make clear that if any rural resident wants to build his own home, he must submit the construction plan for approval and acceptance check. In principle, each rural household is allowed to own only one residence, and the application for home building should be made public in the village. The government should fully mobilize rural residential land resources, advance village planning in a systematic way, and guide villagers to build homes in an orderly manner.

Rural development planning should consider moderate concentration and the original natural conditions of the urban-rural fringe, and preserve them as much as possible. Specifically, special efforts should be made to create public space such as ancestral temples, squares, ponds and ancient trees where villagers can interact and bond with each other. Local traditional festivals such as dragon boats, lion dances and sport meetings should be reserved if possible, to strengthen the cultural identity of local residents.

Existing rural industries should be transformed and upgraded. The focus should be on the extension of the industrial chain. Experts and scholars in the fields of history, geography, culture and folk customs should be invited to study and sort out rural cultural resources such as historical buildings and cultural heritage sites, so that cultural and creative industries could grow based on them. Reception halls should be built to convey the town's historical and cultural heritage to visitors and investors. The government should fully integrate industrial development with cultural and tourism development, and balance the production, people's livelihood and ecological environment as much as possible.

Guangzhou should be active in building specialty platforms. It should learn from Zhejiang's experience in developing specialty towns, make full use of existing industrial and space conditions in each rural town, and produce the synergy effect by pooling municipal and district-level development platforms. To build industry-led specialty platforms with distinctive characteristics and diverse players, the government should make use of local natural conditions and historical and cultural resources and strengthen rail transport and ecological restoration in rural areas.

Guangzhou should introduce original modes to develop specialty platforms. Local governments at all levels should be responsible for coordinated planning, resource integration and the supply of supporting services, streamline procedures for land reutilization, encourage enterprises to take part in joint-stock cooperative operation of land resources, and perfect the collectively-owned construction land circulation market as soon as possible by incorporating the markets for the use right transfer, lease and mortgage of state-owned land. Government departments concerned should establish the coordination mechanism to prevent repetition and chaotic competition among specialty platforms.

4. To effectively increase the concentration of population and industry and accelerate integrated industrial-urban development in Nansha

The following suggestions are put forth based on the economic and social reality in Nansha and with the aim to build Nansha into Guangzhou's sub-center and to boost the development of the Guangdong-Hong Kong-Macao Greater Bay.

First, by drawing Beijing's experience in developing Tongzhou as its sub-center and Xiong'an New Area through regional coordination, the provincial government of Guangdong and the municipal government of Guangzhou should lean resource allocation towards Nansha, and in particular fully mobilize medical, educational, healthcare and cultural resources in Yuexiu and Tianhe and state-owned enterprises, local companies and factories in the central area to move to Nansha, so as to significantly strengthen Nansha's urban development.

Second, municipal human resources, land planning and housing authorities should introduce preferential policies for Nansha to increase its permanent population. For example, they should encourage government organs and public institutions and some state-owned enterprises in downtown Guangzhou to move to Nansha, allocate some land to build government-subsidized apartments, lower the threshold for permanent residence registration in Nansha, encourage downtown residents to buy homes in Nansha, increase the subsidies for high-level specialists, and provide differentiated government subsidies to specialists of different levels based on their tax bracket, to lure more talents to Nansha.

Third, Nansha should seize the opportunity presented by the development of the Guangdong-Hong Kong-Macao Greater Bay, and establish and consolidate its status as its heartland. In terms of industrial development, it should strive to foster the radiation and absorption capacity of existing industries, extend the industrial chain of traditional advantageous industries, form industrial clusters of regional characteristics, and build up regional influence in the Pearl River Delta in the development of the headquarters economy and the transformation and upgrade of traditional industries. Based on existing industrial conditions, it should actively attract engineering parts, auto parts and customer services of the automobile industry to settle in Nansha, improve the supply chain, strengthen regional coordination and market exploration, develop preferential policies, and actively lure companies of traditional advantageous industries in Shunde, Zhongshan, and Dongguan to move to Nansha, and enhance its industrial agglomeration on the whole.

Fourth, special attention should be paid to small- and medium-scale planning and design in Nansha's urban development to make it more concentrated and intensive.It should consider (1) building an expressway network connecting Nansha to downtown Guangzhou such as Tianhe district to remarkably reduce the travel time; (2) building expressways bound to Shunde, Zhongshan and Dongguan with Nansha as the regional transport hub; (3) significantly increasing the public transport capacity and the travel frequency of public buses for the convenience of local residents; (4) planning and designing more small- and medium-scale lanes to connect to main roads; (5) considerably increasing the public space at the neighborhood level where people can interact and bond with each other, so as to enhance the sense of community, the sense of belonging, and the community vitality.

Fifth, consumer service facilities should be developed to boost local entertainment and consumption industries. To attract consumers and elevate the consumption amount and quality, Nansha may consider introducing landmark projects of Universal Studios, Disneyland, Sheraton Macao Hotel, Chimelong, or Wanda, and building Nansha Harbor City to attract medium- and high-end consumers from the mainland, Hong Kong, Macao and overseas markets, and boost local consumption in culture, entertainment, games, leisure and shopping as a supplement to the currently-dominating real estate industry.

Analysis of Guangzhou's Urban Management in 2016 and Prospects for 2017*

Research group of Guangzhou Development Research Institute,
Guangzhou University**

Abstract: In 2016, Guangzhou did a good job in the following aspects of urban management: institutional design, integrated governance, and the improvement of the living environment and quality. But it also faced the traffic bottleneck, the conflict between urban management and the quality of urban life, and the challenging task of establishing a sustainable mechanism to build a clean, safe and orderly city, and of pushing ahead the reform of law enforcement system for integrated urban management. In 2017, Guangzhou should continue to refine urban management for better effect by promoting urban renewal and mini-reconstruction as well as the reform of urban law enforcement system, strengthening grid and digital management, and promoting the compulsory waste classification mechanism, etc.

Keywords: Urban management, progress, current situation, countermeasures

I. Main Progress of Guangzhou's Urban Management in 2016

The year of 2016 marked the beginning of Guangzhou's implementation of the "13th Five-Year Plan." Throughout that year, aspiring to build a clean, tidy, safe and orderly city, Guangzhou continued to improve the urban-rural environment, carry out the three-year action plan for urban management improvement, adopt the philosophy of "innovative, intelligent, coordinated and pioneering" urban management, consolidate the city's status as a demonstration city in the classification of domestic waste, promote the upgrade and transformation of old plants in downtown and

---

*   This research report is a fruit of the collaboration between Guangzhou Development Research Institute of Guangzhou University - a provincial key research base for humanities and social sciences, "Guangzhou Studies" Collaborative Innovation and Development Center under Guangdong Provincial Development of Education, and the decision-making consultancy and innovation team for integrated development of Guangzhou - a provincial university innovation team of Guangdong.

**   Head of the research group: Tu Chenglin, researcher, doctoral supervisor, and head of Guangzhou Development Research Institute of Guangzhou University.Members: Tan Yuanfang, Ph.D., deputy director, professor of the Institute; Zhou Lingxiao, Ph.D., deputy director, associate professor of the Institute; Huang Xu, Ph.D., associate professor of the Institute; Yao Huasong, Ph.D., associate researcher of the Institute; Wang Wenjiao, Ph.D.; Zhou Yu, Ph.D.; Liang Huaxiu, master, assistant researcher of the Institute. Author: Tan Yuanfang.

mini-reconstruction of old neighborhoods and villages, and refine urban management. Remarkable progress has been achieved so far. See below for details.

i.The regulatory framework governing urban management continued to be perfected.

In 2016, Guangzhou released or put into effect at least 25 municipal regulations, departmental rules and normative documents (see Table 1). Among them, Administrative Measures on the Disposal of Animal Remains and Waste Meat Products and Detailed Rules on the Collection of Urban Domestic Waste Disposal Fee, adopted in March and June in 2016, respectively, and the Detailed Rules on the Interim Measures on Regional Ecological Compensation for Domestic Waste Terminal Treatment Facilities and Administrative Measures on Emergency Scheduling of Domestic Waste Terminal Treatment Facilities, both adopted at the end of 2016, were supplements to Guangzhou's Interim Regulations on the Classification of Urban Domestic Waste, the first municipal ordinance on classified waste management issued in China during the 12th Five-Year Plan period. In 2016, the No.7 waste-to-power plant, one of the five such plants in Guangzhou, started its No.1 boiler and the No.4 waste-to-power plant was also ready to put its No.1 boiler to work, basically solving the colossal problem of urban waste. The above local regulations and rules, in particular those about the terminal treatment of domestic waste, have set a great example in classified waste management for the rest of urban China. At the end of 2016, Guangzhou began to refine its own standards in this regard, promoted mandatory waste classification and reinforced legal guarantee for it.

In 2016, Guangzhou Municipal Commission of Transport took the lead in formulating and refining the Implementation of Municipal People's Government of Guangzhou of the Opinions Issued by the State Council General Office on Promoting the Healthy Development of the Taxi Industry through Reform, Interim Administrative Measures on Car-Hailing Services, and Opinions on Determining Illegal Car-Pooling Services Involving Small Private Passenger Vehicles. These three documents were made public after review and approval, representing the local transport industry's initiative to adapt to the "Internet+transport" trend. Later, based on the latest progress in the state-level reform, Guangzhou refined its regulations governing the taxi industry and car-hailing services and started to make practical explorations, attracting extensive public attention with little controversy. In addition, the Notice on Banning Electric Bicycles and Other Non-Motor Powered Vehicles from Roads, the Code of Conduct for Passengers of Urban Rail Transit Vehicles, and the Notice on Restricting the Use of Motorcycles on Road were put into effect in 2016. These local regulations and policies align with the city's original regulatory framework on the one hand and add to its institutional design for urban development.

Table 1 Guangzhou's Normative Documents on Urban Management Issued in 2016 (Part)

No.	Title	Status
1	The Request List for the Municipal Urban Management Authority to Handle Classified Letters and Complaints through Statutory Channels	Issued and put into effect by Guangzhou Municipal Commission on Urban Management on February 1, 2016
2	Municipal Administrative Measures on the Development of Circular Economy Industrial Parks	Issued by Guangzhou Municipal Commission on Urban Management on February 25, 2016
3	Municipal Administrative Measures on the Disposal of Animal Remains and Waste Meat Products	Issued by the General Office of the Municipal People's Government of Guangzhou on March 1, 2016
4	Municipal Regulations on Discretion over Administrative Punishments of Comprehensive Law Enforcement for Urban Management (revised in 2016)	Issued by Guangzhou Municipal Commission on Urban Management on March 14, 2016
5	Municipal Plan for Comprehensively Deepening the Patriotic Health Campaign in the New Era (2016-2020)	Reviewed and adopted at the executive meeting of the Municipal People's Government of Guangzhou on May 9, 2016
6	Municipal Detailed Rules on the Collection of Urban Domestic Waste Disposal Fee	Issued by Guangzhou Municipal Commission on Urban Management on June 24, 2016
7	On Issues Regarding the Calculation of Pipeline Nature Gas Consumers per Household under the Tiered Pricing System	Issued by Guangzhou Municipal Commission on Urban Management on July 26, 2016
8	Municipal Tentative Administrative Measures on Manhole Covers	Issued and put into effect by the Municipal People's Government of Guangzhou City on July 29, 2016
9	Municipal Regulations on Discretion over Administrative Punishments of Comprehensive Law Enforcement for Urban Management (second revision in 2016)	Issued and put into effect by Guangzhou Municipal Commission on Urban Management on August 3, 2016
10	Notice on Investigating and Cracking down on Some Gas Facilities Built and Owned by Enterprises	Issued and put into effect by Guangzhou Municipal Commission on Urban Management on August 16, 2016
11	Notice on the Management of Temporary Outdoor Advertising Setup for the 120th Canto Fair and Auto Guangzhou 2016	Issued and put into effect by Guangzhou Municipal Commission on Urban Management on September 12, 2016
12	Municipal Measures on Cost Accounting for the Transformation of Old Villages	Issued by Guangzhou Urban Renewal Bureau on September 22, 2016 and put into effect on October 1, 2016
13	Guidelines on Administrative Punishment for the Protection of Petroleum and Natural Gas Pipelines	Issued and put into effect by Guangzhou Municipal Development and Reform Commission on October 12, 2016

14	Notice on Comprehensive Control on Stock Yards along the Pearl River and the Liuxi River	Issued and put into effect by the Municipal People's Government of Guangzhou City on October 31, 2016
15	Notice on Banning Electric Bicycles and Other Non-Motor Powered Vehicles from Roads	Issued and put into effect by the Municipal People's Government of Guangzhou City on November 2, 2016
16	Notice on Standardizing the Collection of Residential Property Management Service Fees in Guangzhou	Issued and put into effect jointly by Guangzhou Municipal Development and Reform Commission and Guangzhou Municipal Housing and Urban-Rural Development Commission on November 9, 2016
17	Code of Conduct for Passengers of Urban Rail Transit Vehicles	Issued and put into effect by Guangzhou Municipal Commission of Transport on November 11, 2016
18	Municipal Administrative Measures on Vehicle Transportation Manifests for Construction Waste	Issued and put into effect by Guangzhou Municipal Commission on Urban Management on November 14, 2016
19	Municipal Tentative Administrative Measures on Car-Hailing Services	Reviewed and adopted at the executive meeting of the Municipal People's Government of Guangzhou on November 18, 2016
20	Implementation Opinions on Promoting the Healthy Development of the Taxi Industry through Reform	Issued and put into effect by the Municipal People's Government of Guangzhou City on November 28, 2016
21	Master Plan on Urban Renewal in Guangzhou (2015-2020)	Reviewed and adopted at the executive meeting of the Municipal People's Government of Guangzhou on November 28, 2016
22	Detailed Rules on the Interim Measures on Regional Ecological Compensation for Domestic Waste Terminal Treatment Facilities	Jointly issued by Guangzhou Municipal Commission on Urban Management and Guangzhou Finance Bureau on November 23 and put into effect on December 1, 2016
23	Municipal Administrative Measures on the Gas Business License	Issued and put into effect by Guangzhou Municipal Commission on Urban Management on December 2, 2016
24	Notice on Restricting the Use of Motorcycles on Road	Issued and put into effect by the Municipal People's Government of Guangzhou City on December 18, 2016
25	Opinions on Determining Illegal Car-Pooling Services Involving Small Private Passenger Vehicles	Jointly issued by Guangzhou Municipal Commission of Transport, Municipal Development and Reform Commission and Public Security Bureau on December 21, 2016
26	Notice on Strengthening Road Transportation of Hazardous Chemicals	Issued and put into effect by the Municipal People's Government of Guangzhou City on December 29, 2016
27	Municipal Administrative Measures on Emergency Scheduling of Domestic Waste Terminal Treatment Facilities	Issued and put into effect by the Municipal People's Government of Guangzhou City on December 29, 2016

The above regulations and normative documents share the following characteristics.

First, they reflect Guangzhou's special efforts in building local standards of urban management. For example, the Request List for the Municipal Urban

Management Authority to Handle Classified Letters and Complaints through Statutory Channels released in February and Municipal Regulations on Discretion over Administrative Punishments of Comprehensive Law Enforcement for Urban Management released in August restrict and regulate the exercise of powers by law enforcers for urban management. Municipal Detailed Rules on the Collection of Urban Domestic Waste Disposal Fee and Detailed Rules on the Interim Measures on Regional Ecological Compensation for Domestic Waste Terminal Treatment Facilities, released in June and December, respectively, are institutional guarantees for urban domestic waste treatment. **Second, they all aim at establishing a detailed, sustainable urban management system.** In particular, On Issues Regarding the Calculation of Pipeline Nature Gas Consumers per Household under the Tiered Pricing System released in July was the answer to the question of how to price natural gas for large-sized households, and the Guidelines on Administrative Punishment for the Protection of Petroleum and Natural Gas Pipelines issued in October provided clear institutional guarantee for the normal operation of natural gas pipelines. Besides, Municipal Administrative Measures on the Disposal of Animal Remains and Waste Meat Products (March), Notice on Restricting the Use of Motorcycles on Road (November), Municipal Tentative Administrative Measures on Manhole Covers (July), Notice on Strengthening Road Transportation of Hazardous Chemicals (December) and Notice on Standardizing the Collection of Residential Property Management Service Fees in Guangzhou (December) each governs a specific aspect of the urban life. They make urban management more law-based, detail-oriented and sustainable. The Master Plan on Urban Development in Guangzhou (2011-2020) (with approval from the State Council in February 2016), Municipal Plan for Comprehensively Deepening the Patriotic Health Campaign in the New Era (2016-2020), Master Plan on Urban Renewal in Guangzhou (2015-2020), and the Five-Year Action Plan for the Renewal and Reconstruction of Old Neighborhoods in Guangzhou (2016-2020) that is under preparation are all medium- and long-term plans. **Third, they all show the initiative to adapt to the "Internet+" trend for urban development,** especially the Implementation Opinions on Promoting the Healthy Development of the Taxi Industry through Reform, Municipal Tentative Administrative Measures on Car-Hailing Services and Opinions on Determining Illegal Car-Pooling Services Involving Small Private Passenger Vehicles.

ii.Efforts were made to promote comprehensive environmental improvement and reconstruction and explore the way to make the city more suitable to live and work.

In 2016, Guangzhou actively explored the way to make the city a better place to live and work via comprehensive environmental improvement and reconstruction.

First, the Xicun model of integrated domestic waste treatment took shape. On December 9, 2016, the People's Daily published an article entitled "Besieged by Waste? Not in Xicun", reporting on the integrated domestic waste treatment scheme of Guangzhou. It examines Xicun's integrated solution to domestic waste classification and reduction and discusses Guangzhou's progress from "East Lake sample" to "Xicun model" in urban domestic waste treatment and its social influence. Under the Xicun model, a general survey is conducted to understand the origin and destination of domestic waste, residents are guided to classify their domestic waste, and the first classified waste database is established in Guangzhou. Meanwhile, waste collectors and recyclers are matched to promote the circular utilization of resources and generate profits from waste. It is led by the government, participated in by the general public, operated by enterprises and pushed ahead by social organizations, setting an example for the introduction of social capital into waste classification and treatment.

Second, the sustainable and coordinated mechanism for the construction of gas pipelines was formed. In 2015, Guangzhou issued the Three-year Development Plan for Gas Pipelines, speeding up the construction process of urban gas pipelines, significantly promoting energy conservation and emission reduction, and improving urban air quality. In 2016, based on that, Guangzhou issued a number of local regulatory documents regarding the development of pipeline gas, including the development of pipeline gas and the control over bottled liquefied gas into the content of safety oversight for urban villages, and extending the gas pipelines to 598,000 additional households. In particular, the "Internet +" technology was employed to monitor, regulate gas pipeline construction and inspect gas pipelines after construction, as an attempt for intelligent energy management. In particular, the use of liquefied gas cylinders with a two-dimensional code and smart chain-locked filling guns was gradually promoted city-wide so that the gas filling, transportation, delivery, use, recycling and testing of gas cylinders could be monitored electronically. In the second half of 2016, RMB seven million was spent on patrolling all the urban gas pipelines to chart all the potential safety threats and explore real-time energy monitoring.

Third, urban comprehensive governance proved effective, and the living environment was improved significantly. In recent years, Guangzhou has been striving to build a clean, tidy, safe and orderly city. In 2016, Guangzhou made use of "dynamic monitoring with low-altitude remote sensing" to routinely check and dynamically monitor illegal construction activities, so as to strengthen legal concurrence and judicial cohesion for illegal construction and illegal land use. With the help of new technologies, in 2016, Guangzhou demolished a total of 1,149,000 square meters of illegal construction, fined a total of 927,000 square meters, and suspended the construction of 1,011,000 square meters; investigated 910,000 cases of six kinds of illegal and unauthorized use of public space, and fined 35,500 of them; investigated and punished the setup of 36,000 illegal advertising boards; investigated 3,517 cases of illegal construction, 322 cases of illegal transportation of construction waste, and 1,286 cases of sludge spilling; rectified 1,263 unauthorized bottled liquefied gas businesses, and registered and put up the two-dimensional code on 6.31 million gas cylinders. The urban environment was thus much improved. In addition, the Mobike bike-sharing program was widely welcomed in Guangzhou.

Table 2 Objectives of Guangzhou's Patriotic Health Campaignin the Last Three Years

No.	Indicator	Goal	
		Year 2017	Year 2020
1	Harmless treatment rate of urban domestic waste	95.79%	98%
2	Effective Treatment of Rural Domestic Waste	—	100%
3	Classified recycling rate of urban domestic waste	—	40%
4	Treatment rate of urban domestic sewage	93.5%	95%
5	Proportion of administrative towns treating sewage	90%	—
6	Acceptability of urban domestic sewage	93.5%	95%
7	Rural domestic sewage treatment rate	60%	70%
8	Centralized water supply in rural areas	100%	—
9	Acceptability of rural drinking water	70%	75%
10	Rural sanitation coverage	90%	100%
11	Hygienic toilet penetration rate in rural areas	99.3%	99.8%
12	Penetration rate in national and provincial sanitary towns	70%	80%
13	Population benefit rate of provincial and	70%	80%

		municipal sanitary villages		
14	Rural roads separated from fields and residences	—	90%
15	IT-based rodent and insect pest reporting platform and response mechanism	Covering all neighborhoods and towns	—
16	Urban vector density control level	Up to the national standard	—
17	Smoke-free model units	—	An increase of 1,000

Data source: Municipal Plan for Comprehensively Deepening the Patriotic Health Campaign in the New Era (2016-2020)

iii. The "contiguous reconstruction + mini-reconstruction" mode was established to optimize the storage and development of land resources and promote urban renewal in an orderly manner.

In 2016, Guangzhou promoted urban renewal systematically, and realized land consolidation, reserve and development under the "contiguous reconstruction + mini-reconstruction" mode, making the city more suitable for living and working.

First, the urban renewal plan was optimized, featuring systematic guidance, block planning and zoning for implementation. At the beginning of 2016, Guangzhou Urban Renewal Bureau organized a survey on 2,831 old neighborhoods across the city, comprehensively sorted out the registered residential buildings of more than 30 years old, and formulated Opinions on Strengthening the Renovation of Dilapidated Buildings in Urban Renewal Areas in 2016. In addition, a total of RMB 94.13 million was earmarked for mini-reconstruction projects, with matched funds from the district government, to advance 48 mini-reconstruction projects in a coordinated way. In August, Guangzhou started to prepare the Five-Year Action Plan for Renewal and Transformation of Old Neighborhoods (2016-2020), planning to complete the renewal and transformation of 943 old neighborhoods in five years to improve the living environment and quality of life in these areas. Later, the Master Plan on Urban Renewal in Guangzhou (2015-2020) was reviewed and passed, planning to complete the urban renewal of 42-50 square kilometers in the next five years. According to the Master Plan, Guangzhou's urban renewal will involve diverse players with districts as the mainstay and towns and neighborhoods as the basic unit, and stress the strategy of "systematic guidance, block planning and zoning for implementation." Specifically, contiguous urban renewal will be realized in key development zones and mini-reconstruction in scattered areas in an orderly, tiered, block-by-block manner under the guidance of the master plan.

Second, various modes of urban mini-reconstruction were explored in light of local conditions. In 2016, Guangzhou formulated a number of supporting operational guidelines and technical standards for the Master Plan, including the Guidelines for Application and Approval Procedures for Urban Renewal Projects in Guangzhou, and Guidelines for the Preparation of Plans for Urban Renewal Areas in Guangzhou. The Implementation Measures for the Renewal of Old Plants in Guangzhou and the Implementation Measures for the Renewal of Old Towns in Guangzhou formulated in 2015 also went into effect in 2016.In addition, in 2016, Guangzhou started to draft the Regulations on Urban Renewal, which was included in the legislative readiness plan of 2018 and to be deliberated by the People's Congress in 2019, which will serve as the policy basis for the coordinated promotion and phase-in of urban renewal in Guangzhou. In 2016, Guangzhou compiled and implemented its first annual plan for urban renewal, carrying out 58 projects covering 24.3 square kilometers. Among them, 14 were about the transformation of old towns, plants and villages; 38 were mini-reconstruction of neighborhoods, industrial parks and historical buildings; about 40 of them had formulated the reconstruction plan; and a total of RMB261 million was allocated, accounting for 99% of the budget. In addition, in 2016, five more urban renewal projects (including four for the transformation of old factories) and three renewal schemes were approved. Steady progress was made in the renewal and transformation of the four block projects at the Financial Street, Wanbo City, Agricultural Museum and surrounding areas. In the implementation process, Guangzhou continued to sum up its experience and explore pilot projects. In 2016, four projects, namely, Yangzhong Neighborhood of Zhuguang Street, Y.T. Space, Xicun Street and Pantang Wuyue, were selected for the improvement of the living environment, renovation of old industrial buildings and industrial upgrade, community self-governance+mini-reconstruction (community-level experience in self-governance of mini-reconstruction), environmental improvement+preservation of historical and cultural heritage, etc. The purpose was to promote integrated urban renewal that improves both urban and rural living environments, transforms and upgrades industries and protects historical and cultural heritage.

Third, the practice of transforming old towns, factories and villages was perfected through land consolidation, storage and optimized development. In June 2016, the former leading group for the transformation of old towns, factories and villages was renamed the urban renewal leading group, headed by the city mayor and composed of high-ranking officials from the municipal government, eight municipal departments including the development and reform commission, and 11 district governments. It is responsible for coordinating major tasks of urban renewal at the city level. In January 2016, the Measures on Urban Renewal in Guangzhou took effect, officially proposing the urban mini-reconstruction mode. Guangzhou also carried out a pilot data survey in the Tangyong block of Baiyun district, Chentian block of Yongtai district, and Shibi block of Panyu district, to grasp and dynamically monitor the situation of regional land use, demolition and resettlement of project areas, land transfer and transformation progress. These measures proved useful in exploring the mode of urban renewal.

iv. More efforts were made to pursue fine, quality urban management.

In 2016, guided by the overall goal of building into a national central city and a hub-type network city, Guangzhou strived to improve its urban environment and urban management, seeing overall improvement in its urban living environment.

First, the public health environment was improved significantly. In addition to the above-mentioned urban domestic waste treatment, Guangzhou also did a great job in city sanitation and river management in 2016. In environmental sanitation, the discharge of sewage and the emission of odor at 165 waste compression stations in the six central districts were up to standards, and the surrounding environment of 2,503 makeshift domestic waste collection and transportation points was improved. Over 880 regular patrols and purpose-specific inspections were organized, and more than 7,000 environmental cases were investigated, whose rectification was made under supervision. As to river management, Guangzhou vigorously promoted the water purifying program, launched river course management, investigated and controlled sources of water pollution, investigated 3,398 enterprises distributed in 419 villages (neighborhoods), issued 1,189 rectification orders, shut down and rectified 1,156 of them. The amount of work worth RMB9.439 billion was completed for 16 rivers running through Guangzhou and Foshan, with the completion rate of 80.5%; and the amount of work worth RMB3.175 billion was completed for the rest 35 rivers, with the completion rate of 78.2%, improving the water quality of 35 black and stink rivers across the city. Guangzhou also continued to promote the "one view, one park" campaign, built more than 60 spots for urban residents to enjoy flowers, and launched 138 planting projects. So far it has turned itself into a city of flowers blooming in four seasons, with colorful and thematic flowery scenes and highlights in each district. According to a sampling survey by Guangzhou Municipal Bureau of Statistics on the city's residents, more than 90% of the respondents found the urban living environment much improved in 2016, especially in city appearance and environmental sanitation.

Second, remarkable progress was made in urban community governance. In 2016, Guangzhou constantly strengthened the institutional guarantee for fine and quality urban management. Institutionally, the three-tiered grid-based service management system (municipal, district-level and neighborhood/town-level) was basically in place, and the 1,540 urban communities were divided into 16,658 basic grids, 100% covered by grid-based service management. After grid-based management was applied to the first batch of 176 public items within the power of 20 departments, a total of 6,349,700 grid incidents were reported across the city in 2016, including 30,000 incidents concerning urban components, 96,000 concerning a clean and tidy environment, 17,000 concerning management services for the floating population, 2,958 concerning social stability, 2,162 concerning public security, and 1,860 concerning workplace safety, with the settlement rate of 96.2%. Specifically, Guangzhou was active in helping with the floating population's social infusion, investigating social conflicts and disputes, cracking down on crimes and regulating workplace safety. The inclusive community pilot project was launched in five neighborhoods on Dengfeng Street and Dongshan Street of Yuexiu district, Sanyuanli Street in Baiyun district, and Nancun Town and Shiji Town of Panyu district, respectively, to promote urban development, social stability, public security and urban renewal through social inclusion. A total of 60,000 copies of Service Guide for the Floating Population in Guangzhou was printed and distributed to the floating population for free. The city also set up 574,000 video surveillance points, checked and registered 2,439,900 floating population and 410,700 rental apartments, busted 85 theft gangs, nine online P2P platforms engaged in illegal fund-raising, and 47 illegal fund-raising gangs each involving an amount over RMB100 million, cracked several cross-border telecom frauds involving an astronomical amount of money, recovered RMB115 million for 2,619 victims, investigated 293 major conflicts and disputes and solved 271 of them. Besides, it inspected nearly 110,000 enterprises and over 290,000 potential safety threats, imposed 7,474 administrative punishments, rectified 99.86% of the potential safety threats identified, and rated 466 enterprises as Class-I high-risk enterprises and 2,211 as Class-II high-risk enterprises.

Third, the Year of Food Safety campaign achieved the desired effect. The year of 2016 was designated by the city government of Guangzhou as the Year of Food Safety and food safety was placed on top of the government agenda. Statistical data shows that in 2016, the city spent over RMB300 million on food safety, and built Guangdong's first investigation team against food and drug crimes and the first municipal food safety risk monitoring and evaluation center. It checked a total of 84,947 batches of food samples and 1,246,000 samples of agricultural products throughout the year, with the acceptability above 98.5%. According to a survey by the Information Center of Guangzhou Statistics Bureau, citizens were 1.8% and 10.7% more satisfied with public security than in 2015 and 2014, respectively, with the sense of public security at 94.5% and the degree of satisfaction with public security at 94.1%.

II. Problems with Guangzhou's Urban Management in 2016 and Causes

Despite the progress mentioned above, there were still some weakness links and problems to be addressed, in particular in light of the city's 13th Five-Year Plan and ambition to grow into a clean, tidy, safe and orderly city.

i. Guangzhou's urban management philosophy was inadequate to meet the requirements of building itself into a hub-type network city

Specifically:

First, urban planning and management failed to taken into account the general picture. The departments responsible for urban planning and spatial layout failed to communicate or cooperate with other departments concerned, such as the transport department, resulting in the lack of consistency among different urban plans, the existence of dead-end roads and the last-mileage traffic problems, etc. In response, we must combine the urban mini-environment with the mini-transport system, develop the urban rail and road system, modernize the public transport system, and ensure the consistency of spatial development plans.

Second, Internet thinking was obviously absent in urban management, especially traffic management. A case in point was the entry requirements the city has set for car-hailing services. From July 2016, following the release of the Tentative Administrative Measures on Car-Hailing Services by the Ministry of Transport, cities across China started to roll out their own version of measures successively. Guangzhou didn't announce its detailed rules on the implementation of the car-hailing service policy until December 2016, slower than most other cities whose experience and lessons it should have learned from to better serve the industry and passengers. Instead it decided to restrict the vehicle emission standard further from 1.8T or 2.0L to 1.8L, and demand a local hukou or residence permit from the driver. These requirements not only discriminate against the floating population, but also force nearly half of the vehicles providing the car-hailing service off the road, reducing the supply, squeezing the industry's growth space and likely to drive up the service rate.

ii. The urban traffic management had much room for improvement.

First, traffic congestion was serious. According to a survey by Guangzhou Statistics Bureau, local residents list the increase in the number of vehicles as the top reason for traffic congestion. Specifically, 65.9% and 63.1% of the respondents blame "the year-on-year increase in the number of vehicles" and the "continuous increase in the number of vehicles coming from outside Guangzhou" for the traffic problem respectively; 54.7%, "parking chaos"; 43.3% and 45.2%, "road maintenance/construction" and "poor awareness of traffic rules", respectively; and 42.1%, 41.0%, 41.0% and 37.6%, "traffic management not intelligent enough", "unreasonable road planning", "backward roads and supporting facilities", and "poorly designed traffic lights", respectively. Most of the respondents (94.1%) believe public transportation an effective solution to the traffic problem. For the government, in addition to "parking chaos", more efforts should be made to tackle problems such as "unintelligent traffic management", "unreasonable road planning" and "backward roads and supporting facilities", which are vital for fine, quality traffic management.

Second, the urban traffic management should be more intelligent. Most of the problems identified so far can be addressed by smart transportation. For example, to tackle the parking chaos of shared-use bikes, big data analysis can be employed to select more parking sites for the deliberation and approval of the government. In December 2016, Guangzhou Public Security Bureau announced its strategic partnership with Didi in building a big data platform for smart transportation, which can be viewed as a new trend of urban management. The electronic law enforcement pilot project launched by Guangzhou Municipal Commission of Transport at key passenger transport hubs was also well spoken of.

iii. The sustainable mechanism to build a clean, tidy, safe and orderly city was to be perfected.

First, part of the urban environment was still substandard. During the 12th Five-Year Plan period, the water quality of the west channel and the rear channel of Guangzhou section of the Pearl River failed to reach the established standard, and the lower reaches of Baini River and the section of Liuxi River below Lixi Dam were seriously polluted. The water quality of some rivers (sections) has not yet met the requirements for water use in functional areas. In particular, the water pollution of tributaries and urban rivers is more serious because of their limited water resources and concentrated pollutants. For many rivers included in the water quality monitoring scheme in 2015, the water quality was still below Class V level. Moreover, the air pollution in Guangzhou was characterized by compound pollution, secondary pollution and regional pollution. Although the annual mean concentration of fine particles has been declining in recent years in Guangzhou, it is still far from meeting national and provincial targets for air quality improvement. In 2016, Guangzhou launched four joint actions against pollution and dusting above the mild level, and held 265 ships accountable for port pollution. From January to October, environmental protection departments at the municipal and district levels carried 20 joint actions, investigating 3,204 cases of environmental pollution, punishing 2,833 of them, ordering 1,689 enterprises (projects) to suspend, and issuing fines worth RMB87.8216 million. The number of cases filed and the amount of money fined and confiscated increased by 0.03% and 12.66% from the same period of the previous year, respectively. The environmental regulation workload was heavy.

Second, slow progress was made in promoting the sorting of urban domestic waste. It has been five years since Guangzhou first introduced the waste sorting policy, but in 2015, the urban domestic waste recycling rate dropped, instead of rising, from 37% in 2014 to 35.4%. This indicates that waste sorting is still limited to demonstration communities in Guangzhou, not yet promoted city-wide, and exists more in name than in deeds in some of these communities. The automatic sorting system, among other technologies for building the smart city, might increase the sorting efficiency and recycling rate and is thus worth more research. In addition, the September review report by the Standing Committee of the Municipal People's Congress also pointed out that the work of urban waste sorting was behind the schedule and had little effect. For example, among the seven waste incineration plants to be built, only one has been put into operation, the construction of the rest is far behind the schedule set in 2012, and some projects are still in the early stage. In addition, there are many blind spots in the collection and disposal of industrial solid wastes. The centralized disposal capacity of hazardous waste and strictly controlled waste is insufficient to meet the actual needs, especially the disposal capacity of incineration-type industrial hazardous waste, medical waste and urban domestic sewage and sludge. Most of the current disposal capacity is concentrated on the comprehensive utilization of valuable waste, and some hazardous waste such as used lead-acid batteries and cold-rolled sludge need to be disposed of outside the city.

iv. The law enforcement system was to be further reformed.

In December 2016, Guangdong issued Implementation Opinions on Deepening the Reform of Urban Law Enforcement System and Improving Urban Management, demanding comprehensive institutional setup at the municipal and county levels in the field of urban management by the end of 2017, providing policies and directions for Guangzhou's urban management and highlighting its institutional weaknesses.

First, the front-line law enforcers were in severe shortage. In 2016, Guangzhou registered only over 3,000 urban management wardens and over 6,000 assistant wardens, serving a total of over 18 million permanent and floating population combined, that is, one law enforcer for 1,800 citizens. The workload is imaginable. Another survey shows that most of the neighborhoods in Guangzhou are only about two square meters each, with only 10 government-paid wardens. Take Baiyun district for example. It has about 100 vacancies for urban management wardens, about 20% of the total. In comparison, the law enforcement task for urban management is colossal, involving 376 items in 12 aspects of eight departments, including city appearance & sanitation, urban-rural planning, urban-rural development, environmental protection, administration of industry & commerce, water affairs, civil air defense, and the administration of Baiyun Mountain. The complicated, fine work demand is in sharp contrast with the manpower shortage. Moreover, the law enforcement team is aged about 47 on average, which is not so good for job efficiency.

Second, the law enforcement effect was to be improved. Take the demolition of illegal buildings as an example. The inefficiency of demolition has become the center of public complaints. Many illegal buildings continue to exist despite being reported repeatedly. It's reported in the media that an illegal building standing at the intersection of Shuichang Road on Nanpu Avenue, Panyu district, grew to three floors high after receiving 13 demolition orders from the urban management authority in eight months. After the news came out on January 16, 2016, Luopu Neighborhood organized a joint law enforcement team to demolish the building, but in less than one month, the work quietly resumed at the construction site. In fact, such phenomena are not uncommon in Guangzhou. In Tianhe district alone, in 2016, urban management wardens of Fenghuang Street were charged of taking bribes and acquiescing in illegal construction; the law enforcement team in Yuancun was punished for buck-passing when complained against for their inefficiency in demolishing illegal buildings. This shows that the law enforcement effect needs to be improved. Especially when it comes to team building, it is necessary to strengthen education and training, establish and perfect various systems and mechanisms, and actively build an urban management team which "boast a firm political stance, a fine style of work, and strict disciplines, respect the law, and enforce the law in a pragmatic and honest way."

Third, the crisis response capacity was to be improved. In August 2016, a citizen named Huang Wengang came across violent law enforcement by urban management wardens on the street, and filmed it with his mobile phone. That night he had asthma at home, was taken to the hospital, but unfortunately died. The media exposure of the incident reduced Guangzhou's urban management force into a very passive position. It shows that on the one hand, it's imperative to strengthen the law enforcement team, especially their work attitude; on the other, it's imperative to raise their awareness of crisis response. In particular in the age of information technology, the image of urban management officials is closely associated with the city image, and the crisis response capacity should be viewed vital for building Guangzhou into an international metropolis. While efforts should be made to prevent any more such incidents from happening, Guangzhou should establish the crisis response mechanism and contingency plan through training to raise law enforcement officials' crisis awareness, the spokesman system and media communication.

III. Development Prospects of Guangzhou's Urban Management in 2017 and Suggestions

On December 21, 2016, Guangdong issued Implementation Opinions on Deepening the Reform of Urban Law Enforcement System and Improving Urban Management, which means that 2017 will be an important year for the institutional reform of urban management in Guangzhou. On October 11, 2016, the Ministry of Housing and Urban-Rural Development set up the Urban Management Supervision Bureau, a state-level authority overseeing all urban management teams in all Chinese cities. Later, the provincial government of Guangdong also required that the regulation and standard system governing urban management and law enforcement must be in place across the province by 2020. All these have required Guangzhou's urban management team to work harder in "strengthening the foundation, transforming the work style and building up the image," stay problem-oriented, launch pilot projects, take the lead in institutional setup, refine local regulations and policies, straighten the law enforcement system, and strive to lead the country and produce substantial effects in various aspects of urban management.

i. Development prospects of urban management in Guangzhou in 2017

In 2017, Guangzhou should implement not only the Guiding Opinions on Promoting the Reform of Urban Law Enforcement System and Improving Urban Management issued by the Ministry of Housing and Urban-Rural Development, but also Implementation Opinions on Promoting the Reform of Urban Law Enforcement System and Improving Urban Management in Guangdong Province. In view of both documents, Guangzhou's urban management in 2017 will display the following obvious trends:

1. The reform of urban law enforcement system will be further promoted.

In the Implementation Opinions on Promoting the Reform of Urban Law Enforcement System and Improving Urban Management released in October 2016, Guangdong proposed to straighten relevant systems and mechanisms, strengthen team building, improve the law enforcement capacity, build a coordinated mode of urban management and introduce innovative ways of urban governance. In particular, inter-departmental law enforcement will be promoted in areas concerning people's life and production, closely related to urban management, troubled by duplicate law enforcement, and requiring modest technical support, frequent law enforcement, and the centralized exercise of power to impose administrative punishment. On top of the reform of urban management and inter-departmental law enforcement system initiated at the end of 2014, Guangzhou is expected to further integrate services, management and law enforcement and establish the urban management mode involving multiple departments. In 2017, with a view to the latest deployment of the central, provincial and municipal governments, Guangzhou will further optimize the urban management system and mechanism, scientifically define the responsibilities of urban management and law enforcement, issue implementation opinions, balance the outstanding contradiction between the manpower shortage and the excessive workload, improve the institutional setup for urban management and law enforcement at the municipal and district levels, define functions and prepare for transition, so as to advance towards the goal of growing into a national central city and a national innovation hub.

2. Urban renewal will become the new normal of urban development.

In 2017, urban renewal of Guangzhou will continue to catch up with the world advanced level, focus on generating comprehensive and long-term benefits in the optimization of urban space, improvement of living environment, inheritance of historical and cultural heritage, social and economic development, and in particular significantly improve the life quality for local residents amid the process of building Guangzhou into a hub-type network city. **First, urban renewal efforts in Guangzhou will be more diversified, producing effects in more aspects.** Since the Urban Renewal Bureau was established in 2015 to replace the Office of the Leading

Group for the Transformation of Old Towns, Factories and Villages, it has been pursuing fine, quality urban management and tried to build a platform involving the government, the market and the residents in a reasonable, orderly way. Second, more and more new modes of urban renewal will be introduced and explored. Guangzhou put into effect Municipal Measures on Urban Renewal on January 1, 2016, and has accumulated much experience in community self-governance plus mini-reconstruction as in the case of Xicun. Survey data shows that there are 2,831 old neighborhoods in Guangzhou, housing about one million households and three million residents; there are 2,195 depilated residential buildings in urban areas, covering 316,700 square meters. Thus the reconstruction plan would never be accomplished without the collaboration between the public and private sectors. Meanwhile, urban renewal involves the development and utilization of land stock, repair and maintenance of existing buildings, conservation of cultural heritage, maintenance of good neighborliness, and representation of the historical look of the city, extends from physical aspects of buildings, functions, and economy to non-physical aspects of culture, history, neighborliness, and folk customs, and thus needs to take into account both social and economic benefits. Therefore, the urban renewal work should be differentiated and systematic and form a network. **Third, more efforts will be made to incorporate urban renewal into urban management.** Urban renewal involves urban planning, urban transport and the improvement of the urban living environment, all of which can be integrated into each other to make the city a better place to live and work. For example, urban renewal can be combined with the development of the pedestrian system - the nerve ending system of urban traffic management, to create living circles accessible within 15 minutes of walk; the transformation of old neighborhoods and the renewal and conservation of historical and cultural blocks can be combined with the improvement of the city landscape; the renewal of industrial towns can be combined with the development of specialty towns.

3. More efforts should be made to build up the "clean, tidy, safe and orderly" city image.

After years of hard work, Guangzhou's urban management is reputed for the "clean, tidy, safe and orderly" city environment, but it needs a sustainable mechanism to continue the efforts and consolidate the progress made so far. According to the first meeting of the 15th Municipal People's Congress of Guangzhou, the People's Congress will deliberate on eight laws and regulations in 2017, including those governing the sorting of domestic waste and the development and management of parking lots. Fueled by these macro policies and institutional reforms, Guangzhou is expected to make the city cleaner, tidier, safer and more orderly in 2017. It will not only establish the incentive and evaluation mechanism to sustain and routinize efforts to improve the urban environment, but also work on related technical details and develop plans to publicize role models and make overall advancement simultaneously.

4. Much progress will be made in environmental protection.

In 2017, Guangzhou will go deep in its own way of domestic waste treatment on top of establishing and perfecting relevant systems and mechanisms and refining relevant regulations and policies. First, Guangzhou will formulate and refine local regulations and policies on environmental protection and form a complete policy system for it. In 2017, the city plans to formulate and revise Regulations on Inter-departmental Law Enforcement for Urban Management, Regulations on Wetland Conservation, Administrative Regulations on the City Appearance and Environmental Sanitation, and Administrative Regulations on Domestic Waste Sorting, and will prepare for the formulation of Regulations on Urban Renewal and Administrative Regulations on Energy, which will tighten the control over the city appearance and environmental sanitation. It is also expected to roll out Administrative Regulations on the Setup of Outdoor Advertising Boards and the Technical Specifications for the Setup of Outdoor Advertisements and Signboards (2016-2020), to include environmental protection into government regulation. Second, Guangzhou will enforce waste sorting and seeks to develop its own model of domestic waste treatment. In 2017, Guangzhou will go further in waste sorting, enforce it in certain areas, and focus on reducing the amount of waste generated. It will issue Administrative Regulations on Domestic Waste Sorting as the legal basis for waste sorting. It's reported that waste sorting will be phased in, first in Party and government organs as well as public institutions and meanwhile public education campaigns will be organized to raise the public awareness of waste sorting. The sorting criteria will be simple: separating the kitchen waste from other waste, and the wet from the dry. It will continue to encourage residents to place household waste at fixed points at fixed hours, improve the evaluation and supervision system for waste sorting, and strive to help more than 30% neighborhoods (towns) meet the standards of demonstration sites in waste sorting. At the same time, it will step up efforts in the recycling of low-value recyclables, improve the sorting, collection and transportation system of domestic refuse, and advance the construction of seven circular economy industrial parks, five waste-to-power plants, seven comprehensive utilization plants for construction waste, seven kitchen waste treatment facilities and 35 temporary waste disposal plants. By

2020, the harmless treatment will be applied to all the urban domestic waste generated across Guangzhou.

5. The "smart city" program will provide vital support for Guangzhou's aspiration to grow into a hub-type network city.

Smart urban management will be more relevant to people's daily life and more detail-oriented. In 2017, Guangzhou will focus on the delivery of fine urban management and targeted livelihood services, vigorously push ahead the development of smart urban management, smart transportation, smart communities and smart governance, and create demonstration sites for the smart city program. In particular, the smart urban management project will integrate functions of government services, transport, emergency response, and grid management and build a comprehensive database on urban management. Information technologies such as big data, the Internet of Things, and cloud computing will be employed to transform from digital urban management to smart urban management. Measures to be taken include establishing standards and specifications concerning the development, operation of and administration over smart urban management, applying big data, Internet of Things and cloud computing to urban management, and accelerating the development of the digital urban management platform and its function integration.

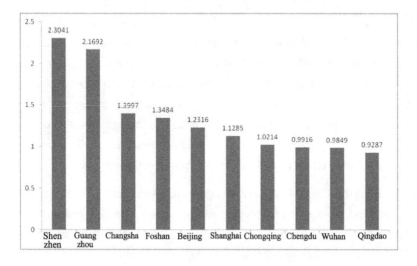

Figure 1 Top 10 Internet+ Smart Cities in China in 2016

Data source: The Internet+ Index in China in 2016

ii. Suggestions on strengthening urban management in Guangzhou in 2017

The year of 2016 saw significant progress in Guangzhou's urban management, making a good start for the 13th Five-Year Plan. Below are some suggestions on how to score further progress in 2017.

1. Seizing the opportunity presented by the massive urban renewal campaign to promote fine urban management

In 2016, the Ministry of Housing and Urban-Rural Development issued a five-year action plan on cracking down on illegal buildings in built-up urban areas, demanding to identify and handle all the illegal buildings in these areas in five years; and started to apply satellite remote sensing to monitor illegal construction activities across the whole country randomly. In 2017, while advancing urban renewal, Guangzhou should vigorously promote fine and quality urban management to improve the quality of urban life.

First, it should be more active in building an urban renewal platform involving the participation of the government, the market and local residents. Urban renewal requires continuous, repeated efforts, as in the case of demolishing illegal buildings. But the government is not as sensitive to and concerned about the progress as local residents. Thus Guangzhou should promote the Xicun mode, and allow residents to play an active role in managing urban renewal and assume their corresponding responsibilities.

Second, Guangzhou should address issues concerning illegal buildings, rental apartments, mobile stalls, and pollution caused by the catering industry amid the course of urban transformation and renewal. To do so, it needs to define the public and private space, strictly abide by relevant laws and regulations, and engage the general public. Shared governance by residents - through consultation and the government - through coordination, with clearly defined responsibilities for each side, is a sign of a better urban life and a stronger sense of wellbeing.

Third, Guangzhou should actively engage state-owned and private enterprises in urban renewal so that it can play a role in boosting market consumption. The enthusiasm of the government, enterprises and citizens should be aroused via the public-private partnership (PPP). An important way to transformation old neighborhoods and factories in urban areas is to have the government develop the development plan and operating rules and provincial- and municipal-level state-owned enterprises and private enterprises jointly take care of market operation. The government may guide enterprises by issuing supporting policies, define the scope of development and conservation, reform the financing mode for urban renewal, actively introduce social capital into it, develop the market, boost consumption through urban renewal, foster new business forms, and attract the settlement of enterprises. Only in this way can urban renewal be sustained and thrive.

2. Vigorously promoting fine urban management while advancing the law enforcement system reform

In 2017, Guangzhou should introduce detailed rules on following the provincial government's opinions about reforming the urban law enforcement system and improving urban management. It should define the rights and responsibilities regarding urban management and law enforcement, explore the inter-departmental collaboration and support mechanism, improve relevant regulations and standards, and straighten the law enforcement system. In particular, it shall strengthen team building, improve the effect of urban governance to the greater satisfaction of citizens, and open up a new situation of modern urban management.

The key is to establish a mechanism for fine urban management through the implementation of detailed rules. Macro policies and specific work procedures should aim at fine urban management and pursue excellence at it. For one thing, we suggest promoting Tianhe's "135 degumming method" and the "no more than cigarette butts in each ashtray" policy to the whole city. For another, skill competitions, such as the skill competition for sanitation workers organized by Tianhe district, should be hosted in the spirit of fine urban management.

3. Vigorously promoting fine urban management through grid management and digital means

First, a dynamic equilibrium mechanism should be in place to make sure grid services are relevant to people's daily life. It is suggested that the smart city campaign be launched and "Internet +" applied to grid services in 2017, to improve the work efficiency and timeliness. The city should also consider how to incorporate "Internet + grid" work into the "Internet + urban management" and "Internet + government affairs."

Second, digital means should be employed to improve the grid service management. Guangzhou should earnestly implement the Tentative Administrative Measures for Grid-Level Items, do a good job in managing the 176 items of 20 departments in the first batch and basic data, and explore the way to blend the district-level own grid information management system and the municipal-level urban management control and command platform, to realize uniform and centralized management. Besides, the "one employee for one square" policy should be strictly obeyed and municipal, district-level and neighborhood/town-level grid service management centers should be established.

4. Promote fine urban management by enforcing waste sorting

At the 14th meeting of the Central Leading Group on Financial and Economic Affairs on December 21, 2016, President Xi Jinping pointed out that the popularization of waste sorting would help improve the living conditions, reduce and recycle waste and promote harmless treatment of waste. Hence, we should speed up in building the waste sorting system that covers disposal, collection, transportation and treatment, is law-based, promoted by the government in both urban and rural areas and supported by residents, and reflects local conditions, and extend it to more areas.

Guangzhou has been leading Chinese cities in the treatment of domestic waste, but as it picks up the urbanization pace, it's generating more and more domestic waste year after year. In 2017, the Xicun Model should be promoted, under which citizens are rewarded by enterprises with points or other incentives for their waste sorting behavior, shifting the focus from the government alone to the public-private partnership. Moreover, Guangzhou should accelerate its smart urban management, develop a mobile app featuring "Internet+waste sorting+recycling", and actively try to incorporate the recycling system with the waste collection and transportation system.

Strategies to Make Guangzhou an International Hub City of Networks

Tu Chenglin*

Abstract: Given its efforts to become a global city, the goal of becoming a hub city of networks is both necessary and feasible for Guangzhou. This report examines the challenges the city needs to address urgently so as to achieve this goal and proposes fundamental principles and policies that may be formulated.

Keywords: hub city of networks, top-level design, Guangzhou

I. A Hub City of Networks Viewed from the Perspective of Global City

In August 2016, *the Opinions on Further Strengthening the Management of Urban Planning and Construction*, adopted by the 9th Plenary Session of the 10th CPC Guangzhou Municipal Committee, for the first time made the strategic plan of "building a hub city of networks that connects people, logistics, information flows and capital flows by integrating the hub of aviation, shipping and scientific and technological innovation". The Eleventh Congress of the CPC Guangzhou Municipal Committee, held in Guangzhou in December of the same year, once again stressed that "building a hub city of networks is a major strategic move that will consolidate and enhance the city's status as one of the country's important central cities" and further specified the goal of "basically completing the building of the hub city of networks within the next five years".

In the world system of cities, hub cities of networks refer to those that are able to gather and regulate the flow of such high-end elements as people, logistics, information, and capital globally. Such cities are supported by swift and well-functioning networks of talents, information, traffic, science and technology, industries, markets and urban managements and therefore, combine the development momentum of a hub and the interconnectivity of a network. Such cities usually start with an urban transportation hub and gradually develop the hub of logistics, business, information, culture, international exchanges and resource allocation through a dynamic process. In the meantime, such cities actively integrate into external city

---

*This report is the joint outcome of studies by Guangzhou Development Research Institute of Guangzhou University, a Key Research Institute of Humanities and Social Sciences in Universities of Guangdong Province and the Collaborative Innovation and Development Center for "Guangzhou Studies" of Guangdong Provincial Department of Education, the Guangzhou Urban Integrated Development Decision-making Consulting Team under the Innovation Team Program for Guangdong Regular Institutions of Higher Learning.

The author is Tu Chenglin, Dean, Research Fellow, and Ph.D. Tutorat Guangzhou Development Research Institute of Guangzhou University.

networks by strengthening the interconnectivity and the flow of resources with neighboring cities and the world system of cities. Gradually acquiring the ability to allocate resources on a global scale and finally become part of the global system of urban competition and cooperation.

In fact, cities of a certain size generally have one or more transport nodes and thus can be referred to as hubs. They also form networks of communication, aggregation and radiation with surrounding areas. However, the goal of building a hub city of networks, as currently proposed by Guangzhou, aims to build a global city (or world city) that can directly influence global social, economic, cultural, and political issues. International academic circles have reached the consensus that a global city represents a higher level of development of cities and enjoys global influence in the world. It should be the home to headquarters of global enterprises, high-end talents and international activities.

A comparative study of a global city and the hub city of networks that Guangzhou strives to build shows many similarities. First, both are nodes in the world city system. Both are control centers in the global economic system and organizational centers in the network of world cities. Second, both seek to fulfill dual functions. On the one hand, they will control the possession and redistribution of global strategic resources, industries and channels. On the other hand, they will influence global politics, economy, and culture. Third, both aim to realize three goals, namely, robust economy, massive flows and transactions of high-end international resource, and global influence.

Build Guangzhou into a hub city of networks from the perspective of global city is historically inevitable and feasible. First, as centers for the circulation and allocation of resources, cities are playing an increasingly important role in the current international competition. Development level, resourcefulness, and connectivity with other parts of the world are often the main factors that determine the success of a city in the competition. Second, after more than 30 years of reform and opening up, Guangzhou now possesses the favorable conditions for becoming a world-class hub city. The timely proposal of building a hub city of networks will further empower the city with more incentives to growth, more channels to influence, and more platforms to lead. Third, it is said that China plans to build Beijing, Shanghai, Guangzhou, and Shenzhen into global cities and another 11 cities into national central cities. If it is true, it is not only natural but also imperative for Guangzhou to follow the lead of other global cities and strives to build a hub city of networks.

II. What Challenges Guangzhou Needs to Address in Building a Hub city of networks

i. The slow progress in developing integrated transport hubs affects the city's connectivity with the outside world

First, although Guangzhou has proposed to build a network of integrated transport hubs through the construction of three internal and three external road rings, it fails to complete the hubs in the east ((Xintang) and the south (Wanqingsha), which seriously affects its connectivity with the outside world. Second, the interconnectivity between existing transport hubs is far from sufficient. Guangzhou East Railway Station, Guangzhou West Railway Station, and Guangzhou Railway Station are located too close to allow the diversion of people or promote the development of adjacent areas. Guangzhou South Railway Station, Nansha Port, and Guangzhou Baiyun International Airport are respectively located at the southwest, north, and south ends of the city, with inadequate supporting transport systems in between. With subways, buses, and taxis always in short supply, it is inconvenient, time-consuming and costly for the transportation of passengers and cargos. Third, Guangzhou Port is a long-established inland river port still in the process of turning into a seaport. Therefore, it faces many obvious problems such as the outdated facilities, fewer berths for large-scale container terminals and low-level bulk cargo terminals. Nansha Port, on the other hand, is a relatively new port with its ground access system not fully established, market not fully open and a joint river-sea transportation terminal not yet available. It thus needs to seize the opportunity of developing the free trade zone and promptly improve its capacity. Fourth, unlike New York, Tokyo, and other global cities which have more than one airport, Guangzhou has only one airport. With its facility always overloaded and terminals always crowded, Guangzhou Baiyun International Airport suffers from a significant shortage of airspace and parking bays. Moreover, the low-altitude airspace is not open yet, the aviation capacity is to be further improved, and there are not enough international routes. The obstructed city traffic is unable to support seamless transfers among the three hubs and it is urgent to build a second airport. Fifth, there are more north-south high-speed railway lines than east-west lines, resulting in many dead-end lines. Guangzhou's connectivity to the east regions needs to be improved. For example, the Ganzhou-Shenzhen High-Speed Railway bypasses Guangzhou, while Shenzhen-Zhongshan Sea Tunnel and Shenzhen-Maoming High-speed Railway virtually block the city's eastern passages. Beijing-Kowloon High-Speed Railway will directly connect to Beijing via Ganzhou-Shenzhen High-Speed Railway. Moreover, the high-speed railway network to its west is yet to be fully developed. There are no direct lines from Guangzhou to Chengdu, Chongqing, or Xi'an at present.

ii. There is no sufficient support for technological innovation which affects the city's technological influence

In order to make up for its deficiency in technological innovation, Guangzhou has introduced a series of policies in recent years to create a more favorable environment. However, due to the delayed impact of policies, no substantive results have been achieved other than mere slogans. In the meanwhile, the city's scientific and technological progress has been undermined by "old diseases" and "new illnesses". "Old diseases" are reflected in the insufficient investment in research and development, the incompetence for original innovation, the low output rate of scientific deliverables, the absence of high-end innovation teams, and the relatively outdated research systems and mechanisms. As a result, the city has far less patent achievements than Beijing, Shanghai and Shenzhen, etc. "New diseases" include the lack of an optimal environment for innovation, the fragmentation of innovative resources, and the difficulty in implementing innovation policies and attracting high-end talents. Compared with other cities of the same type, Guangzhou still has much to do to attract more talents to come to the city where they can settle down and start their own business or career. The problem is further complicated as the city's different districts not only show imbalanced competence for innovation, but also engage in homogeneous competition. For instance, Tianhe, Nansha, and Huangpu are all competing to be the core area of the science and technology hub. This self-oriented approach which ignores the integration of resources and the fully functioning of the hub, hinders the flow of resources among different districts in the city.

iii. The lack of a robust economy affects the city's international influence in the economic aspect

First, Guangzhou lags far behind other global cities at home and abroad in terms of the economic scale. Guangzhou's GDP is not only significantly smaller than that of Tokyo, New York, Paris, and other global cities but also fails to match that of Beijing and Shanghai. Always in the third position of domestic cities, Guangzhou is unable to leverage sufficient resources to support its development. Second, despite some progress in upgrading its industrial structure in recent years, the city fails to develop its high-end industries adequately. As a result, Guangzhou has a lot of small and medium-size enterprises while industrial leaders are few in number. In terms of industry composition, Guangzhou has a considerably smaller number of top 100 information technology, biomedicine, and new energy companies, an obvious disadvantage to its development. Third, Guangzhou fails to develop its modern service industry properly. This is especially obvious when it comes to the development of the headquarters economy and the financial industry, both typical features of hub network cities. Such deficiencies, especially in the financial industry, hinder the allocation of international capital in Guangzhou and further obstruct the development of its headquarters economy.

iv. The weak connectivity of internal and external hubs affects Guangzhou's influence as a global city

In terms of internal connectivity, the serious lack of transport infrastructure and the incompatibility between existing urban planning and the building of a hub city of networks have not only severely hindered infrastructure development and the proper functioning of transportation hubs, but also led to the dislocation of the city's functions and driving forces for growth. The overlapping of administrative bodies creates loopholes and blind spots and Guangzhou is not immune to environmental pollution, traffic congestion, garbage siege, smelly rivers, and other urban diseases. In terms of connectivity with adjacent areas, there is still room for improvement as places in this area tend to "run their own courses" and "mind their own businesses". The connectivity between transportation hubs and the coordination among adjacent cities are far from satisfactory. With a limited service radius, the city is unable to exert much influence on or provide many incentives for the development of adjacent areas. In terms of domestic influence, the global recession combined with fierce competition from the Yangtze River Delta region has significantly undermined Guangzhou's dominant position in foreign trade and exchanges and reduced its strength in the provision of overseas service. In terms of international influence, despite flights to Asian, European, American, and even African countries, Guangzhou fails to connect directly to South America. Therefore, the city still needs to forge deeper ties with certain regions in the world.

III. What Principles Guangzhou Needs to Follow in Building a Hub City of Networks

i. Strengthen top-level design and plan in advance

The city should not only formulate a master plan for building a hub city of networks but also specific plans for developing different hubs such as transportation, industries, logistics, trade, commerce, information and human resources. During the process of top-level design, it is imperative for the city to ensure coordination within the city, between the city and adjacent areas, and fully consider the international landscape for competition.

ii. Start with easy issues and gradually make up for all deficiencies

Building a hub city of networks is a long-term systematic project involving tremendous efforts and huge investment. The city should neither expect overnight results nor rush for success. The city should start with easy issues and gradually make up for all deficiencies, thus creating new driving forces for its growth. As the first step, it may strive to optimize its internal transportation system by addressing blind spots within the city and in its surrounding areas. Then it may continue to solve the "last mile" issue by addressing dead-end or irregular lines that obstruct its connection to adjacent areas. Gradually it may launch some major infrastructure projects that will upgrade the scale and overall functioning of the city's transportation system and hub network.

iii. Proceed step by step to build a network of circles

The city may subdivide the overarching goal of building a hub city of networks into different levels of circles, which will facilitate the optimization of its internal resources and the expansion of its external influences. It is a gradual process and requires efforts step by step. It may start with the intra-city circle and focus on optimizing its urban development and inherent functions. The second step is to set up the inter-city circle by focusing on strengthening interconnectivity and expanding mutual influence. The third circle is at the regional level which will focus on making Guangzhou a fully functioning national central city that supports national development strategies. The fourth circle is at the international level through which the city shall comprehensively enhance exchanges with other global cities and improve its international influence. The ultimate goal is to make Guangzhou a well-functioning global city that leverages the benefits of globalization and the development of networks.

iv. Introduce foreign capital, establish domestic connections, and leverage global resources

Developing a hub city of networks involves all-round efforts to improve Guangzhou's urban functions so that it can provide better support for regional development and more effectively participate in international competition. It is not a task for the city alone, nor can it be accomplished by the city itself. The city should strive to achieve shared growth and prosperity through collaboration with neighboring cities, leverage major projects of national significance for a leapfrog development, and introduce foreign capital, establish domestic connections, and use international and public resources for long-term growth.

IV. Recommendations for Building Guangzhou into an International Hub City of Networks

i. Make plans, build consensus, and strengthen top-level design

First, the city should make full use of external wisdom and consulting services. It should invite foreign and domestic experts to form innovation teams and formulate *Plans for Building Guangzhou into a Hub City of Networks* and relevant subproject plans. Second, public officials at all levels should change their thinking pattern and refrain from "minding their own businesses". Concerted efforts should be devoted to accomplishing the shared task of building a hub city of networks. The government should build consensus among the public and make use of all available resources.

ii. Start with easy issues, focus on major transportation infrastructure, and accelerate the flow of factors

First, the city should strive to build an international aviation hub by further expanding its international routes. It should increase air routes to Europe, North America, and Africa and open new routes to South America. It should speed up the construction of its second international airport and build more terminals. It should improve the passenger transportation system that connects the airport with adjacent areas and expand the airport's scope of influence. Second, the city should devote concerted efforts to the development of Nansha Port and further enhance its cargo transportation capacity.

Measures may include: renovating outdated facilities in inland river port terminals to create new strength; strengthening the development of the international shipping service system and providing tailor-made services for enterprises; and expanding cooperation with other international ports by actively developing new shipping lines for foreign trade containers and establishing stable relations in joint delivery, production and trade. Third, the city should improve the layout of its railway hub so as to ensure the separation of passenger and cargo lines. It should construct more railways that strategically connect with neighboring cities, such as the Guangzhou-Foshan Loop Track and Guangzhou section in the Huizhou–Dongguan–Shenzhen Intercity Railway and build a comprehensive transportation hub in the east. It should speed up the transformation of Guangzhou Railway Station into a high-speed railway station and build an express transport system around it. Fourth, the city should further leverage actual and potential strengths of existing transport hubs. For example, it may speed up the construction of terminals at Guangzhou Baiyun International Airport and further open the low-altitude airspace so as to develop the airport economy. It may cut toll stations between Guangzhou and neighboring cities and promote joint customs clearance and sea-land-air joint delivery in the Pearl River Delta Region. It may also strive to solve the "last mile" issue by reducing traffic congestion points and offering more options of transfers and more accessible facilities.

iii. Pool resources and make up deficiencies, so as to enhance the city's comprehensive innovation strength

On the one hand, it is necessary to bring together national innovation resources to make up for the city's deficiencies in innovation and accelerate the construction of an international science and technology innovation hub. First, to improve its influence, the city should focus on attracting innovative talents and high-end science and technology companies. It should accelerate the construction of mass innovation, crowd-sourcing, collective support, and crowd-funding platforms and encourage people to start their own businesses and to make innovations. Second, it should focus on building the urban innovation corridor and make Tianhe the center of the international science and technology innovation hub. It should promote the coordinated development of the innovation zone and the creativity zone, optimize mass innovation, crowd-sourcing, collective support and, crowd-funding platforms, and integrate innovation companies, incubators, and industrial parks. Third, it should strengthen international cooperation to pool global innovation resources, establish platforms and expand channels for regional partnerships, and build a science and technology innovation trading center with international influence. One the other hand, the city should continue to promote industrial restructuring and upgrading, make up for deficiencies in industrial development, and create new industrial strength. First, it should vigorously develop the modern service industry and enhance the city's catalytic role. Second, it should vigorously develop the headquarters economy and increase its capacity for pooling urban resources. Third, it should vigorously develop the financial industry and increase its capacity for capital allocation.

iv. Seize opportunities and build platforms to enhance the international image

First, by implementing the Belt and Road Initiative, Guangzhou can actively engage in urban public diplomacy, further cooperation with neighboring countries to enhance its international influence. Second, Guangzhou should seize the opportunity of hosting Guangzhou International Award for Urban Innovation to actively expand exchanges and cooperation with international sister cities and other pioneering cities, further improve urban marketing and enhance the city's image. Third, Guangzhou should seize the opportunity of hosting Canton Fair and other international exhibitions to promote exchanges and cooperation with merchants from all countries on an equal footing and enhance the city's international appeal and influence.

Guangzhou Government's WeChat Public Accounts: Current Operation and Future Development

Zhou Lingxiao[1]

Abstract: Using Guangzhou government's WeChat public accountsas an example, this report surveys what problems exist for account holders and subscribers, and provides recommendations for the future development of Guangzhou government's WeChat public accounts.

Keywords: government's WeChat public accounts, subscribers, demand analysis, Guangzhou

I. Current Operation of Guangzhou Government's WeChat Public Accounts

i. The supply side

According to the *2015 Annual Report of Guangdong Government WeChat Public Accounts* released by Guangdong Internet-based Governance Forum, Guagndong has more than 1,700 government WeChat public accounts, ranking first among Chinese provinces. With 51 government-run subscription accounts and 16 service accounts, Guangzhou ranks among the top three of all cities in the province. These accounts cover a wide range of areas including culture, transportation, security, political parties, education, and public services, etc. Almost all government agencies have opened their own WeChat public account.

However, when it comes to actual operation, not all accounts are enjoying the same rapid development as those on the Top 10 List of Accounts with Greatest Communicative Influence like Guangzhou Education, Guangzhou Library, Guangzhou Health Pass, Guangzhou Public Security, and Guangzhou Integrity or those winning the Award of Intelligent Public Service like Guangzhou Subway. Despite the initial growth and progress, some government-run accounts remain anonymous at low ebb, with few subscribers, scarce feeds, and even less hits. In fact,

---

[1] This report is the joint outcome of studies supported by Guangzhou Development Research Institute of Guangzhou University, a Key Research Institute of Humanities and Social Sciences in Universities of Guangdong Province, the Collaborative Innovation and Development Center for "Guangzhou Studies" of Guangdong Provincial Department of Education, and the Guangzhou Urban Integrated Development Decision-making Consulting Team under the Innovation Team Program for Guangdong Regular Institutions of Higher Learning.

The author is Dr. Zhou Lingxiao, Deputy Dean and Associate Professor at Guangzhou Development Research Institute of Guangzhou University.

these are common issues faced by most Guangzhou government's WeChat public accounts.

In a survey where participants were asked to choose the adjectives that best described their impression of Guangzhou government's WeChat public accounts, "pragmatic and democratic" won the most votes while "humorous and interesting" the least. It shows that in the eyes of the public, such accounts are steady and practical, but lack vigor and vitality. Some participants also provided their own descriptions, such as "too pretentious" and "inefficient", to name only a few. When running such accounts, government agencies more than often follow the top-down management philosophy. The condescending gesture of the officials creates a sense of distance.

We have chosen six accounts as samples and studied the distribution of feeds. The six accounts, including China Guangzhou Release, Guangzhou Transportation, Guangzhou Government Website, Guangzhou Customs, Guangzhou Culture and Safe Guangzhou, cover current affairs, transportation, politics, service, culture, and security. The observation period was 15 days from February 24, 2016 to March 9, 2016. The observation content was the distribution of feeds by these sample accounts. Findings are shown in Table 1.

Table 1 Distribution of Feeds by Sample Public Accounts

Sample Government WeChat Public Accounts	Service	Government Affairs	Policy News	Events Promotion	Total	Daily Average
China Guangzhou Release	50	7	20	6	83	6
Guangzhou Transportation	27	1	10	10	48	3
Guangzhou Government Website	16	4	21	2	43	3
Guangzhou Customs	6	5	0	3	14	1
Guangzhou Culture	9	5	6	15	35	2
Safe Guangzhou	12	3	23	9	47	3

From the table above we can see that Guangzhou government WeChat accounts mainly focus on pushing service feeds to subscribers, followed by interpretations of policy news. Feeds related to government affairs are the least pushed. Different accounts vary significantly in the number of daily average feeds.

ii. The demand side

Our survey showed that public demand for Guangzhou government WeChat public accounts presented the following features:

1. Preference for practical information and functions

Most subscribers said that they want service information and practical information concerning urban living. Only a small number of interviewees responded that they would like to know government and administrative information. These results showed that when people subscribe to a government account, their first aim is to gain access to practical and useful information, because the most prominent feature of a government account is accessibility and practicality. It is their hope to receive the needed administrative services anywhere and anytime when they click a functional button on the account platform. .

Another frequently chosen function is "to know cultural features of the city", accounting for 55%. In many cases, government's WeChat public accounts focus too much on functions and information that are closely related to the mandate of a specific agency that they give no importance of promoting the city's culture. In fact, subscribers to Guangzhou government accounts not only include locals but also people who have come to the city to work or study. If government accounts had laid more emphasis on promoting the city's culture, it would have created a stronger sense of belonging in these people and helped them better relate to the city. It would also have helped build the government's image as "not only a political establishment but also an active promoter of local culture".

2. Preference for people-oriented and user-friendly services

When asked about their ideal government's public accounts, nearly 85% of the participants said that an ideal account should provide more interactive functions and be more attentive to public opinions. It is clear that a friendly and people-oriented WeChat public account is what the people look for. Different from government portals, government's WeChat public accounts are not mechanical tools whose only function is to release political information. People expect them to be true-to-life and down-to-earth. However, compared with government microblogs, such accounts are often found lacking interactivity. Many administrators only see such accounts as more casual and relaxing platforms for pushing feeds and forget the fact that WeChat is ultimately a messaging communication platform. That explains why most government accounts fail to install interactive functions with the public.

3. Preference for time-saving and easily-accessible feeds

When asked about their favorite type of feeds, 53% of the respondents chose pictures, which was also the most frequently used format to communicate information by government accounts, because pictures are often colorful and easily understood. The second welcome format was video, as 26% of the respondents expressed their willingness to receive video feeds. However, despite their ability to integrate images, sound, text, and graphs in impressive and funny ways, videos are seldom used by government-run accounts.

II. Existing Issues in the Development of Guangzhou Government's WeChat Public Accounts

i. Lack of authority, promotional efforts and subscribers

Of the 107 people surveyed, only 38 had subscribed to any WeChat public accounts run by Guangzhou government agencies, accounting for 36%. Nearly half of the 38 people responded that they only subscribed to a very limited number of such accounts, ranging from 1 to three. The author also discovered that feeds pushed by the city's government accounts normally did not generate many clicks. For example, in the past week the most popular account Guangzhou Subway generated 11692 clicks per feed on average while the figure for China Guangzhou Release was only 3781. In comparison, studies by the author showed that the public account run by a local restaurant had generated 8383 clicks per feed in the same week. It is clear that when it comes to visibility and communication efficiency, Guangzhou government accounts still have much room for improvement.

Such accounts may also want to significantly improve their promotional efforts. 64% respondents who had not subscribed to any government WeChat accounts said that they had no idea about the existence of such accounts. Other than its portal or microblog, a government agency usually resorts to no platforms to make the QR Code for its WeChat account known to the public. Moreover, even within the government itself accounts run by different agencies fail to help each other build visibility. For example, although Guangzhou Government Portal displayed links to all relevant microblogs run by the city's government agencies, it only displayed the QR Code for one WeChat account, i.e. Guangzhou Government Website to facilitate public subscription. It is necessary that the portal follow its practice with microblogs and add a specific button for all government WeChat accounts.

74% respondents also indicated that they would be more likely to subscribe to accounts that had already been authenticated because information released by such accounts was believed to be more authoritative. However, some government agencies still have not had their WeChat accounts authenticated even until today, which greatly undermines their influence and authority.

ii. Confusing account names, functions and the existence of zombie accounts

In some cases, users are bewildered by confusing account names and functions. For example, if you enter "Guangzhou education" in WeChat's search box for public accounts, you will see displayed below two accounts with the identical name of "Guangzhou Education", both having been authenticated by Guangzhou Bureau of Education. If you enter "Guangzhou railway", you will get two accounts both using the logo of Guangzhou Subway as their profile photo. One account is named Guangzhou Subway and the other named Guangzhou Subway WeChat Service. Although the first account is designed as a subscription account and the second a service account, they fail to distinguish themselves because of the many similarities in function. Moreover, there are also some zombie accounts which seldom push feeds or provide service. Subscribers often feel at a loss as they never get the desired service. Such accounts undermines the overall service quality of government WeChat accounts.

iii. Official-oriented thinking still dominates

According to my observation and study, the official-oriented thinking still dominates in various Guangzhou government WeChat public accounts. Only 10% of the respondents said that such accounts had performed very satisfactory interactions with the public. In the eyes of government account administrators, such accounts are only tools to release government information rather than platforms to interact with the people. Consequently, administrators view themselves as government officials to manage the society rather than providing service for the public. WeChat is the product of a new era and its users are mainly young people. It is necessary that government accounts keep up with the trends of the Internet, adopt more cyber-speak in their daily feeds and interactions with subscribers, and try their best to shorten the distance with users.

iv. Failure to properly respond to public emergencies

Of the few public emergencies that took place in Guangzhou in recent years, most were related to panic over public transportation. The author finds that government agencies tended to publicly respond to such panic events through government microblogs or press conferences. WeChat public accounts were seldom an option. In fact, WeChat accounts can deliver information more speedily than microblogs, since such accounts can push feeds directly to subscribers' mobile phones while microblog postings are only read when users turn on their computer. Therefore, the city's government should give full play to the role of government WeChat accounts in responding to public emergencies. The timely and one-on-one communication features of WeChat accounts will enable every single subscriber to know the latest development and progress in the event in time.

III. Recommendations for the Future Development of Guangzhou Government's WeChat Public Accounts

i. Strengthen promotional efforts and account authentication

First, the city should promote e-governance as a whole and platforms should help each other in attracting more subscribers. As the three major types of e-governance platforms, government portals, microblogs, and WeChat public accounts have differences as well as similarities. None should develop on their own. WeChat public accounts, as newly adopted tools for governance in recent years, cannot develop without the support of portals and microblogs. If the three major platforms can be combined to support each other, all will enjoy breakthroughs in their development. Promotional efforts should be given due consideration to the overall effectiveness of the e-governance system.It is suggested that each government portal add a "Government WeChat Account" button to its interaction section and each government microblog display QR Code for the corresponding WeChat accounton its home page.

Second, government WeChat public accounts should promote each other. Instead of being completely independent, government accounts are somewhat related to each other. Increasing their inter-connectivity will attract new subscribers while cementing the ties with old ones. Since WeChat users tend to subscribe to a very limited number of government accounts at the same time, it is suggested that each government account open a "Related Accounts" section where the QR Code or ID of other government accounts are provided to facilitate subscription.

Third, the city should explore multiple platforms to promote government accounts. Both traditional and modern communication platforms should be used. While advertisinggovernment WeChat accounts on TV, newspapers, magazines, and other traditional media forms, it may also keep up with the development of science and technology and explore new platforms to strengthen promotional efforts.

Fourth, the city should advance the authentication of government-run accounts. It is suggested that such accounts be formally authenticated as soon as possible. In the case that some accounts fail to get authenticated because of the small number of subscribers, the WeChat administration should be immediately contacted so as to prevent fake government accounts from impeding the interests of the people.

ii. Provide practical information services by optimizing account names and functions

First, overlapping functions should be integrated. To develop WeChat accounts, government agencies should focus on quality rather than quantity. Too manygovernment WeChat accounts will not only waste resources but also bewilder users and easily lead to confusion. It is suggested that certain accounts should be merged if their work scope and functions are similar or largely overlapping.

Second, account names should be managed in a unified way. The city should go through authenticated government WeChat accounts and make sure that they are named according to their category so as to prevent occurrence of duplicate names and similar names.

Third, functions and mandates should be clearly defined. Each account should have their functions clearly defined so as to provide services to the public more effectively. Each account should have their mandates clearly defined so as to ensure their feeds and services are targeted and every aspect of public life is duly covered.

Fourth, government microblogs and WeChat accounts should complement each other in functions. While people expect microblogs to be more interactive and lively while gaining more speedy access to practical information through WeChat accounts.

Fifth, zombie accounts should be cleared up. Those accounts that are explicitly abandoned should be canceled. A management system should be established to regulate the functions, frequency of feeds, and interactivity of government's WeChat public accounts.

iii. From the people, for the people

First, interaction should be strengthened. In the future, Guangzhou government's WeChat public accounts should set up interactive functions such as message boards or comment mailboxes so that the public can leave their comments on the operation of such accounts and the performance of relevant government agencies. Government officials administering WeChat accounts should put aside their official title and more actively respond to public comments so as to narrow the distance from the people.

Second, the operation of accounts should be people-oriented. Always bear in mind users' preferences and more frequently use pictures, mini-magazines, and other formats to push feeds so as to allow users to spend less time and flow in gaining more and clearer information. Functions should be optimized according to the needs of users. Only when every single subscriber is treated with care and every single subscriber gets what he or she wants can the government truly be called from the people and for the people.

iv. Let government accounts play a better role in responding to public emergencies

Government WeChat accounts should be included as major platforms for releasing emergency information. As soon as a social emergency takes place, such accounts should be entrusted to release correct, detailed, and authoritative information and provide guidance for public opinions so as to effectively prevent the spread of rumors that may undermine public order. Government WeChat accounts should take the lead toguide public opinions and relieve public panic. They can also serve as major platforms for releasing people-seeking notices and medical aid information in follow-up actions as the huge customer base of WeChat will guarantee the effective dissemination of information and the speedy solution social emergencies.

References:

[1] Gao Hongcun, Yuzheng. Practical Methods, Techniques and Case Guides for Running Government WeChat Public Accounts [M]. Beijing: People's Publishing House, 2015.56-58

[2] Edited by Lin Daliang, Cheng Xiaoyong, Chen Jun. Marketing and Operation Strategies forWeChat Public Accounts [M]. Beijing: Mechanical Industry Press, 2014.146-150

[3] Tencent Penguin Intelligence. 2015 WeChat Platform Data Research Report [Z], http://www.iyunying.org/news/5561.html (2015/1/27)

[4] *gd.qq.com*. 2015 Annual Report of Guangdong Government WeChat Public Accounts [Z], http://gd.qq.com/a/20151126/033899_2.htm (2015/11/26)

[5] Lv Lu. Current Development, Challenges, and Recommended Solutions of Government WeChat Public Accounts in China [D] .Hebei: Hebei University, 2014.21-23

[6] Wang Yue, Zheng Lei. Study on Government WeChat Public Accounts in China: Characteristics, Content, and Interaction [J]. E-Governmence, 2014 (133) .72-74

[7] Li Hongke, Sun Jianli. How Government WeChat Public AccountsLead Public Opinions in Crisis [J]. NewsCommunication, 2015 (7) .110-111

[8] Zhang Qingna. An Analysis of the Development Strategy of Government WeChat Public Accounts [J]. Today's Media, 2014 (11) 122-123

[9] Chen Haichun, Li Xinxin, Zhao Yufan, Hui Mei. Study on How Government WeChat Public Accounts Transform Traditional Governance Pattern: Using the WeChat Public Account"Guangzhou Public Security" as an Example [J]. Journal of

Modern Information, 2015 (5).143-145

[10] Yan Yan. Study on the Credibility of Government Microblogs [D]. Nanjing: Politics and Law Forum of Nanjing University, 2013.15-20

[11] Guo Zede. How Government WeChat Public Accounts Promote Innovation in Social Governance: Using the WeChat Public Account"Shanghai Release" as an Example [J].E-Governmence, 2014 (4) .80-83

[12] Yin Hongyan. Study on WeChat Users' Experience and Satisfaction [D]. Zhengzhou: Zhengzhou University, 2013.13-15

[13] The Institute of Journalism and Communication of Chinese Academy of Social Sciences. Blue Book on New Media: Report on the Development of China's New Media No. 6 [M]. Beijing: Social Sciences Academic Press, 2015.52-60

Recommendations on Promoting the Structural Reform

of Taxi Industry in Guangzhou

Tan Yuanfang*

Abstract: Two major structural problems are currently facing the taxi industry in Guangzhou. The first is the monopoly of taxi companies and the formation of a profiteering class. The second is that government authorities lack the spirit of reform and fail to take a proactive approach. The author, on the basis of good international practices, proposes measures to address these problems, which include promptly enacting regulations on reforming the taxi industry in Guangzhou, encouraging the transformation and upgrading of taxi companies and strengthened branding efforts of operators, and establishing information-based regulatory platforms.

Keywords: taxi industry, monopoly, structural reform

On July 28, 2016, the General Office of the State Council issued the *Guiding Opinion on Deepening Reform and Promoting the Healthy Development of Taxi Industry*, pointing out that it is necessary to "actively and steadily promote the reform of the taxi industry to better meet the travel needs of the people". This document not only gives local governments greater autonomy in decision-making, allowing them to formulate their own implementation plans according to local conditions but also tests their courage and ability in responding to new situations. To Guangzhou, the current reform of the taxi industry is a serious challenge as well as an important opportunity.

I. Structural Problems Currently Facing Taxi Industry in Guangzhou

As one of the first cities to benefit from China's policy of reform and opening-up, Guangzhou witnessed the earliest development of the taxi industry in the country, which testified to the city's reform spirit and dedication to innovation. In the 1970s, while taxis in all parts of the country only picked up passengers at fixed times and

*This report is the joint outcome of studies supported by Guangzhou Development Research Institute of Guangzhou University, a Key Research Institute of Humanities and Social Sciences in Universities of Guangdong Province, the Collaborative Innovation and Development Center for "Guangzhou Studies" of Guangdong Provincial Department of Education, and Guangzhou Urban Integrated Development Decision-making Consulting Team under the Innovation Team Program for Guangdong Regular Institutions of Higher Learning.

The author is Dr. Tan Yuefang, Deputy Dean and Professor at Guangzhou Development Research Institute of Guangzhou University.

places, Guangzhou took the lead to set up the first private taxi company named Baiyun Taxi Company, which offered 24-hour regular and reservation services. Passengers could either hail taxis on the road or call for a reservation in advance. Billing was based on distance. This operation pattern made Guangzhou a pioneer and model in the national taxi industry reform. In 1998, Guangzhou took the lead again by becoming the first city to eliminate taxi franchise fees paid to the government.

However, it should also be noted that despite the industry's role in improving the city's traffic structure and meeting citizens' travel needs, the past 40 years has also witnessed the formation of many structural problems in the taxi industry, such as the monopoly of interest groups and inflexible systems, to name only a few. Among them, the lack of progress in reforming the administration system and encouraging public supervision are the most frequently criticized by the media and the public. According to media reports, low-standard examination for obtaining a driving license for taxis in recent years caused backdoor deals; non-local taxi drivers often get lost themselves or deliberately take detours; and relief drivers are dominating the market. However, limited by institutional obstacles, relevant government authorities are seldom heard to have responded with any reformative measures. Generally, many problems facing the taxi industry in Guangzhou can be categorized into two groups:

The first is the monopoly of taxi companies and the formation of the profiteering class. Currently, the drivers are required to rent a licensed taxi from a large taxi company with certain corporate qualifications, social status, and market strength before they are allowed to operate. This leads to the lack of competition in the industry and the formation of interest groups and a profiteering class. The unequal contractual relationship between taxi companies and drivers further results in the absence of vitality, efficiency, and quality service that permeates the whole industry.

According to relevant documents issued by Guangzhou Municipal Government in 2010, drivers have to pay the taxi company RMB8, 850 per month as management fee in the first year and enjoy a 500 yuan deduction every year thereafter. However, findings of this research group show that drivers, or contractors of taxi licenses, still have to pay for their own social insurance and provident fund which amount to RMB1,955.12 at least as well as RMB90 for personal income tax. All put together, a first-year contracted driver will have to pay at least RMB10,895.12 per month to the taxi company so as to cover its operating costs and risks, which may include vehicle administration fees, security testing fees, traffic tax, and driver uniforms. However, such services and support are not clearly defined or assessed; taxi companies can easily overcharge them and benefit from price differences.

In addition, the maintenance of vehicles as well as the possible time and economic costs resulting from accidents or holiday leaves are required to be borne by drivers themselves, who normally have no right to change the contract period. In taxi companies, however, the unwieldy management is well paid for the few functions that they perform: administering the renting of licensed taxis and assisting in the procurement of "Five Insurances and One Fund" (namely, endowment, medical, unemployment, employment injury, and maternity insurance and housing fund). Instead of engaging in direct production activities and bearing related market risks, they rely on taxi drivers for high returns and form the profiteering class. When visiting a large taxi company in Guangzhou, the research group found that every driver had to pay at least RMB5,000 to the company for every shift (taxi drivers often work on two shifts) every month. When it came to the monthly maintenance of vehicles or replacement of parts, drivers were required to visit designated shops whose services were 30% to 40% higher than those of average 4S stores.

Second, the government administration lacks the spirit of reform and acts passively. The scarcity of taxi operation rights and the absence of an exit mechanism have made them a highly profitable investment, which can easily lead to rent-seeking relationship between taxi companies and competent authorities. On the one hand, government assessment of corporate qualifications and license issuance is not subject to open and transparent public supervision, creating loopholes for off-table deals. For example, it was reported a few years ago that new drivers rushing to get a license generally paid facilitation fees. On the other hand, government authorities often lack the courage to initiate profound institutional changes in the face of prevalent malpractices, such as subcontracting licenses to non-registered or relief drivers, illegal operation of fake or unlicensed taxis, deliberately taking detours, illegal carpooling or refusing to take passengers with no ground, overbilling, dominating the market, and even obstructing justice. Instead, government responses often take the form of vigilance actions or kind recommendations. For example, the Division of Passenger Traffic Management of Guangzhou Municipal Commission of Transpiration calls on taxi companies to send special inspectors to check on drivers between 10:00 pm and 5:00 am, distribute proposals on law-abiding operation to drivers, and giver service cards to passengers. These measures, which address symptoms instead of root causes, not only waste governance resources, but also result in the decline of the taxi industry. Public and media criticism of such malpractices is especially severe when passengers generally find it difficult to hail taxis when travelling in extreme weathers, during important occasions such as the

Spring Festival or national college entrance examination days, or from remote hubs like Tianhe Coach Terminal or Baiyun Airport.

The monopoly of taxi companies and the lack of courage of government authorities are the two major structural issues that lead to the recession cycle of the taxi industry in Guangzhou. The profiteering class, the rigid management system, and the declining services all point to its fall. Gradually, no one will want to take a taxi. Drivers, who cannot make money, will not want to drive taxis. Unable to rent their taxis to qualified drivers, companies will have to settle for unqualified ones, who will provide even worse services. In the end, there will be no one taking taxis. Moreover, interest groups tend to maintain the current pattern and have thus become the biggest obstacle to reform.

II. Models and Options for Promoting Structural Reform of Taxi Industry in Guangzhou

The monopoly of taxi licenses means that people's travel needs are controlled by a few people, which clearly runs counter to the principles of coordinated, green, open and shared development. Moreover, traffic management authorities fail to take comprehensive policy measures against existing issues, which has in effect led to more confusion in administration. For example, in order to reduce the no-load rate, authorities have imposed artificial control over taxi numbers, an interest-driven measure that fails to take into full consideration the city's population structure, economic development, and consumption level, especially the composition of its floating population and the structure of its road network. When making decisions on the number of taxis allowed to operate, the government more than often only considers the size of the city's static population, leading to the difficulty in hailing taxis in Baohua Road, Guangfu Road, and Shangxiajiu Pedestrian Street in the old downtown area. It also creates room for rent-seeking. On the one hand, it is difficult to stop tricycles, electric cars, and other unlicensed vehicles from picking up passengers on the road. On the other hand, taxi licenses have become scarce resources. As is widely criticized by citizens and the media, licensed taxi drivers now earn less, passengers suffer more, while taxi companies and licensees make a fortune.

However, a glimpse at the international practice will find that most developed cities have adopted an open management system and incorporated taxis into their public transportation system for overall planning. While ensuring necessary priorities, their operations are regulated by the market. London, Tokyo, Hong Kong, Taipei and many other cities have never artificially controlled the number of taxis or taxi companies. Individuals can either join a taxi company or apply for a license plate themselves. The management fees are never fixed but subject to market fluctuations. In some cases, taxi fares are divided between the company and the driver by a certain proportion. For example, a taxi driver in Taipei will have to pay his company NT $1,000 (about RMB200) as management fee every month in addition to a certain portion of fares. These fees combined, however, only account for about one third of the company's total revenue. Therefore, the taxi company still has to develop other profit-making businesses, such as offering wrap advertising, running call centers, and providing maintenance services, etc. In Hong Kong, taxi licenses are freely traded in the market as investment tools. While everyone is entitled to buy licenses at auctions, the government also takes measures to prevent monopoly and encourages free competition. As a result, although there are more than 90 taxi companies in Hong Kong, each company maintains an average of about 200 taxis.

Guangzhou's current practice of license control reflects a management philosophy of planned economy rather than market economy. Relying too much on the artificial control of licenses or the total number of taxis, one will easily neglect market's selection and self-regulation functions as well as the interests of taxi drivers and passengers. This typical inactivity of the government will further encourage the formation of the profiteering class in an industry.

It was against this background that the General Office of the State Council issued the *Guiding Opinion*, which required all governments stop issuing perpetual licenses and charging franchise fees for new taxis and take active measures to encourage, support, and guide taxi companies, industrial associations, labor unions, and drivers to properly determine and dynamically adjust license fees or commissions through equal consultation. The decision to abolish franchise fees will reduce the operation costs of taxi companies and reduce the monthly burden of drivers. However, it will not free drivers from any management fees. In fact, Guangzhou eliminated taxi franchise fees paid to the government as early as 1998. However, taxi drivers still have to hand over a considerable portion of their monthly income to companies in order to share their operating costs. In some cases, these fees are misappropriated to cover the salaries of unnecessary management staff or their recreational activities. Running taxi companies has almost become a "special industry" that is always profitable.

At present, Guangzhou has made some efforts to reform its taxi industry. There are generally four patterns regarding the distribution of income. The first pattern is to split taxi fares between companies and drivers; the second is for companies to hire drivers as employees who shall receive a basic wage plus a certain portion of operation revenue; the third is to establish partnerships between companies and drivers; and the fourth is for companies to give subsides or return a portion of contract fees to taxi drivers so as to relieve their financial burden. BaiyunTaxiGroup has adopted the third pattern and allows drivers to buy new cars themselves on the condition that RMB2, 800 is handed over to the company as monthly management fee. If drivers prefer to rent new cars from the company, they will have to pay a monthly RMB2, 800 as contract fee. Another company that has adopted the fourth pattern promised to return RMB3, 000 to drivers for every RMB5, 000 they have paid. It should be admitted that these measures are of certain significance for protecting the legitimate rights and interests of taxi drivers and breaking the monopoly and closure of the taxi industry.

However, faced with growing competition from ride-sharing services, the taxi industry should focus its reform efforts on maintaining its business space and defending its exclusive market. Compared with ride-sharing, taxis face a higher risk of no-load (cruising) and have to bear relevant costs. However, this is also where their strength lies, i.e. the ability to provide convenient, economical, comfortable, and safe services for passengers with special needs (e.g. non-mobile Internet users, people affected by emergencies, and those who want to take short trips, etc.).This makes taxis somewhat similar to public transportation. In London, while requiring all taxis to use clean energy, the government also helps them install high-speed WiFi service and gives them priority over private cars on roads. These demonstrate the "quasi-public-transport" attribute of taxis. Therefore, reform measures should take into consideration the diversified and differentiated travel needs of the people and strive to establish a rational benefit distribution mechanism between taxi companies and drivers, where taxi companies can transform from monopolistic and profit-oriented enterprises into service-oriented, platform-based, and regulatory enterprises. This should be a major direction for the structural reform of the taxi industry in Guangzhou.

III. Recommendations for Promoting Structural Reform of Taxi Industry in Guangzhou

As mentioned above, the enclosed system and the conservative administration form the two major structural problems facing the taxi industry in Guangzhou. Reform measures mainly include transforming the business model to break the oligarchy of taxi companies and highlighting the public attribute to win market share from the ride-sharing industry. In order to effectively improve taxi services in Guangzhou and establish a diversified and differentiated travel service system to better meet the travel needs of the general public, the city may devote its efforts to the following areas:

First, the city should issue documents to guide the reform of the taxi industry as soon as possible. The public attribute of taxis should be further highlighted to create a new market image. For years, the local government has been a talker rather than a doer when it comes to the reform of the taxi industryBoth government authorities and taxi companies are too engrossed in protecting their own interests to take active reform measures. The longer the old system is maintained, the more their interests will be protected. The city should seize the opportunity as the central authority makes it clear in the *Guiding Opinion* that local implementation plans should be developed within three months. Speedy and effective reform measures as well as supervisory and supportive efforts should be taken to highlight the semi-bus attribute of taxis and incorporate them into the public transport system of this modern city.

As an international metropolis, Guangzhou is home to 120,000 international citizens and another large number of transnational migrants. Like members of ethnic minorities, they are not familiar with the ride-sharing industry. To a large extent, taxis will remain their first choice of travel for a long time to come. Taken into consideration its influence on the city's image, the local government should pay special attention to the right positioning and sound development of the taxi industry.

Second, the city should encourage the transformation of taxi companies and support the upgrading of their profit model so that contract fees will not be the only source of their revenue. The development of mobile Internet technologies has made the upgrading of operation and management model an inevitable choice for taxi companies. Instead of relying heavily on contract fees, they should put their bargain chip on the establishment of a modern corporate system, the rebranding of its market image, and the provision of quality services so as to realize integrated development. Growing competition from taxi-hailing firms with ride-on-demand services also makes the transformation from rent collectors to service platforms necessary for traditional taxi companies. Contract fees should gradually be replaced by applicable taxation, royalties, and commissions. The Internet and information technology should be better used to ensure the integration with the modern service industry and other emerging industries. Moreover, the abolition of contract fees and the subsequent loss of ensured yields will force taxi companies to devote themselves to providing better services for drivers and passengers.

Third, the city should make it easier for drivers to obtain licenses and encourage companies to strengthen branding efforts. China's current taxi management system is characterized by stringent market entry requirements and one-directional distributions of a limited number of licenses, which can easily lead to the oligarchy of taxi companies and rent-seeking activities. The city should encourage social forces to take part in the taxi business so as to improve the taxi ownership per thousand people, break the oligarchy of taxi companies, solve the shortage of supply and the difficulty of hailing taxis, and increase the efficiency of travel. The advent of such taxi-booking apps as Didi and Yidao has turned the taxi industry virtually into an individually-run business. Against this background, Guangzhou may follow the advanced experience of other international metropolises (for example, 17% of the taxis in Tokyo are operated by individuals) and allow taxi drivers to personally own licenses. In the meantime, an evaluation system can be established to ensure the quality of services provided by drivers. The ultimate aim is to ensure the free access to taxi driving rights and the free circulation of taxi licenses. For taxi companies already in the business, the city should encourage them to strengthen brand building, ensure public access to service standards, and improve service quality. The ultimate goal is to create a healthy competition environment where market forces are allowed to play their role.

Fourth, the city should establish an information-based taxi regulatory platform anda public supervisory and advisory board so as to ensure public oversight. The closure of the taxi industry in Guangzhou can be attributed largely to its lack of necessary social supervision. Our world is dazzled by the rapid development of information technology. The reform of the taxi industry should also follow technological trends and use big data analysis to establish an integrated regulatory platform. In order to improve taxi services, the platform will not only allow the public to access drivers' violation records (such as refusing to take passengers, bargaining, and overcharging) online, but also incorporate such information into individual driver' s credit record. In the meantime, a public supervisory and advisory board will be set up to exercise effective oversight over taxi companies and their administrators. Civil society should be properly engaged to act as a third-party supervisor over government agencies, taxi companies, and drivers and further break the closed and conservative system of the taxi industry in Guangzhou.

Analysis of Guangzhou's Science and Technology Development in 2016 and Prospects for 2017*

Research Team of Guangzhou Development Research Institute of
Guangzhou University **

Abstract: 2016 was a year when the benefits of sci-tech policies were fully unveiled in Guangzhou. The city made significant progress in strengthening the leading role of companies in innovation, introducing high-end talents and projects, and improving platforms and incubator systems, etc. However, challenges still existed, such as the long absence of sufficient investment, the inadequate development of high-tech sector, and the gradual loss of strength in resources. As the city continues to enact the innovation-driven development strategy, the growth of science and technology is likely to retain the momentum observed in 2016. The city is expected to make new breakthroughs in improving companies' research, development, and innovation capacity and further developing incubators and makerspaces.

Keywords: Science and technology, international sci-tech innovation hub, innovation policies, Guangzhou

I. General Development of Science and Technology in Guangzhou in 2016

On the basis of the "1+9" ("1" refers to the *Decision of the CPC Guangzhou Municipal Committee and Guangzhou Municipal People's Government on Accelerating the Implementation of Innovation-driven Development Strategy*; "9" refers to 9 supporting documents) policy frameworks for scientific and technological innovation established in 2015, Guangzhou further enacted a series of supporting rules and regulations in 2016, including the *Measures for the Administration of Science and Technology Business Incubators in Guangzhou*, the *Implementation Measures for Better Supporting One Hundred Benchmark Companies of Innovation*

---

* This report is the joint outcome of studies supported by Guangzhou Development Research Institute of Guangzhou University, a Key Research Institute of Humanities and Social Sciences in Universities of Guangdong Province, the Collaborative Innovation and Development Center for "Guangzhou Studies" of Guangdong Provincial Department of Education, and the Collaborative Innovation Project for "Guangzhou Studies" of Guangzhou Municipal Bureau of Education.

**Team leader: Tu Chenglin, Dean, Research Fellow, and Ph.D. Tutor at Guangzhou Development Research Institute of Guangzhou University.

Team members: Dr. Tan Yuefang, Deputy Dean and Professor at Guangzhou Development Research Institute of Guangzhou University; Zeng Henggao, Deputy Research Fellow at Guangzhou Development Research Institute of Guangzhou University; Zhou Lingxiao, Deputy Dean and Associate Professor at Guangzhou Development Research Institute of Guangzhou University; Dr. Wang Wenjiao at Guangzhou Development Research Institute of Guangzhou University; Dr. Huang Xu, Associate Professor at Guangzhou Development Research Institute of Guangzhou University; Ding Yanhua, Distinguished Fellow at Guangzhou Development Research Institute of Guangzhou University; and Liang Xiuhua, Research Assistant and Master Candidate at Guangzhou Development Research Institute of Guangzhou University. The report is written by Tu Chenglin.

in Guangzhou, the *Measures for Promoting the Commercialization of Scientific and Technological Research Findings in Guangzhou*, and the *Opinions on Further Attracting Leading Industrial Talents* together with 4 supporting policy documents (thus the "1+4" talent policy framework). These documents further contributed to a favorable policy environment for scientific and technological innovation. As the benefits of policies continued to unveil in 2016, Guangzhou witnessed new breakthroughs in nurturing corporate innovators, introducing high-end talents and projects, improving platforms and incubator systems, developing sci-tech finance, and promoting the commercialization of science-tech research findings.

i. Companies play a leading role in sci-tech innovation, resulting in growing input and output.

2016 was the second year since Guangzhou decided to double its 2013 government spending on science and technology by 2017. That year, the local government invested RMB11.287 billion in the science and technology sector, accounting for 5.81% of the total government expenditure and realizing the goal ahead of schedule. The growing financial input was accompanied by increasing support for corporate research and development. 2,307 Guangzhou-based enterprises received a total post-R&D subsidy of up to RMB1.201 billion and another RMB937 million was awarded to 937 enterprises with a R&D department. Statistics showed that 2, 100 municipal-level or higher-level companies had their own R&D department, of which 755 were industrial enterprises above designated size. With the number doubling that of 2014, companies were exercising an increasingly dominant role in science-tech innovation.

The steady growth in financial input and the enhanced leading role of companies has led to a rapid increase of the city's sci-tech innovation, contributed to its expanded scale and improved quality in 2016. Statistics showed that the city received 99,070 patent applications in 2016, up 56.52% over the same period of 2015. The number of applications for the patent of invention reached 31,850, registering a 58.7% year-on-year growth. 2016 thus became the fastest growing year in the past five years (see Table 1), while Guangzhou topped the list of the 19 cities at the sub-provincial level and above in terms of growth rate. Invention, utility, and design accounted for 32.2%, 41.8%, and 26.0% respectively of the total applications received. While invention and utility applications rose 0.5% and 2.7% respectively as compared with the same period in 2015, design applications dropped 3.2%, further optimizing the patent structure (see Table 2). The number of patent grants amounted to 48,313, registering a 21.28% year-on-year growth. Among them, 7,669 were invention patents, up 15.8% over the same period of 2015, making 2016 the second fastest growing year in the past five years. 1,642 international patent applications were filed under the Patent Cooperation Treaty (PCT), an increase of 163.6% over the same period of 2015 and five times that of 2012, making

Guangzhou the second fastest growing city among the 19 cities at the sub-vice provincial level and above. The number was larger than that combined from 2013 to 2015 (see figure 1). The number of valid invention patents reached 30,305, an increase of 25.5% over the same period of the previous year and 2.4 times that of 2012. Every one million people owned 2,244.8 invention patents, 2.3 times that of 2012 (see Figure 2) and outstripped the target set in the *Outline of the Plan for the Reform and Development of the Pearl River Delta* by a large margin. One China Patent Golden Award and 29 Excellent Awards were received, the largest number in history.

Table 1 Comparison of Received Domestic Patent Applications and Granted Patents in Guangzhou in the Past Five Years

Year	Number of Received Applications	Year-on-Year Increase	Number of Granted Patents	Year-on-Year Increase
2012	33421	18.99%	22045	20.20%
2013	39751	18.94%	26156	18.65%
2014	46330	16.55%	28137	7.57%
2015	63366	36.77%	39834	41.57%
2016	99070	56.52%	48313	21.28%

Source: Statistics released by the Intellectual Property Office of Guangzhou

Table 2 Changes in the Composition of Received Patent Applications in Guangzhou in the Past Five Years (Unit: %)

Year	Invention	Utility	Design
2012	29.4	35.4	35.2
2013	30.6	36.7	32.7
2014	31.5	34.1	34.4
2015	31.7	39.1	29.2
2016	32.2	41.8	26.0

Source: Statistics released by the Intellectual Property Office of Guangzhou

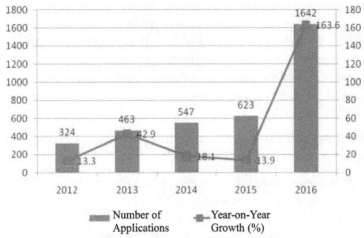

Figure 1 Changes in the Number of International Patent Applications Filed under the Patent Cooperation Treaty (PCT) in Guangzhou in the Past Five Years

Source: Statistics released by the Intellectual Property Office of Guangzhou

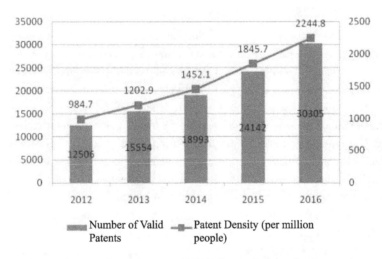

Figure 2 Changes in the Number of Valid Domestic Invention Patents in Guangzhou in the Past Five Years

Source: Statistics released by the Intellectual Property Office of Guangzhou

In terms of the source of sci-tech innovation output, colleges and research institutes continued to play a dominant role in 2016. Statistics showed that colleges took up seven seats on the top 10 list of entities that had filed the largest number of patent applications. South China University of Technology, Guangdong University of Technology, and Sun Yat-sen University topped the list with 2,654,1,650 and 916 applications respectively. In the meantime, companies were playing an increasingly important role, a much welcome development. Statistics showed that the number of invention patent grants by Guangzhou-based enterprises amounted to 16,174, an increase of 84.3% over the same period of 2015. It was the first time that companies contributed more than half of the total granted patents (50.7%). The performance of private companies was particularly eye-catching, which took up seven seats on the top 10 list of companies that had filed the largest number of invention patent applications.

ii. Optimize top-down design for innovation and create a further integrated environment for greater regional cluster effect

Following the *Implementation Plan for the Development of the National Innovation Demonstration Zone in Guangzhou* (2016-2020) and the *Spatial Plan of the National Innovation Demonstration Zone in Guangzhou (2016-2025)*, Guangzhou started to build the sci-tech innovation corridor and satellite matrix in 2016, with special emphasis on Guangzhou Hi-tech Industrial Development Zone, Sino-Singapore Guangzhou Knowledge City, Guangzhou Science City, Tianhe Smart Town, Pazhou Internet Innovation Cluster, International Bio-Island, Guangzhou University City, International Innovation City, Private Science and Technology Park, and Nansha Pearl City of Science and Technology, etc.

Located along the city's sci-tech innovation corridor and the Pearl River Innovation Belt and endowed with rich innovation resources, such as colleges, research institutes, incubators, and high-tech companies in Tianhe, Huangpu, Panyu, Yuexiu, Baiyun, Huadu, and Haizhu played a relatively active role in sci-tech innovation 2016. The number of received patent applications and of patent grants in the seven districts combined accounted for 83.0% and 88.6% of the city's total respectively. Tianhe, Huangpu, Panyu and Yuexiu far outstripped the other eight districts on the list, thanks to the significant clustering effect. Panyu contributed the fastest growth among all the districts and for the first time outran Tianhe to top the list with the largest number of patent grants. However, the quality of innovation still needed to be improved as invention patent applications and grants from the district were both lower than the city's average (See table 3). 30.5% (2,336 patents) and 23.5% (1,799 patents) of the city's total patents granted for inventions came from Tianhe and Huangpu respectively, accounting for 27.1% and 26.5% of each district's total patent grants. With their innovation quality and efficiency significantly higher than those of other districts, Tianhe and Huangpu had become the major engines for promoting innovation in Guangzhou.

Table 3 Comparison of Received Domestic Patent Applications and and Granted Patents in Guangzhou by District in 2016

District	Received Patent Applications			Granted Patents		
	Number	Year-on-Year Increase	Percentage of Invention Patent Applications	Number	Year-on-Year Increase	Percentage of Invention Patent Applications
Tianhe	19767	67.8%	48.9%	8613	14.9%	27.1%
Huangpu	13863	69.7%	42.0%	6796	25.6%	26.5%
Yuexiu	10348	18.2%	32.9%	5864	7.4%	13.9%
Panyu	14907	76.3%	20.9%	8677	61.6%	9.3%
Haizhu	4993	29.8%	39.1%	2629	-0.2%	21.2%
Baiyun	9129	48.8%	15.6%	5458	12.8%	7.1%
Nansha	3256	66.0%	38.0%	1539	19.4%	24.8%
Huadu	9200	40.9%	15.6%	4751	19.1%	5.8%
Liwan	10044	83.9%	31.0%	2024	11.8%	9.2%
Zengcheng	2293	80.4%	22.8%	1068	35.7%	7.9%
Conghua	1223	39.0%	14.5%	866	18.1%	5.1%
Others	47	-6.0%	8.5%	28	47.4%	3.6%
Average		56.5%	32.2%		21.3%	15.9%

Source: Statistics released by the Intellectual Property Office of Guangzhou

iii. Significant progress made in the development of innovation platforms contributed to a further improved innovation and entrepreneurship incubation system.

In 2016, Guangzhou continued to strengthen the development of new R & D institutions, especially in emerging strategic sectors. In joint efforts with renowned domestic and foreign enterprises, universities, and research institutes, the city became home to a considerable number of high-level R & D institutions such as Sino-Singapore International Joint Research Institute, the Institute for Advanced Materials and Technology under the University of Science and Technology Beijing, and ZTE Guangzhou Research Institute. Moreover, 16 Guangzhou-based institutes including the Research Institute of Tsinghua (Pearl River Delta) and the Computer Network Information Center under the Chinese Academy of Sciences successfully entered the second list of new R&D institutions of Guangdong Province in 2016. At the end of 2016, there were 44 provincial-level new R&D institutions in Guangzhou, accounting for 25.9% of the total of the Province and helping Guangzhou maintain its leading position. 10 municipal-level key laboratories were established and applications were filed for the recognition of 34 provincial-level key laboratories. At the end of 2016, Guangzhou was home to 357 key laboratories, including 19 state-level laboratories, 191 provincial-level laboratories, and 147 municipal-level laboratories, covering a wide range of cutting-edge technologies such as biological health, new energy, energy conservation, environment protection, and new-generation information technology. These laboratories formed a rather complete three-tier research system, focusing on materials science, engineering calculation, biological computing, and personalized medical services. The National Supercomputer Center (Guangzhou) set up six major platforms on super cloud computing and offers services to over 1, 600 corporate users in 28 provinces (including municipalities directly under the Central Government), Hong Kong SAR, Macao SAR, and Taiwan.

The plan to double incubators was successfully implemented. It also devoted active efforts to setting up a full-process service system that covered cultivation, incubation, and accelerated growth. Both the number and the quality of makerspaces and incubators improved considerably. With 80 makerspaces joining the family in 2016, the total number mounted to 115, thanks to the impressive year-on-year growth rate (229%). 45 such makerspaces were included in the national incubator management and support system. The city also became home to 73 new sci-tech incubators as the total number reached 192, of which 21 were at the national level. Such incubators covered a total area of 8.4 million square meters, hosting more than 10,000 companies and projects. While the number of incubators increased rapidly, Guangzhou took the lead nationwide in establishing an index system to evaluate the performance of sci-tech incubators and improve their services. While continuing to stress their basic functions, the city further highlighted their performance and social contribution. In 2016, the city topped the national list with the largest number of national outstanding incubators for sci-tech companies for the second year. Moreover, because of its innovative cluster practice for sci-tech company incubators, Guangzhou Development Zone won the Special Science and Technology Progress Award of Guangdong Province.

New breakthroughs were registered in setting up collaborative innovation platforms that combined efforts of industries, universities, and research institutes. At the end of 2016, there were 103 such cooperative platforms or alliances, covering a variety of sectors such as the new generation of information technology and biological health. Throughout the year, the prime operating revenue of such cooperative platforms and alliances reached approximately RMB47 billion while the output value of their high-tech products amounted to about RMB30 billion. 25 research findings were commercialized, 1,438 patent applications were field and 674 granted. Winning 16 honorary titles at the national, provincial, and city levels, these cooperative alliances served as important innovation platforms for the research, development, application, and commercialization of key and cutting-edge technologies.

iv. Sci-tech finance demonstrated significant leverage effect while innovative industries gained greater momentum of growth.

Statistics showed that by the end of 2016, Guangzhou had managed to attract approximately RMB29 billion of social capital for sic-tech finance, nearly 30 times that of its fiscal investment (RMB1.019 billion) in this area. Thanks to its pioneering role in adopting the two-way incentive subsidy scheme, a total of RMB146 million had been invested in science and technology since 2015 and 212 newly started technology enterprises were able to bring in RMB 2.432 billion of social capital. Since it formally launched the credit risk compensation fund pool for small- and medium-sized sci-tech enterprises in early 2016, Guangzhou had issued loan confirmation letters to 418 enterprises, resulting in a credit volume of RMB4.247 billion, the largest among domestic cities. With an initial investment of RMB180 million, Guangzhou Venture Capital Guidance Fund set up four sub-funds including Hongtu Kexin, together with Shenzhen Capital Group and other established investment agencies. The total venture capital eventually amounted to over RMB1.5 billion. They were also able to engage social capital to invest in 26 local sci-tech innovation projects and the total investment reached RMB5.4 billion.

Due to the strong leverage effect of sci-tech finance, innovative industries gained greater momentum of growth in 2016. It witnessed a stunning increase of 2,821 new high-tech enterprises, almost ten times that of 2015 (263 new enterprises). Guangzhou topped the list of cities above the sub-provincial level in the country in terms of the growth rate and ranked second in terms of the net increase. With the total number of high-tech enterprises surging to 4,740, or 2.5 times that of 2015 (1919 companies), Guangzhou successfully entered the top four list of major cities in China. Guangzhou had the third largest number of companies on the top 50 List of Best Innovation Companies in China, with nine Guangzhou-based enterprises including Miniso and Homekoo. The city had more than 120,000 sci-tech innovation companies. With 203 companies newly listed on the New Three Board, China's share transfer system for medium and small sized companies, the total number of companies listed on the Board amounted to 347, making Guangzhou the champion among capital cities nationwide in terms of increase and the total number. Guangzhou also had the highest net asset value of an average newly listed company among the first-tier cities (Beijing, Shanghai, Guangzhou, and Shenzhen). With high-tech enterprises and small giant enterprises accounting for 80% of all the listed companies, Guangzhou-based sci-tech companies began to make a considerable presence on the New Three Board.

In 2016, the output value of high-tech products of industrial companies above designated sizein Guangzhou reached RMB903.526 billion, an increase of 7.3% over the same period of the previous year, which was faster than that of the industrial average (6.5%). The output value of high-tech products accounted for 46% of the total industrial output above designated size, up 1.0 percentage point over the same period of the previous year (45.0%), driving the growth of industrial companies above designated size by 3.0 percentage points.[1]

v. With new progress in the introduction of high-level innovative talents and large foreign-funded innovation projects, Guangzhou was able to bring in high-end factors of innovation in a faster manner

In order to better engage high-level innovative entrepreneurs and entrepreneurial teams, Guangzhou issued the *Opinions on Better Engaging Leading Industrial Talents* and four supporting documents in February 2016, which made it clear that from 2016 onwards the city would allot RMB3.5 billion from its fiscal budget to support 100 leading innovation and entrepreneurial teams, 500 leading innovators and entrepreneurs, 5,000 high-end industrial talents, and 10,000 urgently needed industrial professionals. The city further launched its *Green Card Policy for Talents* in May, which gave residents from abroad and other parts of China the same rights and services as locals, meaning they could buy property and cars and their children could attend public school, etc. Those entitled to apply for the card include Chinese academicians, experts selected by the Recruitment Program of Global Experts (known as "the Thousand Talents Plan"), top foreign talents, and people with foreigner expert permit, etc. 2016 marked the first year of implementing the new talent policy in Guangzhou. 11 leading entrepreneurial teams, 10 leading innovation teams, 10 leading innovators and entrepreneurs, and 30 top industrial talents were initially identified. Meanwhile, the city intensified its implementation of the Pearl River Science and Technology Nova Program and increased the number of yearly "stars" (outstanding public and private sci-tech entities) to 200 from 2016 onwards. Statistics showed that 46 experts from Guangzhou entered the Thousand Talents Plan in 2016, accounting for 47.9% of the total number of the province; 52 experts from Guangzhou were included in the National High-Level Talent Special Support Plan, or the Ten-Thousand Talents Program, accounting for 74.3% of the province's total; and 249 Guangzhou residents entered the Guangdong Special Support Plan for High-Level Talents, accounting for 75.2% of the province's total. 16 talents were recognized as Outstanding Talents by the Special Support Program ("South Guangdong Hundred Talents"), accounting for 94.1% of the province's total. A total of 1220 Green Card were issued throughout the year. For the fourth time, Guangzhou entered the list of the 10 Most Attractive Chinese Cities for Foreigners, according to a survey conducted on foreign professionals living in China nationwide.

As for introducing world-class sci-tech innovation and commercialization projects,

---

[1] Source: "Follow New Philosophy and Lead New Development: Economic Conditions of Guangzhou in 2016", Guangzhou Statistics Bureau, http://www.gzstats.gov.cn/tjfx/gztjfx/201701/t20170124_25528.html

as many as 1,600 foreign-funded projects were established in Guangzhou in 2016, an increase of 23% over the same period of the previous year. The projects covered a wide range of areas including new-generation information technology, bio-medicine, smart manufacturing, and cross-border e-commerce. From January to November, the total amount of foreign capital utilized in the information and software sector, the transportation and warehousing sector, and the property leasing and commercial service sector increased by 10.84 times, 7.05 times and 1.06 times respectively over the same period of the previous year. The number of large innovation projects with a total investment exceeding UDS30 million, including those funded by Cisco, Microsoft, Qualcomm, and Foxconn reached 150, accounting for over 90% of the total contractual foreign investment in the city. Nearly 800 projects in Guangzhou were invested by 288 enterprises on the Fortune Global 500 List of the World's Largest Companies, contributing to a total foreign investment of more than USD50 billion.

vi. A multi-level property righttransaction system was established to promote the commercialization of scientific and technological findings.

2016 was the second year to fully implement the *Three-year (2015-2017) Action Plan for Science and Technology Services in Guangzhou*. In this year, the city adopted a series of policies including the *Measures for Promoting the Commercialization of Scientific and Technological Findings in Guangzhou* and the *Measures for Subsidizing Transactions of Scientific and Technological Findings in Guangzhou*. These policies aimed to better introduce advanced scientific and technological findings from home and abroad to Guangzhou through a robust transaction subsidy system. Local companies that had successfully brought in and commercialized scientific and technological findings of domestic and foreign colleges and research institutes were entitled to a subsidy that equaled 5% of the total technological transaction volume as shown in the contract.

At the same time, it actively supported the development of various technology trading platforms such as Guangzhou Intellectual Property Exchange, Guangzhou Technological Equity Trading Center under Guangzhou Enterprises Mergers and Acquisitions Services, and Guangzhou Science, Technology, and Innovation Service Centre and continued to improve the multi-stakeholder technological property rights trading system which consisted of research and development institutions, enterprises, intermediaries and agencies, etc. In 2016, Guangzhou identified five model agencies for the successful commercialization of scientific and technological findings and another 20 agencies for outstanding science and technology services. Each of the five model agencies was rewardedwith RMB1 million from the fiscal budget while each of the 20 agencies was rewarded with RMB500,000. After successfully hosting China Innovation and Technology Fair in 2015, Guangzhou managed to persuade China Association for Science and Technology and became a permanent host of the annual fair, which was then renamed as China Innovation and Entrepreneurship Fair. In 2016, with a total area of more than 20,000 square meters, the fair provided platforms for more than 1,700 domestic and foreign programs, covering information technology, bio-medicine, new materials, new energy, and intelligent equipment manufacturing.

Statistics showed that 12 state-level technology transfer service agencies and 58 agencies (enterprises) on the top 100 list of provincial-level technology services were located in Guangzhou as of the end of 2016, accounting for 53.7% of the province's total. Guangzhou also supported the establishment of 18 technological contracting service centers to provide specialized transaction contracting and tax policy services for buyers and sellers.The city's total turnover of technological contracts reached RMB28.958 billion in 2016, up 8.86%. The growth rate was 1.1 percentage points higher than that in 2015.

vii. The adoption of institutional measures and the introduction of brand programs contributed to the popularization of science and technology and to the steady improvement of citizens's scientific literacy.

On March 1, 2016, Guangzhou formally enacted the *Regulation of Guangzhou on Popularization of Science and Technology*, followed by a series of supporting policies such as the *Management Measures for Guangzhou-based Social Sciences Popularization Bases (Trial)* and the *Measures for Implementing the Outline of the National Scheme for Scientific Literacy (2016-2020)*. Together, they paved the way for the institutionalized popularization of science and technology in Guangzhou.

As the major local platforms for science education, the 11 municipal-level science popularization bases followed standard operation procedures and received over 9 million visits in 2016. The community-based popularization program "Science for All" was fully implemented, significantly improving the awareness-raising and other service capacity of communities. 15 communities including Guangzhong Community (Shayuan Street, Haizhu District) were recognized as national models, 34 communities including Sanyanjing Community (Hongqiao Street, Yuexiu District) won the honorary title of provincial model communities and 29 communities were identified as municipal models for science popularization. A wide variety of activities were organized. On the National Science Day, 315 events sponsored by 268 government agencies attracted more than 2 million participants across the city. Some of the most popular brands included Pear River Science Lectures, Science and You, One-day Tour of Science, and Free Tour in the World of Science, etc. Mass media were playing an increasingly prominent role in bringing science and technology to the common people as radio-, TV-, newspaper-, and Internet-based popular science programs and columns gained influence.

These programs and activities contributed not only to the popularization of science but also to citizens' rapidly improved scientific literacy. According to the *Survey Report on the Scientific Literacy of Chinese Citizens (2015-2016)* released by China Association for Science and Technology, which studied situations in six provinces (cities) including Beijing, Chongqing, Guangzhou, Heilongjiang Province, Hunan Province, and Shaanxi Province, Guangzhou registered a literacy rate 25.59%, right after Beijing (30.69%) and Shanghai (28.8%). Findings of five surveys on the local scientific literacy conducted by Guangzhou Association for Science and Technology between 2003 and 2015 showed that 11.7% of the citizens were literate in science, a substantial increase from 5.5% in 2010 and 4.8 times that of 2003 (see Figure 5). That figure made Guangzhou the unquestionable champion in the province and a top 4 in the country. It was equivalent to that of an average developed country at the turn of the century. With that, Guangzhou accomplished the goal of having a scientific literacy rate greater than 10% as proposed in the *Decision of the CPC Guangzhou Municipal Committee and Guangzhou Municipal People's Government on Accelerating the Implementation of Innovation-driven Development Strategy* ahead of time.

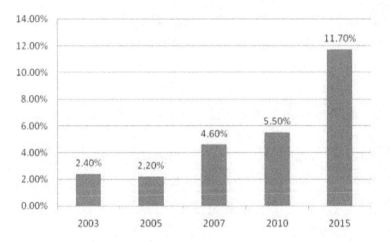

Figure 3 Changes in Citizens' Scientific Literacy in Guangzhou in Recent Years

II. Major Issues Undermining the Development of Science and Technology in Guangzhou in 2016

i. The long absence of sufficient investment in research and development remained a major obstacle for fast-track expansion of the city's independent innovation capacity

The absence of sufficient investment in research and development had been a long standing problem for Guangzhou in recent years. According to the *2010 Statistical Communique of Guangdong Province on Investment in Science and Technology*, the city's fiscal investment in research and development only accounted for 1.79% of its GDP, slightly higher than the provincial average (1.76%). In the following years, the figure hovered between 1.8% and 2.0% until it barely reached the minimum requirement (2.0%) of building a national innovation city in 2014, but still far below the average of Guangdong (2.4%). The gap with cities like Beijing, Shanghai, Shenzhen, Tianjin, Hangzhou, and Suzhou was even more obvious (see Table 5). Although Guangzhou enacted its innovation-driven development strategy and launched a plan to double its fiscal investment in science and technology in 2015 in an effort to address the longstanding obstacle to independent innovation, its investment in research and development only increased 0.1% over the previous year to 2.1% , still far below the average of the province (2.5%). Despite the lack of accurate public data at present, we were able to roughly assess the actual fiscal investment in 2016 based on the common practice that fiscal investment could normally leverage four to five times the investment of enterprises. That would generate a figure of 2.3%, which was still far less than that of Beijing, Shanghai, Shenzhen, Tianjin, Hangzhou, Suzhou, and other similar cities (see Table 5). Even in the Pearl River Delta region, Guangzhou not only long lagged behind Shenzhen (4.1%), but also was overtaken by Dongguan (2.4%), Foshan (2.65%), and other prefectural cities. In general, the city's fiscal investment in research and development failed to match its strategic positioning as the leading city and engine for building National Innovation Demonstration Zone in the Pearl River Delta region.

Table 5 Comparison of R&D Investment in Major Domestic Cities in the Past Five Years

Year	Beijing	Shanghai	Shenzhen	Guangzhou	Tianjin	Hangzhou	Suzhou
2012	5.79	3.37	3.81	1.93	2.7	——	2.6
2013	6.16	3.60	4.0	1.89	2.8	2.6	2.95
2014	6.03	3.66	4.0	2.0	2.8	3.0	2.7
2015	5.95	3.73	4.05	2.1	3.0	3.0	2.68
2016	5.94	3.80	4.1	——	3.1	——	——

Source: statistics concerning Beijing, Shanghai, Shenzhen, Tianjin, Hangzhou, and Suzhou between 2012 and 2015 cited from the *Statistical Communiqué on National Economic and Social Development* of the respective year; statistics concerning Shenzhen and Tianjin in 2016 cited from the 2017 local government work reports; and statistics concerning Guangzhou cited from *Analysis of Guangdong's Investment in Science and Technology* over the years.

The long absence of sufficient investment in research and development seriously affected the scale and quality of Guangzhou's technological innovation output. In 2016, as the city increased its R&D investment, it witnessed a significant growth in the number of patent applications, especially invention patent applications, ranking first among 19 cities at or above the sub-provincial level nationwide. However, due to the late start and weak basis, it only ranked fifth, seventh, sixth, and sixth among domestic cities in terms of the number of received patent applications, the number of received invention patent applications, the number of invention patent grants, and the number of valid invention patents respectively, which failed to match its position as the third largest economic city in the country. Its gap with Beijing, Shanghai, and Shenzhen can not to be offset in the short term (see Table 6 and Table 7). The city's invention patent density was less than one-third that of Shenzhen and Beijing and far smaller than that of Shanghai, Nanjing, Hangzhou, Xi'an and other similar cities. In terms of the proportion of invention patents, Guangzhou was outperformed not only by Beijing, Shanghai and Shenzhen, but also by Chengdu, Nanjing, Xi'an, and Tianjin (see Table 8). All these pointed to the fact that Guangzhou still had much to do to improve its technological innovation capacity.

Table 6 Comparison of Received and Granted Domestic Invention Patent Applications in Major Cities in 2016

City	Number of Received Domestic Applications for Invention Patents	Year-on-Year Increase	Number of Domestic Grants for Invention Patents	Year-on-Year Increase
Beijing	104643	17.7%	40602	15.0%
Shanghai	54339	15.7%	20086	14.1%
Tianjin	38153	33.8%	5185	12.1%
Chongqing	19981	-43.1%	5044	27.2%
Guangzhou	31892	58.8%	7669	15.7%
Shenzhen	56326	40.7%	17665	4.2%
Nanjing	31556	13.4%	8705	5.3%
Hangzhou	25009	40.4%	8666	4.4%
Chengdu	39431	32.4%	7190	15.9%
Xi'an	18569	30.4%	6686	11.6%

Source: Statistics released by the Intellectual Property Office of Guangzhou

Table 7 Comparison of Valid Domestic Invention Patents in Major Cities in 2016

City	Valid Patents	Year-on-Year Increase	Patent Density per million people
Beijing	166722	25.3%	7681.3
Shanghai	85049	21.5%	3521.3
Tianjin	22663	22.5%	1465.0

Chongqing	16737	30.7%	554.8
Guangzhou	30305	25.5%	2244.8
Shenzhen	95370	13.7%	8365.8
Nanjing	33458	23.1%	4060.4
Hangzhou	36579	20.8%	4064.3
Chengdu	25198	27.5%	1720.0
Xi'an	24368	23.2%	2800.9

Source: Statistics released by the Intellectual Property Office of Guangzhou

**Table 8 Comparison of Composition of Received Domestic Patent
Applications in Major Cities in 2016**

City	Invention	Utility	Design
Beijing	55.3%	34.1%	10.6%
Shanghai	45.3%	43.2%	11.5%
Tianjin	35.8%	59.7%	4.5%
Chongqing	33.6%	53.9%	12.5%
Guangzhou	32.2%	41.8%	26.0%
Shenzhen	38.8%	39.1%	22.1%
Nanjing	48.4%	40.1%	11.5%
Hangzhou	33.9%	43.8%	22.3%
Chengdu	40.3%	38.0%	21.7%
Xi'an	40.3%	39.8%	19.9%

Source: Statistics released by the Intellectual Property Office of Guangzhou

**ii. The critical underdevelopment of the high-tech sector remained the biggest
bottleneck that restricted Guangzhou's innovation-driven development**

While amazed by the surging number of high-tech companies in 2016 (2,821), one
should not become blind to the huge gap between Guangzhou's current development
status and its goals of becoming a national innovation hub and an international hub
for scientific and technological innovation, a gap that could be attributed to the
long-term underdevelopment of its high-tech sectors. Although the total number of
high-tech companies in Guangzhou soared to 4,740, they only accounted for 24.8%
of the province's total.However,in the same year, Shenzhen became home to 2,513
new hi-tech enterprises with the total number of high-tech companies amounting to
8,037, accounting for 42.3% of the province's total and almost doubling that of
Guangzhou. In terms of the number of national high-tech companies, Dongguan far

outperformed Guangzhou as it witnessed a 3.7 times increase from 413 in 2015 to 1,500 in 2016.

More importantly, the rapidly increasing number of high-tech enterprises in Guangzhou was overcast by a much slower growth rate for the output value. The output value of high-tech products throughout the year reached RMB903.526 billion, an increase of only 7.3% over the same period of the previous year, which was 1.6 percentage points lower than its growth rate in 2015(see Table 9). In 2016, the output value of high-tech products in Guangdong Province increased by 12%, which was also 4.7percentage points lower than the average level of the province. It contributed to a 3% growth of industrial sectors above designated size, down 0.6% from 2015. In general, high-tech sectors were playing a lesser role in promoting economic growth.

Table 9 Output of High-tech Products by Industrial Companies above Designated Size (2010-2016)

Year	Output (RMB100 million)	Year-on-year Growth
2010	5327.92	-
2011	6353.38	19.3%
2012	6277.38	-1.2%
2013	7360.14	17.3%
2014	7730.84	5.0%
2015	8420.56	8.9%
2016	9035.26	7.3%

Source: Guangzhou Statistics Bureau

Among them, the growth rate of advanced manufacturing and of high-tech manufacturing was most noticeably slower than that of the provincial average and that of other cities in the Pearl River Delta region. In 2016, the added value of advanced manufacturing and of high-tech manufacturing in Guangzhou increased by 6.6% and 7.5% respectively, 0.1% and 1.0% higher than that of sectors above designated size. In contrast, the added value of advanced manufacturing and of high-tech manufacturing in Guangdong increased by 9.5% and 11.7% respectively, 2.8% and 5.0% higher than that of sectors above designated size. In Shenzhen, the added value of advanced manufacturing and of high-tech manufacturing rose by 8.5% and 9.8%, 1.5% and 2.8% higher than that of sectors above designated size in the city. In Foshan, the added value of advanced manufacturing and of high-tech manufacturing respectively registered an increase of 10.8% and 10.3%, up 3.1% and 2.6% from that of sectors above designated size. In Dongguan, the added value of the two sectors rose by 15.2% and 17.6%, 8.2% and 10.6% higher than the city's average.

iii. The city had long been a follower in enacting policies and its proud strength in sci-tech resources was at stake

Despite the absence of prosperous high-tech sectors as found in Shenzhen and stunning sci-tech achievements frequently encountered in other first-tier cities, Guangzhou was ambitious enough to propose the grand goal of "building a national innovation center with international influence and an international hub for scientific and technological innovation by 2020". To become an innovation center facing the world and significantly influencing south China, Guangzhou's confidence came from its rich sci-tech resources in the region. It was home to 70% of universities and colleges, 97% of national key disciplines, most national key laboratories, and 58% of independent research institutes in the province. According to the *Communiqué of Guangdong Province on Major Data of the Second Survey of National Research and Development Resources*, the number of full-time equivalent R&D personnel in colleges and universities in Guangzhou, as calculated by actual working hour, was 12,346, accounting for 90.5% of the total in the Pearl River Delta region, 78.4% of the province's total, and 24 times that of Shenzhen. The number of full-time equivalent R&D personnel in state-owned research institutes in Guangzhou as calculated by actual working hours was 6017, accounting for 93.9% of the total in the Pearl River Delta region, 89.3% of the province's total, and 353 times that of Shenzhen. However, as Shenzhen, Dongguan, and other cities in the Pearl River Delta region stepped up their efforts to nurture, bring in, and co-found scientific and technological research institutions and actively participated in the global competition for high-level innovative teams and talents in recent years, Guangzhou's long-established monopoly of research infrastructure and personnel was threatened to a certain extent. Of the eight major national scientific installations in Guangdong at present, only one was located in Guangzhou. The other seven were distributed in Shenzhen (three), Huizhou (two), Dongguan and Jiangmen (one). Moreover, although the city had stepped up its efforts to develop national key laboratories, engineering laboratories, engineering technology research centers, and corporate technology centers, their proportion continued to decline. Take national innovation platforms for example, although Guangzhou had 71 such platforms, they only accounted for 33.3% of the province's total. In contrast, with 210 innovation platforms joining the family in 2016, Shenzhen was now home to 1493 national, provincial, and municipal key laboratories, engineering laboratories, engineering technology research centers, and corporate technology centers. Its gap with Guangzhou was rapidly narrowing.

Another rapidly narrowing gap was observed in high-level innovation teams and talent. Of the seven newly elected academicians from Guangdong Province in 2016, six were based in Shenzhen. While Guangzhou managed to engage 33.9% (44, 800) and 34.4% (447, 00) of long-term Guangdong-based foreign experts in 2014 and 2015 respectively, Shenzhen followed closely with 30.2% (39,900) and 32.5% (422,

00) of the province's total foreign experts[2].

The main reason lied in the fact that Guangzhou had long been a follower in enacting sci-tech related policies in recent years but failed to fulfill its mission as a pioneering reformer. It was not in a position to compete with Shanghai, Shenzhen, Hangzhou, and other cities whether in terms of the vision, system, or effectiveness of policies. The absence of robust policy initiatives was largely responsible for the city's loss of competitive edge and development opportunities in a new round of competition for high-end innovation platforms and top innovative talents.

III. Development Trend of Science and Technology in Guangzhou in 2017 and Recommendations

i. Development trend of science and technology in Guangzhou in 2017

1. With state-owned enterprises becoming increasingly active in innovation, companies will consolidate their leading role in this regard

In order to realize the 2017 growth goal of "bringing in over RMB59 billion of social investment in research and development with over RMB10.8 billion of fiscal investment in science and technology", Guangzhou will continue to enact the plan to double its fiscal investment in science and technology and fully implement supportive policies such as weighted pre-tax deduction and post-tax subsidy of enterprise research and development expenses in the coming year. Thanks to the uninterrupted enactment of the scheme to double fiscal spending on science and technology, local companies are more willing to invest in research and development nowadays. Since 2015, there has been a steady increase in the proportion of R&D facilities, the scale of R&D investment, the number of patent applications, and the number of patent grants in companies above designated size. Therefore, it is safe to predict that Guangzhou-based companies will demonstrate a rapidly improved innovation capacity and play an even greater part in innovation in 2017.

Considering the large proportion of state-owned enterprises in Guangzhou, the General Office of Guangzhou Municipal People's Government issued *Several Opinions on Accelerate Innovation-driven Development of Municipal-level State-owned Enterprises* in September 2016, which made it clear that municipal state-owned industrial companies and groups and their major subordinates should all set up R&D facilities before 2020. It also proposed to reward a certain number of projects and companies every year for outstanding performance and significant progress. The enactment of these policy incentives in 2017 will further invigorate municipal-level state-owned enterprises and substantially increase their R&D investment and improve the scale and quality of their innovation-related output.

---

[2]Source: "Strengthen Talent Programs to Build a Moderately Prosperous Guangdong: Findings and Analysis of Foreign Experts in Guangdong in 2014 and 2015", Service Sector Division, Guangzhou Statistics Bureau, http://www.gdstats.gov.cn/tjzl/tjfx/201604/t20160427_327208.htm

2. With a better financing environment for sci-tech companies, the total output of high-tech products is expected to exceed RMB1 trillion for the first time

In 2017, while continuing to implement the *Action Plan for Cultivating Small Giant Enterprises for Scientific and Technological Innovation and High-tech Enterprises*, Guangzhou will further optimize the development environment for science, technology, and innovation companies by providing targeted services for 100 model companies and industrial benchmarks. Meanwhile, Guangzhou is taking speedy actions to set up its RMB5 billion guidance fund for the commercialization of research findings and China Construction Bank has formally opened its Sci-Tech Finance Innovation Center in the city. As a financial service system that fully covers the growth cycle of sci-tech companies continues to improve, the local financing environment will be greatly optimized. Recently, Huangpu District and Guangzhou Development Zone, the two clusters where most sci-tech innovation companies were based, gained approval to use 30 square kilometers of urban land. A much more supportive development space will effectively address longstanding issues and provide favorable conditions for bringing in large-scale high-end sci-tech innovation projects in 2017.

Therefore, it is expected that Guangzhou will register a faster growth of high-tech sectors in 2017. The output value of high-tech industrial products above designated size is expected to exceed the threshold of RMB1 trillion for the first time. The output value of high-tech products will take up a larger proportion of the total industrial output of companies above designated size, while the added value of the high-tech manufacturing sector will account for a greater part of that of manufacturing above designated size.The number of high-tech enterprises and sci-tech companies listed on the New Three Board will continue to rise rapidly. It is estimated that there will be more than 1,000 new high-tech enterprises in 2017 while over 200 companies will be listed on the New Three Board. The total number of science, technology, and innovation companies will exceed 140,000.

3. The city enters the second phase of implementing the plan to double sci-tech incubators and will place more emphasis on service capacity

In 2014, Guangzhou started to enact the scheme to double incubators for sci-tech companies. The target of the first phase was to "house 10,000 incubating companies in 120 incubators and 1,000 incubated companies with an area of 8 million square meters by 2016". The target of the second phase included "further improve incubation services that lead to more than 2,000 incubated companies and over 500 high-tech companies; an incubation service system that covers the whole growth cycle of companies and support the development of national brands; and a Guangzhou-based incubator group with significant influence". From the data released by Guangzhou Science, Technology, and Innovation Commission in 2016, we can see that the target of the first phase has been fully completed. Starting from

2017, incubators and makerspaces will enter a higher level of development where more emphasis will be given to professional service rather than number and land area.

The revised *Measures for the Administration of Guangzhou-based Incubators for Science and Technology Companies* were enacted in April 2016, which required annual performance evaluation, data collection, and dynamic administration of incubators, proposed a performance evaluation index system based on service capacity, incubation performance, and social contribution, and a quantitative evaluation method. The full implementation of the policy in 2017 will surely end the "savage growth" of local incubators and makerspaces and usher in a new round of competition. Compared with the previous two yeas, incubators and makerspaces will experience a noticeably slower growth in number but improved service and profitability.

iv. The city will speed up the development of the sci-tech innovation corridor, where Tianhe, Huangpu, and Panyu function as the three pillars

Following the *Implementation Plan for the Development of the National Innovation Demonstration Zone in Guangzhou* (2016-2020), the city will speed up the construction of major infrastructure projects in 2017 such as the Innovation and Entrepreneurship Park for Academicians and Experts and the GE Bio-Campus. It will further strengthen the development of its sci-tech innovation corridor and the Pearl River Innovation Belt with special emphasis on Guangzhou Hi-tech Industrial Development Zone, Sino-Singapore Guangzhou Knowledge City, and other major innovation and entrepreneurship platforms. The three districts of Tianhe, Huangpu, and Panyu, where major platforms are currently based, will further accumulate technology, talents, capital, industrial sectors, and other innovation factors and thus become the three pillars for the city's innovation-driven development.

Tianhe District with the largest number of universities and financial institutions and highly-development makerspaces and sci-tech services, and Huangpu District with the greatest number of high-tech companies, are the two major players in the battlefield of science, technology, and innovation. For a long time, the two districts have far outrun other districts both in the quantity and quality of outcomes and output value of high-tech companies. However, Panyu has been steadily walking towards the center of the battlefield in recent years as it assumes a more important part in the city's plan of building an international innovation city and becomes the home to the University City, Tianhe-2 Supercomputing Center, and a large number of major industrialization projects sponsored by Cisco, Inspur, and other technological providers. The rapid rise of Pangyu will eventually break the dominance of Tianhe and Huangpu in Guangzhou's sci-tech development and 2017 is expected to mark the beginning of a three-pillar era.

5. With more top innovators and entrepreneurs coming to Guangzhou, the Convention on Exchange of Overseas Talents will assume a more prominent role in attracting overseas talents to the city

Thanks to the establishment of the "1+4" talent policy framework, in particular, the enactment of the Green Card Policy for Talents, Guangdong Special Support Plan for High-Level Talents, Guangzhou High-End Foreign Experts Project, Guangzhou Elite Project, and other talent programs, as well as the accelerated development of national post-doctoral stations, expert stations, and municipal bases, Guangdong-Hong Kong-Macao Demonstration Zone for Talent Exchange in Nansha, the National Innovation and Entrepreneurship Platform for Top Overseas Talent in Guangzhou Hi-tech Industrial Development Zone, and other talent platforms, Guangzhou is expected to offer a further optimized environment and maintain its strong appeal for high-level innovators and entrepreneurs in 2017. It will remain in the first echelon in the present fierce competition for top sci-tech talents among domestic cities.

Guangzhou Convention of Overseas Chinese Scholars in Science and Technology, which had long served as an important talent platform for Guangzhou, was renamed as the Convention on Exchange of Overseas Talents and Guangzhou Convention of Overseas Chinese Scholars in Science and Technology at its 18th session, thus covering a wider range of overseas talents including top foreign experts, overseas scholars, talents from Hong Kong, Macao, and Taiwan, and outstanding representatives of overseas Chinese. The Convention is expected to play a more prominent role in bringing in high-level overseas talents and programs and contributing to the city's innovation and entrepreneurship in 2017.

ii. Recommendations for further promoting the development of science and technology in Guangzhou

1. Vision and horizon are essential for decision-making while courage and sense of responsibility are indispensable for pioneering and reformative policies

In the past two years, Guangzhou has adopted a significant number of policy measures to promote science, technology and innovation that cover a wide range of aspects including research and development, incubation, industrial growth, talents, and commercialization. Statistics show that the number of documents issued during the past two years is even larger than the total of the past ten years. These have indeed contributed to some historic breakthroughs. However, horizontal analysis is as important as vertical comparison when evaluating a policy. We should not only recognize progress from the past but also identify the gap with other cities. In order to narrow its gap with other domestic and foreign cities, Guangzhou should pay special attention to analyzing its policies on R&D investment, industrial development, and top innovation talents and programs, which have long been proven critical for catching up with and even outrunning competitors.

For example, the city's policies on R&D investment, including the scheme to double fiscal investment in three years and other incentives for strengthening corporate R&D, all target 3% of GDP by 2020, which is indeed a major breakthrough from the past. However, this target was a reality for Beijing, Shenzhen, and Shanghai a decade ago. Even Tianjin and Hangzhou realized the goal two years ago. Countrywide, innovation-driven development is a national policy that has been implemented throughout China. With almost all cities substantially increasing their investment in science, technology, and innovation, recent policies adopted by Guangzhou seem unable to accommodate its position as a major national central city. If we turn to top talents and major projects, we will find that Guangzhou has indeed adopted a series of more competitive policies than 2010. However, these policies are in no position to compete with those enacted in Shenzhen, Shanghai, and Hangzhou, especially when we consider the current economic decline and the fierce rivalry for talents among cities undergoing transition.

In order to stop being a follower, Guangzhou has to be more courageous and dare to initiate institutional innovations, especially in areas critical for catching up with and even outrunning competitors. After completing the three-year scheme to double fiscal investment in science and technology by 2017, the city should continue with another three-year (2018-2020) program and once again double its fiscal investment in this area. It should further expand its subsidies, rewards, and other forms of financial aid for corporate R&D efforts so that more companies will join follow suit. It should adopt institutional measures to evaluate the efficiency of fiscal aid for R&D and offer subsidies in a more targeted manner so as to effectively guide the innovation of companies. In terms of better engaging innovative talents and bringing in entrepreneurial projects, local competent authorities should better track and study the evolution of sci-tech policies adopted by domestic and foreign cities and adjust local policies accordingly. It should also pay close attention to change in the external environment and amend policies in a timely manner so as to maintain their competitive edge.

However, more competitive policies never mean reckless subsidies or fiscal investment. Rather, competitive edge is only gained through a future-oriented vision and the full utilization of one's resources. Taking into consideration its shortage of fiscal resources and suitable land, Guangzhou can only rely on a future-oriented vision, a systematic and sound policy framework, and a set of accessible methods and procedures to win the competition with other cities.

2. A inter-departmental coordination and administration mechanism should be set up to effectively improve the performance and use efficiency of limited fiscal investment in science and technology

Due to the shortage of fiscal resources and the insufficient investment in the beginning, the combined municipal- and district-level fiscal investment in science and technology only amounted to RMB8.13 billion in 2016, despite the implementation of the scheme to double fiscal input for two consecutive years. Therefore, it is necessary to improve the performance and efficiency of limited fiscal investment if Guangzhou hopes to narrow the huge gap with Beijing, Shanghai, Shenzhen, and other cities and become a national innovation central city and an international sci-tech innovation hub. The actual use of fiscal investment in recent years shows that quite a number of issues exist in terms of coordination and efficiency. According to the *Report on the Implementation of the Law of the People's Republic of China on Progress of Science and Technology and the Regulation of Guangzhou on Promoting Science, Technology, and Innovation* issued by the law-enforcement inspection group of the Standing Committee of Guangzhou Municipal People's Congress, the use of fiscal spending on science and technology was not managed in a sound and coordinated manner; overall planning and coordination were compromised with more than one authority overseeing the use of municipal-level fiscal budget, and overlapping application, administration, and investment led to the lack of holistic planning and the difficulty in realizing scale effect and policy guidance.

In order to address these issues, Guangzhou Science, Technology, and Innovation Commission issued the *Reform Plan for Streamlining the Administration of Science, Technology, and Innovation Sectors* in December 2016, with some reformative measures proven to be effective in improving the use efficiency of fiscal spending. However, since the use of fiscal spending on science and technology also involved the Development and Reform Commission, the State-owned Assets Supervision and Administration Commission, and many other authorities, the Science, Technology, and Innovation Commission was not in an ideal position to promote its overall planning and coordination. In fact, the authoritativeness and effect of policies were compromised. Therefore, it is recommended that Guangzhou follow the practice of Shanghai and other cities and enact a cross-board coordination and planning plan for the administration of fiscal spending on science and technology by the municipal people's government. It is advised to set up a uniform information sharing platform and an interdepartmental cooperation and joint administration mechanism so as to avoid overlapping and increase coordination.

3. The explosive growth of high-tech industries requires better support for gazelles and unicorns

A national sci-tech innovation hub is at the center of Guangdong's strategic plan of building a National Independent Innovation Demonstration Zone in the Pearl River Delta region. The CPC Guangdong Provincial Committee and Guangdong Provincial People's Government have made it clear that Guangzhou and Shenzhen, the two biggest cities in the Pearl River Delta region, must play a leading role in establishing an innovation-driven industrial system with global competitive edge. Besides being one of two engines for the regional sci-tech innovation hub, Guangzhou has another two development goals, namely becoming a national innovation central city and an international sci-tech innovation hub. A most important precondition for the realization of these goals lies in the accelerated development of high-tech sectors, a longstanding obstacle to the city's innovation-driven economic and social development.

In order to speedily remove the obstacle, Guangzhou has to realize unconventional leap in economic growth during the 13th Five-Year Plan period (2016-2020). A study of domestic and foreign experience points to two feasible routes. One is to optimize the city's business environment and attract major industrial projects to be launched here. The other is to optimize the local environment for innovation and entrepreneurship and nurture the city's own innovation companies with huge potential for economic jump. In fact, Guangzhou is taking both routes at present. On the one hand, it has intensified its efforts to draw external capital and business, especially major industrial projects. On the other hand, it continues to implement the three-year *Action Plan for Cultivating Small Giant Enterprises for Scientific and Technological Innovation and High-tech Enterprises* in full swing. Major progress was observed in introducing important projects and nurturing high-tech companies in 2016. However, due to the late start and the indiscriminate distribution of limited fiscal subsidies that failed to generate centralized results, the development of high-tech sectors was far from satisfactory. There is still a long way to go before the city fundamentally restructures its industrial pattern, currently crowded with many small companies but no major players.

Therefore, as it continues to implement its *Action Plan for Cultivating Small Giant Enterprises for Scientific and Technological Innovation and High-tech Enterprises*,Guangzhou should also devote concentrated efforts to support the growth of gazelles and unicorns, especially in new information technology, artificial intelligence, biomedicine, and other emerging sectors, in a more targeted manner. Newly-established sci-tech companies with strong innovation capacity and huge potential for robust growth should enjoy special policy support and fiscal aid so that gazelles and unicorns will have a better change of outperforming their competitors. Their potential for economic leap is undoubtedly a possible answer to the city's current difficulty in nurturing leading sci-tech companies and will become an important engine for driving the fast-track growth of its high-tech sectors.

4. The technology transfer and commercialization system should be further improved to support the city's strategic position as regional high-tech transfer center

Home to more than half of the province's national technology transfer services,

Guangzhou is endowed with an exceptionally active technology trading market and rich sci-tech service resources that are unattainable in other cities in the Pearl River Delta region. This is where the city's fundamental strength lies as it strives to become a national innovation central city and an international sci-tech innovation hub. When issuing the *Implementation Plan for the Development of the National Independent Innovation Demonstration Zone in Guangzhou* (2016-2020), the government made it clear that the city should speed up the establishment of a commercialization and transfer system for sci-tech research findings and strive to become a sci-tech service model city. Therefore, it is recommended that the city enact the *Implementation Plan for the Commercialization and Transfer of Science and Technology (2017-2020)* on the basis of *Three-year (2015-2017) Action Plan for Science and Technology Services in Guangzhou*, which shall define the major tasks for the establishment of the system during the 13th Five-Year Plan period (2016-2020). It may even make the bold suggestion of "building a big regional technology trading center that matches its position as national central city and a high-end regional technology transfer center by 2020".

For a certain period in the future, Guangzhou should strengthen its efforts from the following aspects to improve its service system for the commercialization of research findings and establish a regional high-end technology transfer center. First, it should improve the policy framework. While further improving its market-oriented pricing mechanism, profit distribution and incentive system, classified professional title conferring system, "first buy and first use" risk mitigation system, and other institutional arrangements, the city should adopt more effective incentives in a more timely manner so that companies are willing to play a more active role in the commercialization of research findings and allot more corporate funding to those areas, which will eventually remove the obstacles to technology transfer. It should also draw experience from domestic and foreign cities and introduce more competitive incentives for the local commercialization and transfer of research findings from home and abroad. Second, it should set up high-end service platforms. The city should step up its efforts to nurture, co-found, and bring in a number of top professional service agencies that will facilitate the information gathering, trade representation, and value assessment in the commercialization of research findings and transfer of technologies. It should improve its public service platform in this area and strive to build a national demonstration zone for the commercialization of research findings and transfer of technologies. Third, it should strengthen capacity building. The city should support local universities to offer courses on the commercialization of research findings and transfer of technologies, thus strengthening capacity building for professionals and provide the market with richer human resources. The city should strive to pave a career path for professional technical brokers and continue to implement the leading talent support program in full swing. A talent highland can be envisioned with more efforts devoted to their cultivation and engagement.

Current Development of Cross-Border E-Commerce in Guangzhou and Recommendation for the Future

Wang Wenjiao*

Abstract: In recent years, Guangzhou has outrun other Chinese cities in developing cross-border e-commerce and nurturing new business models, thanks to its readiness to seize market opportunities, enact supporting policies, and combine efforts. However, the prospect of cross-border e-commerce in Guangzhou is also foreshadowed by the enactment of new taxation regulations coupled with the city's weak bargaining power, lack of unique local products, insufficient infrastructure, and shortage of professionals. In order to further empower cross-border e-commerce, Guangzhou should devote its efforts to strengthening trade platforms, institutional innovation, product heterogeneity, supply chain management, global settlement, and personnel training.

Keywords: Cross-border e-commerce, new development in foreign trade, Guangzhou

The cross-border e-commerce boom in recent years, as reflected in the high frequency and big volume of transactions, has significantly transformed traditional business models and contributed to the advent of a blue ocean in foreign trade. Guangzhou, a millennium commercial city, has seized the opportunity to launch a cross-border e-commerce pilot zone, which proves to be of great importance to stimulating the market, integrating resources, and nurturing new business models. However, the confidence in its huge future potentials is tainted by suspicions cast over emerging challenges. Therefore, a high priority on the city's agenda is to leverage the strength of the pilot zone and boost the comprehensive competitiveness of cross-border e-commerce through the introduction of institutional measures and

---

* This report is the joint outcome of studies supported by Guangzhou Development Research Institute of Guangzhou University, a Key Research Institute of Humanities and Social Sciences in Universities of Guangdong Province, the Collaborative Innovation and Development Center for "Guangzhou Studies" of Guangdong Provincial Department of Education, and Guangzhou Urban Integrated Development Decision-making Consulting Team under the Innovation Team Program for Guangdong Regular Institutions of Higher Learning.

The author is Dr. Wang Wenjiao, Director and Assistant Fellow at Urban and Rural Development Research Center, Guangzhou Development Research Institute, Guangzhou University.

the transformation of traditional trade models.

I. Development of Cross-Border E-Commerce in Guangzhou: Status Quo and Characteristics

Integrating "Internet Plus" into cross-border trade, Guangzhou has made considerable progress in developing cross-border e-commerce. It topped the list of national pilot cities with the highest import, export, and cross-border trade volume in 2015. It continued to outrun other cities and make big strides in 2016. It not only supported a diversity of cross-border e-commerce business models, but also adopted a unique direct purchase import model that would be applied nationwide.

i. Seize the opportunity to realize exponential growth

Grasping the opportunity of becoming a pilot city for cross-border e-commerce, Guangzhou set up a number of online experience platforms such as meijoybest.com, 891world.com, and funsens.com, etc. In the meantime, the city stepped up negotiation with other cities in the Pearl River Delta on cross-border e-commerce projects. By adopting the fully centralized franchise model, the city not only paved the way for the export of local products, but also sped up the transformation and upgrading of traditional local trade groups and created new growth points for foreign trade. Statistics of Guangzhou Customs showed that in 2016, Guangzhou's total import and export volume of cross-border e-commerce reached RMB14.68 billion, an increase of 1.2 times over the same period of last year, accounting for 29.4% of the whole country. In particular, import and export reached RMB8.65 billion and RMB6.03 billion respectively, up 150% and 83.2%, accounting for 36.3% and 23.1% of the country's total, and helped the city top the list of pilot cities. Of the 1,151 Guangzhou-based companies in the cross-border e-commerce business, 865 were e-commerce platforms, 142 were logistics enterprises, and 44 were payment platforms. Nationally, about 50% of cross-border e-commerce companies were based in Guangzhou, leading to a concentration effect. In general, Guangzhou had ushered in a period of exponential growth of cross-border e-commerce.

ii. Enact favorable policies to integrate resources

A key to Guangzhou's success lay in the timely enactment of favorable policies to release existing advantages. Guangzhou formally launched the 21st-Century Maritime Silk Road Cross-border E-commerce Platform and signed the *Action Plan for Industrial Cooperation along the 21st-Century Maritime Silk Road* with China-ASEAN Business Council in 2015, a great boost to the development of its cross-border e-commerce. At the same year, Guangzhou utilized its advantages in positioning, human resource, and logistics after the establishment of Nansha Free Trade Zone and enacted the *Implementation Plan for Launching Cross-border E-commerce Pilot Project in Guangzhou City*, identifying Huangpu, Nansha, and Huadu as the three pilot zones. After being included into the second batch of cities of Cross-Border E-Commerce Comprehensive Pilot Zones in 2016, Guangzhou had been investing RMB500 million supporting the development of e-commerce and cross-border e-commerce for 5 consecutive years since 2013. A fund of RMB33.2 million was earmarked for setting up Guangzhou's Cross-border E-commerce Public Service Platform. In 2015, the city invested RMB60 million for developing Nansha Free Trade Zone, Airport Economic Zone, and other cross-border e-commerce zones. The series of fiscal policies had significantly released the city's potential for developing cross-border e-commerce.

iii. Joint forces to seek breakthrough development

After the pilot zone was launched, Guangzhou took the lead in setting up a recording system, which effectively lowered the entry threshold and attracted more companies to the cross-border e-commerce business. Government authorities including the administration of commerce and industry, customs, inspection and quarantine, state taxation administration, and foreign exchange administration launched a series of measures to facilitate customs clearance and better meet the sales demand of cross-border e-commerce companies. The mode of "checklist verification and consolidated declaration" was introduced, the cross-border e-commerce retail list of imported goods was faithfully implemented, and supporting settlement policies for cross-border e-commerce were duly enacted. After the Chinese government announced its new tax policy for cross-border e-commerce, Guangzhou intensified its regulatory efforts and encouraged platforms, supply chains, and government authorities to return to the market competition. Within the administration of customs, different functions joined forces to send the message to the general public. Many communication platforms were used including citizen-run media platforms. In additional to government support, companies, association, and colleges formed strong partnerships to explore the future development of the industry and provide recommendations for setting standards on companies' expansion efforts, attracting trade professionals, initiating cross-sector procurement, and promoting brands in overseas markets.

II. Development of Cross-Border E-Commerce in Guangzhou: Challenges

i. The scarcity and weak bargaining power of local e-commerce platforms

As a pacesetter for China's online shopping market, Guangzhou failed to become home to national giants like JD.com and Alibaba. The combined business volume of Guangzhou-based leading e-commerce companies such as gbhui.com and vip.com only accounted for 5% of the national total. If Guangzhou missed the golden opportunity when cross-border e-commerce took off, it would risk losing its position as a leading economic and cultural capital. In addition to the limited number, e-commerce platforms in Guangzhou were generally small in size and mostly belonged to traditional companies or small and medium-sized enterprises. Take Nansha District for example, the offline experience store of cross-border e-commerce platforms seldom had a registered capital of over RMB200 million. Despite favorable policies for bonded zones, super cross-border e-commerce platforms and companies with strong purchasing power were still ideas to be realized. The overall bargaining power of local platforms remained weak.

ii. The stringent "Positive List" and the difficulty in enacting tax refund policies

Guangzhou started implementing the "Positive List" in a very strict manner in 2016 by completely prohibiting e-commerce sales of goods not found on the *Cross-border E-commerce Retail List of Imported Goods*. Cosmetics and other products that used to take a large portion of items purchased by Chinese consumers on e-commerce platforms are excluded from the list and therefore, subject to stringent and complex custom clearance process. Newcomers to the foreign trade sector, cross-border e-commerce exporters could provide neither import vouchers nor VAT invoices. The application of the traditional tax system rendered tax refund almost impossible for Guangzhou-based cross-border e-commerce companies. Instead of receiving tax rebates, they faced even higher tax requirements. As a result, the price advantage no longer existed. On the other hand, although Guangzhou allowed e-commerce platforms and customers to reach online agreements which permitted the payment of a certain percentage of commission after the receipt of goods, this part of commission could not be deducted from VAT as done in the traditional offline retail sector. This led to a higher VAT burden for e-commerce platforms than offline companies.

iii. Serious homogeneity competition and low proportion of cross-border goods

Currently, fast moving consumer goods such as formulas, snacks, and diapers accounted for the largest share of products sold at experience stores of cross-border e-commerce platforms, leading to prominent homogeneity problems. However, luxury brands much favored by consumers had not found the chance to enter the market. It seemed that platforms were simply copying the business model of others instead of exploring their own. The lack of differentiated products and distinctive business features not only bored customers but also undermined the overall attraction of cross-border e-commerce business. The proportion of real cross-border products was also low in these experience stores. Statistics showed that only one ninth of the dutiable products sold in Nansha Cross-border Direct Purchase Experience Center were cross-border products in the real sense. In Panyu Cross-border Direct Purchase Experience Center and the Cross-border E-commerce Experience Store of GrandBuy Department Store, the percentage was only 20%. Although cross-border articles accounted for 40% of products sold in experience stores run by Mopark Department Store and meijoybest.com, consumers were mostly shown by pictures rather than real samples.

iv. Lack of authenticity guarantee and inadequate logistical and warehousing services

Our survey showed that only 48.8% of respondents had actually bought foreign products through cross-border e-commerce platforms[1]. vip.com, a Guangzhou-based giant, was frequently accused of selling counterfeit products and doing little to guarantee quality. Except for those in free trade zones, most platforms required a very long delivery period during which the whereabouts of packages could not be tracked. Take Guangzhou as an example, after a customer ordered a foreign product online, it normally took two days for the platform to process the order and another two days for the platform, the payment channel, and the warehouse to verify the order before the product could be shipped from the bonded zone. If the desired product was not stocked in the bonded zone, then it would take even longer. However, overstocking might also be a problem. Take Nansha for example. The lack of 300 to 500 million square meters of warehouse facilities had become a major obstacle for the growth of cross-border e-commerce. Other issues waiting to be addressed included the difficulty that most consumers faced in accessing after service and returning or exchanging products in the case of damage or loss.

v. Shortage of professionals and decoupling between supply and demand

With 230,000 professionals in demand, cross-border e-commerce platforms in Guangzhou faced severe challenges in discovering overseas suppliers and exploring the overseas market. The rapid growth of cross-border e-commerce was not matched

---

[1] Statistics from *Knowledge and Willingness of Young and Middle-aged Guangzhou Residents to Use Cross-border E-commerce Platforms.*

by a rapid growth in professionals. Not only were there no dedicated programs, but also there were no targeted courses, except in Guangdong University of Foreign Studies and Guangzhou Business Vocational School. Besides, university curriculum generally failed to take into consideration the actual operation of companies. Compared with the domestic e-commerce sector, cross-border businesses involved more players and required more professional expertise. Traditional companies and practitioners in domestic e-commerce found it difficult to address the complexity in international logistics, customs clearance, and intellectual property protection and adapt to the difference in languages and consumer habits, further aggravating the problem.

III. Recommendations for Accelerated Development of Cross-Border E-Commerce in Guangzhou

In 2016, Guangzhou was approved as the second batch of cities in the national cross-border e-commerce comprehensive pilot area and the second-easterly air of cross-border e-commerce took off. Guangzhou should actively connect with the overall goal of "build China's cross-border e-commerce development highlands and Asia Pacific Regional cross-border e-commerce center city ", seize the opportunity to make up for the lack of existing development and accelerate the development of cross-border e-commerce supplier in Guangzhou. Specifically, while cross-border e-commerce in Guangzhou consolidates the development of its existing import business, it can also accelerate export business and increase its efforts to go global. Combined with the Canton Fair, Guangzhou's cross-border e-commerce business has realized a new format of "Internet + Foreign Trade" and promoted the traditional foreign trade in Guangzhou Upgrade and promote the common development of cross-border exports and tourism commodities exports.

(A) Build large scale platforms to enhance the share of local e-commerce supplier

Step up the scale of cross-border e-commerce platform and integrate the existing service platforms, Taking Pazhou as the CBD of cross-border e-commerce to create an e-commerce "Silicon Valley"with billions of assets and improve the overall bargaining power by cooperating with giant e-commerce enterprises such Tencent, Alibaba and Gome. Introduce and nurture a batch of Guangzhou foreign trade integrated service enterprises, give them key support and reward them with RMB5 million from the provincial government budget when they have exported products/services worth over USD1 billion each year. Taking the cooperation between Guangzhou and Portuguese enterprises in the field of cross-border e-commerce as an opportunity, expand Guangzhou's trade in fields of cross-border e-commerce, financial leasing, bonded logistics and market procurement, andencourage domestic enterprises to invest in overseas market and start cooperation with overseas companies in fields of marketing network construction, brand mergers and acquisitions, technology research and development so as to jointly explore the overseas e-commerce market and achieve mutually beneficial and win-win development.

ii. Take initiatives to encourage institutional innovation and develop export tax rebate administration mechanism

The city may adopt a more flexible attitude towards the "Positive List" and give cross-border e-commerce companies more space for development. The "Positive List" itself should be fine-tuned from time to time and customs, inspection, and quarantine processes should be simplified to better meet the demand of consumers and support the growth of cross-border trade. The Internet Plus Export Tax Refund model should be further explored and big data, cloud computing, and other emerging technologies should be allowed to play a bigger role in expanding and strengthening export tax rebate services. Favorable policies should be better applied to cross-border e-commerce retailers, comprehensive foreign trade service platforms, and zero-VAT rated taxable services so that Guangzhou may become a pilot tax rebate city on export of financial leasing goods. It is suggestedto implement a paperless management of export tax rebates (exemptions), improve the management of letter-boxes and complete the procedures for the approval of tax refund (exemption) within 20 working days for eligible export businesses so as to ensure timely and full tax rebates. As cross-border (export) e-commerce is an export trade business, in line with the state's policy of encouraging exports, the turnover tax (VAT) is a tax rebate. It is recommended that Guangzhou implement the tax exemption policy in circulation; in the case of corporate income tax, cross-border e-commerce retail (B2C) industry can enjoy the preferential policies of tax exemption for the first two years and half tax for the third year. Based on the approved tax rate, a 1% corporate income tax will be levied on the e-commerce enterprises with an annual turnover of over RMB100 million.

iii. Apply differentiated business models and push the integration with big data

In order to avoid homogeneity problems and vicious competition, Guangzhou-based cross-border e-commerce platforms are bound to adopt differentiated business models. First, the city should push the integration of mobile internet, big data applications, and cross-border e-commerce platforms. Mobile apps should be strengthened as the dominant sales channel. The 24-hour sales model of vip.com should be applied to other platforms. Big data should be used to accommodate people's differentiated needs. Second, the Belt and Road initiative provides an optimal opportunity for Guangzhou-based platforms to fine-tune their packages. In addition to maternal and baby products and cosmetics, more brands should be imported optimize the product structure. Thirdly, Guangzhou should stick to the segmentation of the market. The example of Alpha Gifts, a cross-border e-commerce experience store opened by a foreign retailer, should be followed to further explore the pharmaceutical and health care niche market and avoid homogeneity. A major way to strengthen exports in the future lies in building Chinese brands in overseas markets. Branding strategy requires the support of overseas warehouses and the expansion of overseas markets needs the integration of services resources.

iv. Comprehensively strengthen authenticity guarantee and optimize supply chain management

The city should help platforms to expand their access to famous foreign brands, integrate procurement channels, strengthen warehouse, logistics, and supply chain management, and establish quality oversight mechanisms. On the one hand, there should be strict entry standards for source suppliers and buyers to ensure products sold on cross-border e-commerce platforms have been imported through perfectly legal channels and are one hundred percent authentic. On the other hand, the city must ensure that the whole delivery process remain an enclosed circle, customs clearance complies fully with legal and regulatory requirements, and consumers can track their packages in an up-to-date manner. Domestic return warehouses should be used to permit online shoppers to return purchases within seven days with no reason, be they purchases sent directly from abroad or from bonded zones. Favorable policies should be properly applied to optimize land use in bonded zones. Warehousing and logistic facilities should be further expanded and strengthened to relieve overstocking.

v. Initiate globalized settlement and strengthen comprehensive financial support

With the support of Guangdong Provincial Branch of the People's Bank of China, Guangdong Sub-administration of China Customs, and Guangdong Department of Commerce, the city should combine domestic and foreign efforts to provide integrated services for cross-border RMB E-commerce on the basis of the successful launch of the cross-border RMB settlement service. Special emphasis should be attached to product innovation and the provision of such globalized financial services as online payment and cross-border settlement, exchange, and cash management. While strengthening large-scale online transaction monitoring and guarding against financial risks, the city should also strive to meet the needs of companies and individuals for cross-border electronic payments both at home and abroad. Meanwhile, the city should also provide comprehensive financial support for cross-border e-commerce platforms by encouraging commercial banks to explore suitable lending models and offering financing and insurance service to foreign trade companies.

vi. Provide training in practical expertise and expand the talent pool

The government should let the market play a dominant role in training professionals. Trainees should target at employment rather than certificates and trainers should focus on practice rather than mere theories. Guangzhou's Cross-border E-commerce Public Service Platform should be fully utilized to realize training programs. A portion of the earmarked fund for e-commerce may be devoted to training talents. Two models are feasible. The first one focuses on the growth of local professionals through third-party programs or partnerships between companies and universities. The second one focuses on attracting external professionals who are well-trained, passionate, and experienced in internet marketing, operation, and management to start their own cross-border e-commerce business in Guangzhou.

Current Status of the Sharing Economy in Guangzhou and Policy Recommendations for Its Development

Wang Wenjiao*

Abstract: The sharing economy is an important Blue Ocean in the new normal of economic development. Guangzhou's shared-use mobility develops rapidly and will become one of the "main battlefronts" of the sharing economy.By combing the present situation and existing problems of Guangzhou's sharing economy, this paper puts forward suggestions on regulating the sharing economy and building Guangzhou into a national model city of sharing economy from the perspectives of the government, the industry and enterprises.

Keywords: Sharing economy, Internet+, collaborative management

In 2015, the 5th plenary session of the 18th CPC Central Committee for the first time put forward the concept of "sharing" and promoted the rise of sharing economy, covering income and wealth distribution, resource and factor allocation, and win-win cooperation among market players. Time saving and efficient in resource allocation, the sharing economy has become an important cutting-edge, challenging economic model, and also an important Blue Ocean to stimulate the vitality of economic development in the new normal. Since 2015, Guangzhou has been witnessing the flourishing of sharing economy represented by car-hailing and bike-sharing programs. The global trend is clear that the sharing economy will bring transformative innovations to the economy. Guangzhou will without doubt grow into one of the key fronts in the competition.

I. The Status Quo of Guangzhou's Sharing Economy

i. The shared economy model is spreading to a large number of industries.

As a new business model, the sharing economy penetrates into all industries in Guangzhou, especially in the transportation industry. Car-hailing, Mobike and car-sharing are three dominant shared-use mobility services in Guangzhou. Among them, the car-hailing service was the first to enter the consumer market. Uber and Didi are the two biggest car-hailing service providers in Guangzhou. They pool private drivers on their platform and allow them to share their ride with consumers. In 2016, bike-sharing services represented by Mobike entered into Guangzhou, providing a solution to the last-mile travel. Following the success of the bike-sharing service, car-sharing appeared in the market. UR-Car and Jiabei launched the car-rental service at the university town where parking is free. In the parking-space-sharing market, EZPark and KAPark launched their intelligent parking service in Pearl River New Town and local neighborhoods to make the most of idle parking spaces via a trading platform. In addition to the transport industry, the sharing economy has spread to areas of public culture and social exchange.

ii. The mode of sharing economy challenges traditional governance

To stimulate the development of sharing economy, Guangzhou is among the first in China to employ information technology to refine its social governance and promote cross-departmental collaboration. For example, Tianhe and Yuexiu districts took actions to address the chaotic parking and man-made damages to shared bikes; a total of 10 neighborhoods in Liwan, Huangpu, Panyu, Baiyun and Huadu districts will set up recommended parking spaces for shared bikes. To create an environment in favor of sharing economy, Guangzhou has accelerated the formation of the public credit system. As of August 2016, it had built a credit database including 1.01 billion entries of data about 273 items of the government, individuals, enterprises, public institutions and social organizations while promoting joint contribution to and sharing of an intelligent city. In 2017, it gradually allowed the public access to government data as appropriate. The management of sharing economy has no administrative regulations or detailed rules to follow. The traditional governance philosophy prefers the wait-and-see attitude towards new things and has no courage to take the initiative, thus failing to truly attend to the needs of the sharing economy baby despite the latter's relentless cry.

iii. The sharing economy calls for more efficient supporting facilities

Take the bike-sharing program for example. Under the old road management mode, there are not sufficient cycle lanes and cyclists are forced to squeeze through the stream of motorists. Besides, it's costly to expand the driveway in old neighborhoods, which further intensifies the problem of traffic jam. As to bike parking, it's common for cyclists to park at will in public areas such as pedestrians' lanes and bus stations. In January 2017, a pile of Mobike bikes appeared at the junction of the South Road of Guangzhou Station and the West Ring Road, blocking the way for local residents. In addition to bike-sharing, the car-sharing program also calls for the city to upgrade supporting facilities. In the current land-rush period, car-sharing service providers are faced with a number of obstacles. They need a lot of fixed parking spaces whose use is well managed.　The reality is that the users are fighting for instead of sharing the car and even if they manage to get one, it's extremely annoying and frustrating to locate one of the limited designated parking spaces to park the car. Therefore, the convenience of car-sharing is still a moon in the water for local citizens.

II. Challenges Facing the Sharing Economy in Guangzhou

i. The boundary of government regulation is not clear, and sharing is more in name than in reality.

A hotspot for sharing economy, Guangzhou determines to create an open, inclusive environment to facilitate its development. But in reality, the regulatory authority whose boundary, rights and responsibilities are poorly defined is in constant friction with players in the sharing economy. On the one hand, government regulation lacks corresponding administrative regulations to follow and has feeble control over market behaviors which seriously disturb the city order and hinder the promotion of sharing economy. On the other, sharing economy businesses grumble about the too-high market threshold and barriers which damage the interests of market players and consumers. For example, Guangzhou's detailed rules on the implementation of the car-hailing policy cap both the number of cars for use and the amount of fare charged, disregarding the spirit of "sharing economy". Under this policy, the cars in service are neither idle nor privately owned.

ii. The business model is immature and the implicit cost of governance is high.

At present, the sharing economy is yet to develop a mature business model that can save social cost and generate economic benefits at the same time, and overcome many operating obstacles. Most players just want a free ride on the wave of sharing economy. In addition, there are concerns about the safety, standardization, quality assurance system and user data protection of shared services and products. This is also the case in Guangzhou. Most local sharing economy businesses are to establish an effective business model yet, the services and products they provide are highly homogeneous, and the competition is chaotic on many fronts. To make it worse, there are many problems with government oversight, the cost-income gap is huge for the sharing economy, many players might not be able to break even, and the lack of administrative measures and supporting facilities might drive up the implicit cost of governance.

iii. The notion of "sharing" is a hype and sharing economy plays a limited role in activating the idle resources.

In the current scene, the sharing economy seems to be an umbrella term for nearly all Internet-based services and products and the notion of "sharing" has become a hype. In Guangzhou, sharing economy businesses extend from transportation to catering, accommodation and finance, but their role in activating idle resources is insignificant. Instead, the marketing hype and the rise of customized services might increase the market supply. For instance, the car-hailing program was originally intended to ease the traffic in rush hours by utilizing unused private cars and off-peak hours, but in reality, driven by the handsome profit, a lot of drivers join the program and hit the road full-time, increasing the market supply and the pressure on road traffic. In most areas of sharing economy, macro planning is absent and copycatting is pervasive, and the services for startups need to be improved.

iv. Credit constraints have limited effects and there is a grey zone of law enforcement.

Given the limited effects of credit constraints, there's no trust between resource owners and users and or effective regulation over the market. On the one hand, there is lack of legislation for regulation. In many areas of sharing economy, players often play the card of "new economy" or "Internet+" to take advantage of legal loopholes and stay outside the regular regulatory system. For instance, though Guangzhou has issued detailed administrative rules to legitimize the status of car-hailing services, it still faces many problems in policy execution. On the other hand, regulation is absent over the users and owners of shared goods and services. The legal risks and disputed division of liabilities of sharing economy are reflected in traffic accidents of errand-runners and Mobike users reported by Guangzhou Daily.

v. The sharing economy squeezes the survival space of traditional economy and monopolizes the industry with data barriers.

The rise of sharing economy poses challenges to the traditional economy which is being squeezed out by unfair competition. In its early days, by taking advantage of legal loopholes, the sharing economy gains extra profits at the expense of traditional businesses. In addition, the low entry level allows many sharing economy businesses to seize the market and grab the market share from traditional economy businesses in no time, breaking the monopoly of the latter. It's also noteworthy that the sharing economy is Internet-based and the data barriers it has will allow its players to establish market monopoly, which won't be challenged in the short time.

III. Policy Recommendations for Promoting the Development of Sharing Economy in Guangzhou

The rise of sharing economy in various sectors is forcing the government to seek innovation in its governance. Guangzhou shall pioneer in the law-based, regulated, healthy and orderly development of sharing economy by promoting repeatable practices and establishing a three-tiered regulatory system comprising the government, industry associations and enterprises.

i. At the government level: strengthening regulation

1. Clarifying the regulatory approach and introducing new regulatory philosophy

The regulatory approach for traditional economy focuses on the setup of barriers to market access and fails to meet the need of sharing economy for whole-process regulation. Thus the city government of Guangzhou shall adopt a new regulatory philosophy and approach, create an inclusive, favorable environment for sharing economy businesses that utilize idle resources, and speed up to foster a mature business model. As for shared services, the government should refine its administration, deliberate on market access thresholds, and tighten regulation during and after the delivery of services.

2. Reconstructing the regulatory system to better regulate and promote the development of sharing economy at the same time

Guangzhou shall tighten control over sharing economy, build a sound regulatory system that not only oversees but also guides and promotes the development of sharing economy, create a favorable environment for sharing economy businesses, and include sharing economy into its grid management system, to prevent either chaotic or stifled development of sharing economy. Guangzhou should also take the lead in establishing a new data collection mechanism, effectively measure and share the impact of sharing economy on GDP and CPI, provide accurate data analysis results for government decisions, and actively guide the orderly development of sharing development.

3. Strengthening practical management and improving legislation

First, administrative measures shall be put forward to tackle specific problems with sharing economy, and corresponding laws and regulations shall be introduced to perfect the top-level design for sharing economy. For example, Guangzhou should actively administer the shared-use mobility market, improve cycle lanes, provide necessary facilities, open public parking lots to sharing economy businesses, increase support and expand the growth space for them. To be specific, the government should employ Internet and big data for regulation, improve the existing social credit system and blacklist system, grant access to public data, realize seamless connection of credit information platforms, and allow businesses to inquire about credit information and business identity online.

4. Stepping up efforts to raise public awareness and encouraging new activities of sharing economy

The government must not reject sharing economy or indulge it with impunity. It should strengthen information sharing among departments and increase the value of information through inter-departmental collaboration. For example, in the case of the car-hailing program, it should recognize it as a useful supplement to traditional means of mobility, guide and regulate its development and publicize its advantages in providing customized services. In the field of public culture, it should promote university and community libraries to share resources. Meanwhile, outside traditional sectors of transportation and housing, new sharing-economy programs such as Walking School Bus and Time Bank are encouraged.

ii. At the industry level: self-regulation

Guangzhou Sharing Economy Industry Development Association shall give full play to its role as a third-party platform and provide trading rules for businesses and consumers. Specifically, on one hand, it should collect the information and transaction records of both parties in a timely manner, and punish dishonest behaviors according to relevant rules to discipline the behavior of both parties. On the other, it should establish a reputation mechanism to reinforce mutual supervision of both parties, such as the current mutual evaluation system adopted by shared-use mobility programs and incentives and punishments that come along with it. At the same time, Guangzhou's transportation industry should be the vanguard in promoting the development of sharing economy, integrate with other industries such as education, culture, medical services, and housing, strengthen inter-sector communication and cooperation, and set up industry norms and standards. The Association should also actively formulate and promulgate the Convention on the Self-Discipline of Sharing Economy Industries in Guangzhou to promote the healthy development of sharing economy businesses, improve resource utilization efficiency and maintain a fair, harmonious market environment. It should also serve as a bridge connecting industries, the academia and the government so that they could work together to promote the rapid, healthy and orderly development of sharing economy and prevent vicious competition and unrestrained growth.

iii. At the business level: practicing the spirit of "sharing"

1. Strengthening communication with the government

As the clash with government regulation intensifies in Guangzhou, sharing economy enterprises should take the initiative to actively work with the regulatory department, respect and balance the interests of stakeholders (including long-term users) as much as possible, answer questions from the regulatory department, build up credibility, and properly handle the relations with the regulator. Moreover, they can contact the regulator via industry alliances or associations or contribute to policy making via third-party platforms to help develop proper policies governing sharing economy and seek for external recognition.

2. Engaging customers into the sharing economy

By actively engaging customers into the sharing economy, businesses can build up their reputation and influence, attract new customers, expand the market share and promote shared products and services. In addition, businesses can share their office space, human resources and technology, effectively combine the supply chain and the consumption chain, and enhance the sharing efficiency. They can seek institutional breakthrough by assembling a task force for certain mission, realizing interactions among departments and sectors or incentivizing employees to tap their unused talents, wisdom and expertise.

3. Actively exploring the mature business model

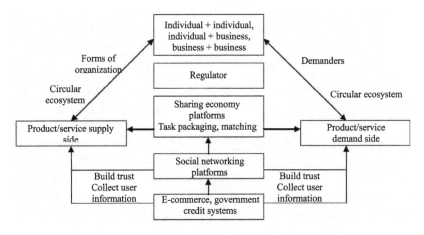

Figure 1 Business Model Evolution of the Sharing Economy

To explore a mature business model that is currently absent in the sharing economy, efforts shall be made in the following aspects. First of all, sharing economy businesses should match supply and demand. The sharing economy rises when Chinese economy enters into the new normal of development. It should actively reflect the consumption behavior, pattern and mindset that appear in the course of supply-side structural reform, try to optimize the supply-side structure, balance and coordinate supply and demand, and efficiently utilize excess capacity and idle resources to meet the demand for customized products and services. Second, they should seek innovation regarding core resources and competitiveness. Sharing economy businesses should make full use of their advantages in "Internet+" and big data, integrate idle and fragmented resources, and employ information sharing platforms and information technology for resource sharing. Third, they should step up efforts to develop innovative operating modes. The reason is that the sharing economy produces no goods, but utilizes idle resources and trades the right to use for the mutual benefits of both sides of the transaction. Fourth, they should establish a sustainable development mode for sharing economy. Specifically, they should integrate with the e-commerce, search engines and social networking platforms, build a credit system and place consumers at the heart of the sharing economy to realize seamless connection between supply and demand of products and services.

Analysis of Development of Makerspaces

in Guangzhou in 2016 *

Zhou Yu**

Abstract: The national call for more people to start their own business and make innovations was embraced by Guangzhou and its districts in 2016. A series of supporting policies were implemented, ushering in a very great startin a new era. The year of 2016 also witnessed the great development of makerspaces in Guangzhou, with significant progress made in the scale, total number, and business models of such spaces. However, a closer examination would lead to some existing issues such as the inadequate implementation of policies, the improper structure of the sector, the unsatisfactory brand quality, and the inefficient services for venture capital investment.

Keywords: Makerspaces, innovation and entrepreneurship, Guangzhou

In 2016, China devoted vigorous efforts to encourage people to start their own business and to make innovations, leading to the establishment of over 4,200 makerspaces[1], which made China the second largest market in terms of the investment scale right after the United States[2]. Following the guidance of the *Guiding Opinions of the General Office of the State Council on Developing Mass Makerspaces and Promoting Mass Innovation and Entrepreneurship*, Guangzhou launched a series of initiatives such as enacting the city-level *Measures on Supporting the Developing Mass Makerspaces* and district-level targeted supporting policies. A surging number of makerspaces made effective use of stock resources, optimized the impact of policies, and provided comprehensive and professional supporting services for the society at low costs. The initiatives were starting to play

---

* This report is the joint outcome of studies supported by Guangzhou Development Research Institute of Guangzhou University, a Key Research Institute of Humanities and Social Sciences in Universities of Guangdong Province, the Collaborative Innovation and Development Center for "Guangzhou Studies" of Guangdong Provincial Department of Education, the Collaborative Innovation Project for "Guangzhou Studies" of Guangzhou Municipal Bureau of Education, Guangzhou Young Scholars Project (16QNXR18), Guangdong ProvincialYoung Innovators Project (2016WQNCX119), and Guangzhou Municipal Institutions of Higher Learning Research Project (1201630526), etc.

** The author is Dr. Zhou Yu at Guangzhou Development Research Institute of Guangzhou University.

[1]Statistics released at the NationalConferenceforScience andTechnologyWork on January 1st, 2017.

[2]-*2016InternetEntrepreneurship andInnovationWhitePaper* released by Tencent Research Institute

their guiding and promotional roles.

I. Current Development of Makerspaces in Guangzhou

i. General information

1. The establishment of new national makerspaces in the city

In 2016, the Ministry of Science and Technology publicized the information of 1, 201 outstanding makerspaces (363 for the first time and 839 for the second time), which had been incorporated into the management and service system of national science and technology business incubators as national makerspaces, after two rounds of careful examination of their business model, profession service, achievement, and operation[3]. Guangzhou was home to 30 new national makerspaces, an increase of 114.29% over the same period of the previous year. However, the 30 new makerspaces only accounted for 2.5% of the national total, a sharp drop from the 10.29% in 2015. As is shown in Figure 1, Guangzhou only ranked the eighth in terms of the number of new makerspaces among the ten cities listed including the four municipalities directly under the Central Government and five cities specifically designated in the state plan.

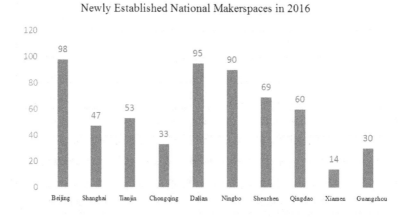

Newly Established National Makerspaces in 2016

Figure 1 Newly Established National Makerspaces

---

[3] G. K. F. H. (2016) No.46 and G. K. F. H. (2016) No.105 released the information in March and September 2016 respectively.

2. The establishment of new provincial makerspaces in the city

In 2016, Guangdong Province witnessed the establishment of 78 new trial provincial makerspaces[4], of which 29.48%, or 23 makerspaces, were located in Guangzhou, far exceeding the number in other cities in the province (Figure 2). Of the 23 new makerspaces, 12 were also included in the second and third batches of national science and technology business incubator management and service system in 2016. The figures are as follows:

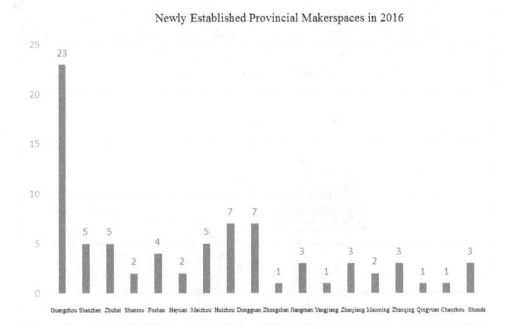

Newly Established Provincial Makerspaces in 2016

Figure 2 Newly Established Provincial Makerspaces

3. Categorization of newly established makerspaces in the city by service type

Based on the types of services, the project team categorizes Guangzhou-based makerspaces into four groups. The first group of makerspaces focus on providing business spaces that can be shared by different teams. This type of open makerspaces increases the opportunity of team-to-team communication and creativity. The second group of makerspaces enjoy special strength in financial capital operation and provide angel funds, equity investments, financing guarantees, and other investment and financing information and services. They are known as investment and financing

---

[4]*Notice on Publicizing Information of 2016 Guangdong-based Trial Makerspaces and National Science and Technology Business Incubator Hotbeds* (Yue Ke Han Gao Zi No. 〔2016〕 1485) released by the Department of Science and Technology of Guangdong Province.

service makerspaces. The third type gives special emphasis to helping new makers. Generously sharing their experience and resources, successful entrepreneurs and experts are functioning as mentors to newcomers. The fourth type specializes in providing professional services for a major technical industry. While supporting upstream and downstream projects, makerspaces strive to establish a complete industrial chain or industrial ecosystem.

In 2016, Guangzhou witnessed the establishment of 41 new makerspaces at the provincial level or above. Following the above mentioned categorization, 8 makerspaces (20%) belonged to the first group (open makerspaces for sharing); 12 (29%) fell under the second group (investment and financing services); 11 (27%) were devoted to helping new makers, thus belonging to the third group; and 10 (24%) specialized in professional and technical fields. Please see Figure 3.

Proportion of Four Types of Makerspaces

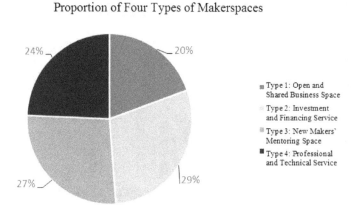

Figure 3 Categorization of New Guangzhou-based Makerspaces at the Provincial Level or Above by Service Type

ii. Distribution and categorization of new makerspaces in the districts

1. Establishment of new makerspaces in the districts

In 2016, the eleven districts of Guangzhou witnessed the birth of 30 new national makerspaces, 23 new provincial makerspaces, and 44 new municipal makerspaces. Their distribution is shown in Figure 4. As can be seen from the figure, Tianhe District saw the largest increase in the total number of the makerspaces among all districts. Moreover, the sound structure supported by seven national makespaces, 13 provincial makerspaces, and 34 municipal makespaces promised even greater future development for Tianhe. Tianhe District was followed Huangpu District (11 makerspaces), Yuexiu District (nine makerspaces), Haizhu District (ten makerspaces), Panyu District (seven makerspaces), Liwan District (two makerspaces) and Baiyun District (two makerspaces), which together formed the second stratum. Districts in this stratum saw a considerable gap with Tianhe District in the number of new national, provincial, and municipal makerspaces. Their future development is also threatened as the number of new provincial and lower-level makerspaces was generally smaller than that of national ones.

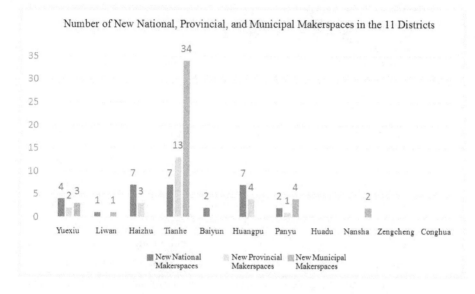

Number of New National, Provincial, and Municipal Makerspaces in the 11 Districts

Figure 4 The Overall Growth of New Makerspaces in the 11 Districts

2. Categorization of makerspaces in the districts by service type

Following the categorization standards mentioned above, the project team worked out the distribution of the 41 new provincial and higher-level makerspaces (including overlapped ones) in the districts as follows. As shown in Figure 5, most makerspaces in Tianhe District focus on providing investment and financial services (seven makerspaces, accounting for 58.3%) or mentoring for newcomers (five makerspaces, accounting for 45.5%), thanks to its highly developed financial industry and cluster of universities and colleges. Benefiting from its long accumulated technical strength ,Huangpu District became the home to the largest number of professional and technical makerspaces (5 in total, accounting for 50%).

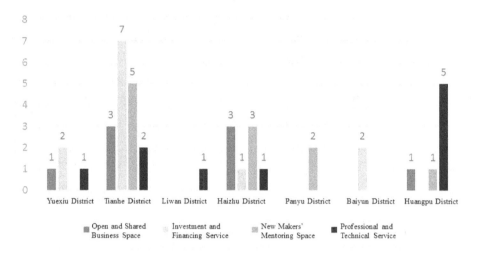

Distribution of Makerspaces in the 11 Districts by Service Type

Open and Shared Business Space | Investment and Financing Service | New Makers' Mentoring Space | Professional and Technical Service

Figure 5 Distribution of Makerspaces in the Districts by Service Type

A closer look at the distribution of professional and technical makerspaces by service sector shows that Yuexiu District and Liwan District both have one makerspace specialized in culture, forecasting the birth of a number of cultural and creative enterprises in the future; Tianhe District, with the most robust economy, witnessed the establishment of Tianhe Guanggu and Zhangyuan Mobile Internet, showing that its future strength would lie in the development of telecommunication and software; and with its five makerspaces covering every sector from telecommunication and software to health and new material, Huangpu District demonstrated its unique advantage in high-tech transformation, which would continue to support of the development of its high-tech industry as an important engine for local economic growth.

Table 1 Distribution of Professional and Technical Makerspaces

District	Name of Makerspace	Service Sector
Yuexiu	Venture Factory	Culture
Liwan	Cultural Makers	Culture
Haizhu	Yichuangshe Makerspace	Health
Tianhe	Tianhe Guanggu (CPLUS)	Telecommunication
	Zhangyuan Mobile Internet	Software

Huangpu	Yueqian Makerspace	Telecommunication
	Da'an Chuanggu	Health
	Guanghao Bio-health Makerspace	Health
	TOPS Makerspace	Software
	Huaxin Park	New Material

3. The number of newly-introduced enterprises in makespaces of all districts

As of December 2016, makerspaces in Guangzhou had become home to 421 new companies. Tianhe District topped the list with 220 companies (52.2%), followed by Haizhu District with 106 companies (25.1%). None of the rest districts hosted more than 100 new companies[5].

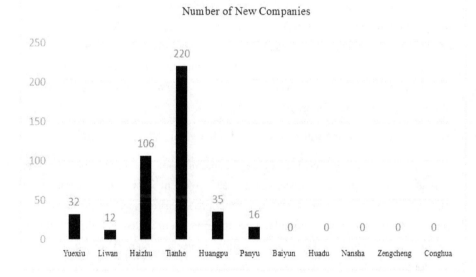

Number of New Companies

Figure 6 Number of New Companies in Makerspaces by District

---

[5]Statistics of Baiyun, Huadu, Nansha, Zengcheng, and Conghua not available at present.

II. Major Issues Facing the Development of Makerspaces in Guangzhou

i. The difficulty in implementation the policy and release of its dividend

Although cities around the country all issue policies to support the development of makerspaces in line with the state requirement, Guangzhou far exceeds Beijing, Shanghai, and Shenzhen as it offers much more generous subsidies to makerspaces, makers, and agencies investing in maker programs or hosting innovation activities in a much more flexible manner. Actually, the city's generous support for the growth of makerspaces is shown in the different types of subsidies it offers. Model makerspaces recognized for their unique characteristics can receive a maximum subsidy of RMB5 million. Agencies providing services for public technology platforms are entitled to a one-time subsidy of up to RMB3 million. Makerspaces supporting college students to start their own business or make innovation can receive an annual subsidy of up to RMB1.5 million. However, statistics show that the growth rate and scale of makerspaces in Guangzhou are far less than the above areas, indicating the policy dividend has not been fully released because of the obstacles such as inconsistent assessment standards, high policy thresholds, complicated procedures, delayed processing of applications, and postponed allocation of earmarked funds, etc.

2. Online platforms and public access to information are far from satisfactory

The project team conducted a special assessment of the online platforms of provincial and higher-level makerspaces established in 2016. Three factors were assessed, including the existence of online platforms (official website, WeChat account, or micro-blog), the completion of information provided on online platforms (such as their service package, representative projects, incoming investments, and development dynamics, etc.), and the timeliness of updated information (whether information is promptly released). Results[6] showed that up to 26 makerspaces, or 63.4% of the total 41 national and provincial makerspaces established in 2016, failed to develop their own online platforms. To be more specific, two thirds of national makerspaces and half of provincial makerspaces had no online platforms.

---

[6] Last assessed on February 25, 2017

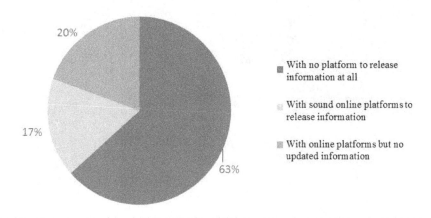

Establishment of Online Platforms

20%

17%

63%

With no platform to release information at all

With sound online platforms to release information

With online platforms but no updated information

Figure 7 Establishment of Online Platforms

3. The city faces an apparent shortage of professional and technical makerspaces

Guangzhou's *13th Five-Year Development Plan for Strategic Emerging Industries* calls for the further development of a new generation of 100 billion-yuan industrial clusters focusing on information technology, bio-health, new materials, high-end equipment, new energy vehicles, energy-saving and environment-friendly projects, fashion, and creativity, etc. As initial breeders for innovative enterprises, makerspaces to a certain extent determine the development direction of Guangzhou's industrial strategy in the future. Statistics quoted above show that more than 80% of the 41 new national and provincial makerspaces fail to develop their own specialized technical and industrial plans. Only Da'an Chuanggu in Huangpu District, Venture Factory in Yuexiu District, and another eight makerspaces chose the path of developing unique industrial clusters. There is still much room for improvement if compared with the present development in Beijing and Shanghai. Please see Figure 8.

Categorization of Makerspaces by Service Sector

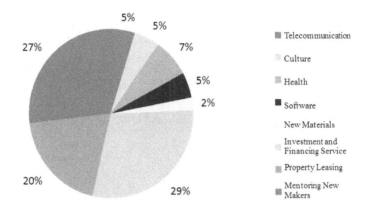

Figure 8 Categorization of Makerspaces by Service Sector

Professional and technical makerspaces are those focused on providing systematical startup services for a certain industry or sector. Their most prominent feature lies in the fact that all their targeted companies are from the same industry or sector, thus the services offered are more professional and specific. Supporting upstream and downstream companies and enterprises in different sectors of the same industry, these makerspaces only attract startups that can complement or form synergy with each other so as to improve industrial competitiveness and reduce homogeneous competition. However, makerspaces, especially those mainly relying on asset leasing for profit, always ignore systematic planning or fail to pay enough attention to the selection of incoming companies as they overemphasize utilization and occupancy rates, which will lead to the lack of clear industrial positioning and decreased professional and technical level. Domestic and foreign experience shows that the future of makerspaces more than ever lies in the development of industrial clusters with unique professional and technical strength. Therefore, it is necessary that Guangzhou speed up the establishment of makerspaces with special strength in forming industrial clusters.

4. The overall brand image of makerspaces needs improving

Makerspaces are generally new to Guangzhou. Except a few highly developed and fully qualified ones, most makerspaces need to improve their brand image. How to end the current free fight and usher in a new era of standard practice remains a pending question.

1. The upgrading of internal management

Makerspaces in Guangzhou generally lack of professional platform managers and intermediaries. Most makespaces can only provide simple primary services, such as asset leasing, office sharing, and official certification application, etc. High-end value-added services, such as technical consulting, market consulting, project liaison, business consulting, risk avoidance and preferential policy application, are beyond their capacity. This is because that most of these low-end makerspaces were originally established as property management companies, book-keeping firms, or commercial agencies. Their transformation into makerspaces was not accompanied by the timely introduction of highly professional and experienced operating teams, which were essential for the provision of entrepreneurship training, management consulting, investment, financing, and other more important supporting services.

2. The establishment of external brand

Makerspaces in Guangzhou suffer from the lack of effective guidance for industrial development. The result is the absence of local makerspaces with famous brands, unique strength, and external influence. So far Guangzhou has exported no local makerspace brands and few overseas projects. The fundamental reason lies in the fact that the brand management pattern, resource integration capacity, creativity, and standardization of local makerspaces have not been recognized by its counterparts from home and abroad. Take Beijing as an example. Its Makerspace Alliance has set up the Volunteer Mentors Board for Capital Start-ups, which is dedicated to integrating resources, encouraging and guiding outstanding makerspaces to establish their brands and export services, and setting up partnerships through chain management, joint listing, and shared investment and financing, etc. This has contributed to the cross-regional integration of resources and utilization of services. Now a large number of Beijing-based local makerspaces are exporting their brands to domestic cities like Shanghai, Tianjin, and Guangzhou. Some of them are even establishing overseas branches.

3. The improvement of self-supporting capacity

At present, government subsidy and property rental payment remain the most important sources of revenue for makerspaces. Government subsidy provides short-term support and is aimed to inject vitality into the market. Therefore, it cannot be counted on as a long-term source. In terms of property rental payment, makerspaces charge much higher than ordinary office spaces. Take a makerspace in Tianhe District for example. One has to pay RMB5,000 every month for an ordinary

20-square-meter eight-person glass cubicle. That means for every square meter, one has to pay RMB250. However, one can easily rent an ordinary office in the same area at RMB100 per square meter. Therefore, rental payment shall not form a long-term source of revenue, either. In order to support themselves, makerspaces need to adopt an effective business model. Government-subsidized public platforms as they are, makerspaces are essentially business platforms that link real estate, venture capital, and real economy. Their sustainable and sound development requires the support of a sound business model rather than favorable policies and property leasing.

III. Recommendations

i. Facilitate policy enactment to release more benefits

First, the city should strengthen the implementation of various supportive policies, especially those designed to attract professionals, and programs aimed to double financial investment in science and technology. It should encourage the districts to develop their own supportive policies that will suit changed conditions and new market demand and promote local economic development. The influence of such supportive policies will be further expanded as they attract more social capital to local makerspaces. The government should pay attention to combining high-end policies for top-notch companies with inclusive policies that bring benefits to all so as to enrich the policy thresholds. It should also combine long-term supportive policies with short-term incentives so as to ensure the coordination and sustainability of the policy system.

Second, the city should encourage all districts to carry out objective and scientific policy performance assessment, carefully examine current gains and losses, and look at the system itself, its supporting mechanism, and implementation measures for decisive influencing factors. It should pay close attention to the needs of entrepreneurs, business platforms, and other stakeholders and strive to meet the market demand. It should set up a proper evaluation system with scientifically designed indicators to select fully qualified and highly competent makerspaces which are also good at integrating resources and enjoy strong development potential for government subsidies. It should strengthen oversight on the implementation of policies and establish an accountability system and a withdrawal mechanism for fiscal subsidies so as to ensure the economical, efficient, and fair investment of finance capital.

Third, the city should streamline the administrative system and improve the efficiency of public services. The Government authorities in charge of industry and commerce, taxation, finance, human resources and social security, and other functions should strengthen coordination and mutual support so as to ensure the full implementation of central policies aimed to encourage more people to start their own business and make innovations. Efforts should also be devoted to raising public awareness and providing better services and guidance. Simplified procedures should be adopted to facilitate the speedy and direct allocation of earmarked funds to targeted receivers.

2. Provide more professional and featured services

First, the city should strengthen capacity building measures and attract more professionals to join makerspaces. The lack of professional and experienced operation teams have led to the current low service and operation level. It should draw upon domestic and foreign development and operation experience, establish a multi-tier training system, promote interactions and exchanges within the industry, and continue to improve the services provided by people work with makerspaces.

Second, makerspaces should further divide service sectors, define service standards, and provide professional and tailor-made services. The city should stick to the development of big incubators and optimize the growth chain of "makerspaces-incubators-accelerators-science parks". Instead of being sublessors, makerspaces should strive to increase the proportion of revenue generated by additional services, optimize self-supporting measures, and find an industrial service pattern with Guangzhou characteristics as soon as possible. Providing sector-specific professional services will be an inevitable choice for the future development of makerspaces.

3. Improve the building and management of online platforms

First, from the perspective of management authorities, an online management platform should be established to integrate citywide resources and information. Third-party online tools may be used to integrate the management of makerspaces and their companies. This will effectively avoid the omission and duplication of corporate information, especially in daily management, information disclosure and registration, authentication, and performance evaluation, etc. New technological tools, such as the internet, cloud computing, and big data should be fully utilized to facilitate the timely and comprehensive understanding of the development of the city's makerspaces and provide accurate statistical support for policy coordination.

Second, from the perspective of makerspace operation, the government should help makerspaces to set up online operation platforms and encourage them to use online tools to effectively attract social resources and build cross-regional and cross-sectoral collaboration and exchange platforms.

4. Guide the development of unique industrial clusters and improve the brand image of makerspaces

First, the city should recognize the differences between districts in terms of the geographic location, natural conditions, applicable policies, and resources, etc. and adopt scientific and rational system so as to fully utilize and integrate resources across districts while exploring their original features. It should pay attention to the scientific development of makerspaces and help them find their position, tap their potential, and amplify their advantage so as to realize differentiated strategic growth.

Second, the city should follow Beijing's practice and better help makerspaces to define standards and export brands. Relevant government authorities are advised to provide continuous guidance and support for their brand building and public communication efforts so as to establish a series of Guangzhou-based makerspaces that serve different industrial clusters, focus on different technical fields, and enjoy different service strengths and a series of start-up service platforms whose influence goes beyond the Pearl River Delta to attract entrepreneurs and venture capital from both at home and abroad.

5. Inject vitality into existing platforms and improve regional competitiveness

First, the government is advised to consider the possibility of enacting policies that support the collaboration between companies, research institutions, and universities for innovative breakthroughs. It should step up the enactment of incentive policies to promote the local commercialization of research findings. It should make full use of the large number of Guangzhou-based colleges and universities and strengthen cooperation with Sun Yat-sen University, South China University of Technology, Jinan University, South China Agricultural University, and South China Normal University, etc., so as to attract more innovation projects to local makerspaces. It should step up cooperation with Hong Kong- and Macao-based colleges and universities and invite more projects to be launched in Guangzhou. The government is also advised to encourage companies, colleges, universities, and research institutions to increase their investment in the infrastructure and facilities of makerspaces through subsidies, rewards, accelerated depreciation, and import tax incentives. The pretax additional deduction policy may be applied tothose meeting the investment requirement so as to reduce the construction and operation costs of makerspaces.

Second, the government is advised to improve the degree of specialization of some makerspaces and incubator parks that used to be factories or industrial parks. Deserted factory buildings, collective village land, and professional markets can be used by makerspaces to upgrade their property, expand their size, and form complete incubator chains and systems.

6. Improve the investment and financing security system

Capital is the blood that ensures the survival and development of start-up enterprises. A smooth flow of capital will contribute to their rapid growth. The platform strength of makerspaces should be fully utilized to attract angel funds, venture capital, and other energies on the capital market, explore diversified investment and financing modes, and continue to make financial innovations.

The government should step up efforts to support the operation of both government-subsidized and social venture capitals and make Guangzhou a development highland that integrates the innovation chain, the industrial chain, and the capital chain. It should also actively integrate social resources and work with commercial banks to encourage the development of customized financial products with technological features for enterprises with credit needs, such as small giant enterprises, high-tech enterprises, and those included in the system of future high-tech enterprises.

This book is the result of a co-publication agreement between Social Sciences Academic Press (China) and Paths International Ltd.

Analysis of the Development of Guangzhou in China
Editors-in-Chief: Qu Shaobing, Wei Minghai
Associate Editors-in-Chief: Zhang Qixue, Luo Jiaowan, Tu Chenglin
ISBN: 978-1-84464-518-3
EBook ISBN: 978-184464-519-0

Copyright © 2018 by Paths International Ltd and by Social Sciences Academic Press, China

All rights reserved. No part of this publication may be reproduced, translated, stored in a retrieval system, or transmitted in any form or by any means, electronic, mechanical, photocopying or otherwise, without the prior permission of the publisher.

The copyright to this title is owned by Social Sciences Academic Press (China). This book is made available internationally through an exclusive arrangement with Paths International Ltd of the United Kingdom and is only permitted for sale outside China.

Paths International Ltd
www.pathsinternational.com

Published in the United Kingdom

CPSIA information can be obtained
at www.ICGtesting.com
Printed in the USA
LVHW062250220519
618269LV00004BA/12/P